Curbing Campaign Cash

Curbing
Campaign Cash

HENRY FORD, TRUMAN NEWBERRY, AND

THE POLITICS OF PROGRESSIVE REFORM

Paula Baker

 University Press of Kansas

© 2012 by the University Press of Kansas

Published by the University Press of Kansas (Lawrence, Kansas 66045), which was organized by the Kansas Board of Regents and is operated and funded by Emporia State University, Fort Hays State University, Kansas State University, Pittsburg State University, the University of Kansas, and Wichita State University

Library of Congress Cataloging-in-Publication Data

Baker, Paula.
  Curbing campaign cash : Henry Ford, Truman Newberry, and the politics of progressive reform / Paula Baker.
      p. cm.
  Includes bibliographical references.
  ISBN 978–0-7006–1863–7 (cloth : alk. paper)   1. Campaign funds—United States—History—20th century.   2. Campaign funds—Law and legislation—United States.   3. United States. Congress. Senate—Contested elections.   4. Ford, Henry, 1863–1947.   5. Newberry, Truman, 1864–1945.   I. Title.
  JK1991.B348 2012
  324.7'80973--dc23
                                                                      2012021650

British Library Cataloguing-in-Publication Data is available.

Printed in the United States of America

10 9 8 7 6 5 4 3 2 1

The paper used in this publication is recycled and contains 30 percent postconsumer waste. It is acid free and meets the minimum requirements of the American National Standard for Permanence of Paper for Printed Library Materials Z39.48-1992.

For my father

CONTENTS

This book has a circuitous history, and it is a pleasure to thank the individuals and institutions that helped move it forward. I began the research as a fellow at the Woodrow Wilson Center for Scholars, when I thought that a bit of additional digging might round out the strange story of an election involving Henry Ford that tested the first federal campaign finance regulations, a case that was part of a wider history of campaign finance. I received good advice at a Social Science History and an American Society for Legal History conference. More good suggestions came with the opportunity to present what was an unwieldy mass at the Miller Center at the University of Virginia. Thanks to Sid Milkis and Brian Balough for the invitation to Charlottesville, along with their comments and those of the audience. Robert Mutch shared his expertise on the history of campaign finance reform, and Allison Hayward and Don Critchlow provided valuable feedback.

As I came to understand that this case worked better standing apart from the general history of campaign finance, research funds from the Ohio State Department of History made possible some extended stays in Michigan and Washington. Along the way, archivists at the Burton Collection at the Detroit Public Library, the Benson Ford Research Library, the Bentley Historical Library, the Library of Congress, and the National Archives were especially helpful. Ralph Mavis and Andrew Haley assured me that I had not gone off the rails, and provided good ideas on style and substance. Donald Ritchie's comments on the entire manuscript saved me from some errors and, more important, pushed me on the book's argument.

Working with the University Press of Kansas has been a delight. Fred Woodward's encouragement, patience, and timely nudges came in just the right mix. I am proud to join the fine political history list Fred has assembled. Kelly Chrisman Jacques moved the manuscript through production with efficiency and good humor.

Steve Thomas read every word, even though he had heard most of them before they made it to paper. His enthusiasm for the project boosted mine, and our conversations are reflected on every page. With all of that, I'm sure he's glad that Truman Newberry is no longer a dinner companion. I'll blame him for the next book; for this one he will have to settle for my love and respect.

My father died as I was finishing the book. He would have liked to have seen the finished product, even if he had never heard of Newberry and was a Chrysler guy. This book is for him.

1

Just Politics

In 1918, Henry Ford quite nearly became a U.S. senator, representing Michigan and, to his mind, all of mankind. Having entered the race at the urging of President Woodrow Wilson, Ford made no campaign speeches or appearances. Such exertions would have been both unnecessary and uncomfortable. Thanks to the early advertising and wild success of the Model T, practically every man, woman, and child in the state and beyond knew his face and what they imagined was his signature. And everyone already knew what he stood for. Campaign literature, newspaper coverage, surrogate speakers, and, most of all, Ford's recent political projects made obvious his opposition to war. Once the United States had joined the bloodbath in Europe, Ford pivoted, enthusiastically supporting Wilson's plan for peace, while his company turned some of its assembly lines to building the instruments of war. He was a nonpolitician—even an antipolitician—who ran in both the Democratic and Republican primaries at a time when Progressive Era suspicions of politics still ran high. There were good reasons to wonder how Ford, terrified of public speaking and accustomed to giving orders that men obeyed, would function in a body known for endless talk and imperious egos. By only 8,500 out of more than 430,000 votes cast in the general election, Michigan denied the country the chance to find out.

The winner was Truman Handy Newberry, son of John S. Newberry, a former Republican congressman and a fixture among the Detroit elite, and grandnephew of Walter Newberry, who had made his fortune in Chicago banking and real estate. Active at the edges of

Republican politics, this Spanish-American War veteran had served as assistant secretary of the navy and, briefly, as secretary under Theodore Roosevelt. Newberry idolized TR, even if his own preferred position was on the sideline rather than in the arena. Business, not politics or adventure, occupied Newberry, and he shifted the family's investments into new areas, including Packard automobiles, one of the top luxury brands. Like Ford's, his campaign did without speeches and, taking Ford's silence one step further, without statements. Serving as assistant to the commandant of the Third Naval District, he was, mostly to his relief, not free to offer his views. But everyone knew where he stood, too. Campaign ads printed in nearly every newspaper in the state told the story. They showed the uniformed commander, a squat man, square straight on but more than a bit round in profile, positioned stiffly by his uniformed twin sons, staring ahead through his pince-nez glasses. Michigan voters would have to imagine what else he was, but they knew he was the anti-Ford: a nationalist who would follow Roosevelt and Senator Henry Cabot Lodge in opposition to the League of Nations in its current form. Whether he was a progressive (he had been a Roosevelt man in 1912) or a conservative or something else entirely (the war was changing the meanings of those labels) was anyone's guess.

Michigan voters would never learn much about his positions on most of the issues thrown up in the turbulent years after the war. Even before the Republican primary, in which Newberry defeated former governor Chase Osborn and Ford, investigators combed the state in search of election irregularities worth prosecuting. Wilson's Department of Justice was especially alert to violations of the federal campaign finance laws. Here was low-hanging fruit: it was nearly impossible in most states to make a credible race in a competitive primary and spend less than the $10,000 limit established by the 1911–1912 Federal Corrupt Practices Act (FCPA). But loopholes in the law ("doorways" might be a better metaphor) made prosecution tricky. The limits covered only the spending of the candidates themselves. Newberry's campaign committee spent nearly $200,000, most of it donated by friends and family. Newberry himself reported contributing and spending nothing. When a grand jury in New York, Newberry's wartime station, failed to return an indictment, Ford's own detective staff took charge. Picking a new federal prosecutor and friendly judge, Ford's assistants produced the evidence and a new theory of the case that resulted in the indictment and conviction of Newberry and members of his campaign committee.

That verdict did not survive the scrutiny of the Supreme Court. Still, Newberry's troubles were not over. Twice the Senate had considered whether seating Newberry would be an affront to its dignity. With another hearing looming after the 1922 elections had thinned the ranks of his supporters, Newberry had neither the stomach nor the votes to endure the next round. He resigned in 1922, satisfied with what he chose to believe was the Supreme Court's vindication, and with the justification that his important work was done. His election had helped defeat the League of Nations, and most of all had kept the madman Henry Ford out of the Senate.

The 1918 elections and the contests that followed were front-page news in Michigan and across the country. There were other close races that year, any one of which would have tipped the partisan balance in the Senate and the vote on the League of Nations, but none of those had the novelty of a celebrity candidate. And Ford was not merely famous. A bundle of paradoxes and, by the late 1910s, unfocused energy, Ford believed in the image he built for himself of a capitalist without greed or guile who embodied a simple, pastoral America. He had ideas, various and disjointed, about how to improve the lot of humanity beyond making a car ordinary people could afford, and an increasingly urgent itch to put them into action. Ford's wealth dwarfed Newberry's, yet he scorned rich men like Newberry as part of a parasitic and self-absorbed elite that created nothing and cheered on military adventures for the profits they generated. Newberry's world revolved around socializing at fancy private clubs, service on corporate boards, summering and wintering in the right places, and most of all, his family and equally prosperous friends. While he lacked the drive and bellicosity of some of his peers—his was not an especially strenuous life—he shared with them the call of military service, as it was the duty of the elite to serve their country. Ford may not have burned to be one among ninety-six equals in the Senate, but to give in and let Newberry take the seat would have been to condone what he believed was surely militarism, fraud, and the machinations of a Jewish conspiracy. Newberry persisted despite his precious name becoming synonymous with corruption. To do otherwise would have been to admit that his campaign had done wrong and to hand the seat to a pacifist loon.[1]

The quirks of the two men—their clashing personalities, politics, and place in upper-class culture—motivated them to press forward beyond where the sting of losing or the threat of embarrassment would have pushed one of them to quit. Each had plenty of money to hire high-priced legal teams (and, in Ford's case, a detective force, too). But the case was also not about them. First the Wilson administration and then the Senate advanced the Ford-Newberry contest for their own reasons. The Wilson administration had eagerly spied on and prosecuted what it saw as enemies of the nation at war—socialists, pacifists, and people who might have said something critical about Wilson or the war. It was not difficult to turn the machinery of investigation on potential enemies of the administration's plans for peace, as the nation and Wilson's plan were the same thing for some Wilsonians. The thought of a Senator Ford made some Senate Democrats queasy, but Ford would be a vote for the League if nothing else. Some insurgent Republicans were among the most adamant opponents of the League, but their well of outrage was deep enough to allow them to fight Newberry's seating, too.[2]

Insurgents had joined Democrats in supporting campaign finance regulations, arguing that big spending threatened free government and the Republic. For Republican regulars Newberry was a cause, a victim of hypocritical and politicized investigations. They fought for Newberry, even if some of them thought that his campaign spending was foolish overkill.

As the political and legal wrangling dragged on, and time removed Ford and the League of Nations from play, other questions took their place. The largest of them were the substance of representative democracy and what counted as justice in politics. Michigan voters had elected Newberry, knowing full well that his campaign had spent a lot of money. They saw the advertising it bought, read about it in the newspapers, heard the charges of excessive spending from the other campaigns, and knew that a grand jury had looked into the matter. If two-thirds of the senators could remove someone they disliked, in this case after numerous tries years after the election, what was the point of voting? Some senators, following Ford's cue, insisted that Newberry's campaign must have spent far more than the hefty sum disclosed, and that surely some of the money must have found classically corrupt uses, such as vote buying. Did Newberry's victory mean that money could buy elections, and that unless he was unseated only the wealthy could consider running for office in the future?

Newberry's campaign had taken pains to operate within the confines of the FCPA. But even if the campaign's spending was completely legal, was it right? Those who sought to remove Newberry argued that his campaign had violated the spirit of the law and commonsense morality, decency, and fairness, even if the spending was technically legal. Newberry's defenders believed that all the talk about political virtue masked a politically inspired persecution. They spent their time on the floor cleaning up after the critics' rhetorical excesses, returning the discussion to the letter of the law and the facts that the hearings had established. They concluded that politics, not righteousness, explained the original and continued interest in the seat Newberry had won. Democrats and insurgent Republicans might get through an appointment what they did not get in an election: a progressive Republican replacement, who might vote with Democrats on many issues. Failing that, Democrats had a safe issue—"Newberryism"—that united all of its sometimes quarreling factions. For Newberry and the regulars who stuck with him, the attacks were just politics, not an attempt to make politics just or fair.

Veterans of the 1910s seating controversies involving William Lorimer of Illinois and Isaac Stephenson of Wisconsin could nearly cut and paste from their earlier speeches. Those cases raised different issues—buying state legislators in the first and substantial spending before the FCPA became law in the second. Still, the major themes remained. One side warned of the dire future of the Republic if money ruled politics, while the other decried abandoning the rule of law in the service of obvious political purposes. One new element in the arguments about Newberry's seat was the FCPA, which had passed with assurances that the country had been protected from expensive campaigns. But the FCPA was never an effective legal or administrative instrument in taming the cost of campaigns. No matter: the Senate could and did judge the fitness of its members. The Newberry precedent inspired hearings examining the circumstances of other Senate elections, which in turn were part of a larger context of partisan and factional investigations in the 1920s. Newberry's resignation allowed him to beat a happy return to private life, but it settled none of the big questions.

This book reexamines the story of the 1918 election and the machinations that followed. It began its life as a miscalculation. I imagined that the Newberry case would supply a bit of background in a chapter on the FCPA, the guiding national legislation from the 1910s through the 1970s, in a larger study of campaign finance. Telling the story eventually overwhelmed the chapter as designed. Getting it as close to right as I could manage turned out to be more challenging and to include more angles than I had anticipated. Attorney Spencer Ervin's 1935 book on the case (the only full-length study) is a reliable guide through the legal morass. Otherwise, many of the secondary sources were thin or misleading. Biographies of Ford generally misremember this episode of his erratic career in public life, largely because they rely either on the archival collections connected with Ford or on Allan Nevins and Frank Ernest Hill's massive biography that did the same. Overviews of the history of campaign finance reform discuss Newberry's spending and the legal fallout, noting their role in rewriting the spectacularly ineffective FCPA. Yet, most everyone involved left records that fill in what happened, why it mattered, and how the stakes changed over time. They open out a case that lays out basic questions in the history of campaign finance and, more than that, post–Progressive Era politics and political culture.[3]

The Ford-Newberry contest generated the first full test of the purpose, meaning, and possible uses of the FCPA, the first national campaign finance legislation that aimed to rein in the amount of money in politics. Reformers claimed that limiting campaign spending was important, even in the absence of classic corruption such as vote buying. Expensive elections hinted at *potential* corruption and influence peddling. But even without real or shadow corruption, even if money bought the labor of campaign workers and advertising, high campaign costs were dangerous. Dollars might substitute for talent, giving mediocre candidates an edge, and advertising could corrupt the minds of voters. Spending limits, the argument went, both encouraged equality among candidates and protected voters from too much seductive publicity.

The early twentieth-century assumptions have persisted in the major attempts to reform the American campaign finance structure since the 1920s. While legislation in recent decades largely has aimed at contributions rather than spending, and the Supreme Court has weighed whether specific limits do damage to constitutional rights to free speech, Progressive Era ideas about money and politics continue to guide campaign finance reform, as political scientist Raymond La Raja points out. Some current reform proposals take their cue from the Court and look to schemes that would enlarge the base of small donors, abandoning concerns about how much money campaigns spend. Others look to create greater equality among campaigns through public funding or other mechanisms. While the methods differ, they share a concern with building citizens' trust in politics and politicians, which, they argue, money erodes by buying access to power, creating the appearance of special favors, or composing a limited menu of possible policy choices. Progressive Era reformers would recognize and applaud both the current reform agenda and the sense that money stands in the way of both better politics and voters believing that their participation matters.[4]

Critics then and now have doubted every one of the reform claims. In addition to their concerns about First Amendment rights, they imply that reform ought to generate mistrust rather than trust. Most if not all of the efforts to tame the "problem" of money in politics have been motivated by partisanship and insulating incumbents, not good government. Some critics have wondered whether money is much of a problem at all. It is difficult to directly link contributions and policy: individuals and groups connected with specific policies tend to bet on winners or to fund candidates who already support their views. Political advertising allows candidates to communicate directly with voters and creates name recognition for candidates who lack it. Before getting too worried, they suggest that we compare the relatively paltry sums spent on political advertising with the amounts companies lavish on getting us to buy beer, soft drinks, and snacks. Critics depict campaign finance reform less as an urgent democratic project than as a masquerade, with plain political self-interest disguised as the public good.[5]

The controversy about the Newberry campaign spending arose before anyone worried about the free speech rights of candidates or contributors. So debate focused entirely on whether or how big-spending campaigns corrupted politics. Some politicians reacted to the Newberry campaign spending with real outrage. They meant what they said: they believed costly campaigns corrupted the electorate in subtle and obvious ways. Yet, if money provided a suspect advantage in winning office, what about fame? Surely it is at least as helpful as cash in amplifying a political message or promoting a candidate. So are many other advantages that have little to do with ability or statesmanship. Putting aside race, gender, religion, and ethnicity, they include good looks, a compelling speaking style, and, most commonly, the perks and recognition that flow from incumbency. The Michigan Senate race put the questions squarely: How is money different from—actually worse than—other advantages candidates bring to campaigns? How exactly does it corrupt elections? Was money necessary to counteract almost perfect name recognition?

The questions lead back to the Congresses that passed the FCPA and debated changes to the law. The discussion of campaign finance reform featured soaring statements about the evils of money in politics but little engagement with substance. Critics who spoke raised quibbles or proposed tougher regulations. The promise was that campaign finance reform would make politics fairer and more representative of the people's real wishes by allowing unbought candidates of ordinary means to succeed. No one piped up to publicly defend the general proposition that big-spending campaigns might be acceptable or necessary. Those arguments only emerged when the Senate considered specific cases such as Newberry's. But drafting legislation that regulated something as fundamental to success on election days as campaign spending inevitably meant that congressmen considered their own interests and the prospects of their parties and factions. Democrats and insurgent Republicans, who anticipated some election day advantages, most loudly supported this round of campaign finance reform. But the votes for FCPA—the law and amendments passed in 1910 and 1911 and the 1920s revision—were usually unanimous. Congress managed both to signal disapproval of money in politics and to allow its members to adapt to the reality of ever more expensive campaigns.

The FCPA nonetheless had its uses in the 1920s, just not those mentioned in the legislation. Congress could investigate accusations of excessive spending while ignoring the pesky legal details that would be raised in a trial. Violators would escape the threat of jail time, true. But the odor of scandal might be attached to the target of investigation, and under perfect partisan conditions it was possible to deny a seat to a winning candidate whose spending threatened the honor and dignity of the Senate. The law need not force candidates to greatly change their campaigns, but capricious enforcement in the political branch was possible. Campaign finance reform proved to be a handy instrument of partisan and factional revenge for Democrats and progressive Republicans.

There was more to the FCPA and the Newberry case that tested and refined it than how well or poorly it contained the amount of money spent on campaigns. Because the FCPA was embedded in a wider effort to remake politics, its implementation illustrates the ironic consequences of the new rules and how politicians responded to the new electoral realities. Progressive Era reformers supported efforts to shift power to the people and away from the parties and their rich allies with laws that included primary elections, the direct election of senators, and campaign finance reform. Historians and political scientists have pointed out that we should not take reform rhetoric at face value. Politicians who knew their business wrote and supported these reforms. They understood what political scientists later codified and theorized: the rules shape which candidates have the best chance to succeed.[6]

Yet neither reformers nor party bosses could completely anticipate the consequences of the new laws. Attempts to weaken the parties and give voters direct control increased the costs of running for office. Money had to be raised for the sorts of things that parties once provided: labor and effective communication with voters. Candidates running in primaries had to purchase their own publicity as well as workers, who might work in general election campaigns as a matter of course but had their hands out for primary elections. Those in tight races had to buy quite a lot. They competed against not only their opponents but also new heroes from the movies, boxing rings, baseball diamonds, and business in gaining the attention of the public, whose participation in politics had been growing more and more fitful. Candidates still used tried-and-true campaign staples for reaching and persuading voters, but they now supplemented speeches, rallies, and literature with advertising and, increasingly, film. Progressive Era election law required hefty campaign budgets while also apparently forbidding them.

When reports of big-spending campaigns surfaced, advocates of campaign finance regulations were outraged, or at least did a convincing imitation. The legal and congressional inquiries they launched allowed them to express their indignation but also provide an insider's view of how reform had changed the business of electoral politics in the years between the party-centered nineteenth century and the candidate- and media-driven period later in the twentieth century. Primary races necessarily focused on candidates, not parties, and campaign managers competed for the best talent, experienced party workers, who in turn made their own calculations about fitness and electability. The FCPA limited candidates' contributions, but their campaigns worked around the law by creating committees that handled fund-raising and spending. Most campaign practices would have been familiar to a late nineteenth-century political professional—producing literature, engaging organizers who figured out how to distribute it, and organizing speaking tours. But in keeping with the trend toward professionalization, managers with expertise in public relations and fund-raising, the forerunners of modern consultants, increasingly took control in high-stakes campaigns.

Part of what drove both the increased costs and the utility of professional campaign management was a new media environment. If most nineteenth-century newspapers worked in tandem with party organizations in supplying the message and the motive for voter turnout, the managers of primary candidates could not assume good—or any—coverage and had to hustle for it. During the first half of the twentieth century, newspapers occupied a bit of a golden age between the dominance of the party press in the nineteenth century and the competition from television after the 1950s. In the 1910s and 1920s, many editors continued to tip their newspapers in the direction of one of the parties, but they were independent, accustomed to relying on advertising, not political patronage, for their revenues. Political writers adopted an above-mere-politics, analytical style. The judgment of editors mattered. Newspaper stories were free advertising, and how writers and editors shaped or slanted reporting might sway voters. Because political coverage no longer occupied the column inches it did in the days of the party press, the value of speeches and campaign events lay in their ability to generate press more than in rallying the faithful. Managers and candidates (some of them newspapermen themselves) cultivated contacts to encourage positive spin.[7]

They also communicated with voters directly through advertising. The advertising that the Newberry campaign bought in abundance struck some observers as doubly corrupt. It polluted voters' minds, an argument that echoed the distrust of a gullible public that went back to the beginning of popular democracy. The spectacle of international enthusiasm for the Great War, ginned up by the propaganda of governments, deepened some social scientists' and intellectuals' doubts about public rationality. Progressives put great stock in generating impartial decisions grounded in facts, and in intelligent voters weighing evidence about public men and questions without the distortion of partisanship. Advertising imperiled the hope for a rational, impartial electorate. And it created a problem beyond its apparent power to persuade. Did one source of such revenue—political advertising—destroy editors' judgment, especially in primaries? Were their endorsements, which mattered a great deal in party primaries, for sale?[8]

The power of advertising—and therefore the power of money—was among the major issues in the Newberry seating controversy and the ones that came before and after. Yet, power and control of the political agenda were also at stake. Senators eyed close elections and campaigns that spent what members deemed too much because the underlying conditions had not changed: Republicans remained factionalized, and insurgent Republicans held the balance of power. Viewed from the Senate, 1920s politics was not a return to normalcy, unless normal is the sort of partisan and factional fighting that we associate with the post-Watergate years.

This book follows the controversy as it unfolded. It begins with progressive reform of the political process and the remaking of campaigns. It then moves through the locations where the Ford-Newberry conflict played out. The first place is Detroit, where the two men's antipathy for each other began both in the city's elite culture and in Progressive Era politics. Next is Michigan. The high stakes of the campaign, the presence of Ford, and the national spotlight— all in a state where the Republican Party was already factionalized—created the expense of the Newberry campaign and the desperation on all sides. The controversy at the end of the exceedingly close general election then moved to Washington, for a recount, argument before the Supreme Court, and Senate hearings. Newberry's terrifically efficient campaign manager demonstrated what could be done even with a silent candidate who took no positions on issues. That might have been unnerving enough to sitting senators. The Newberry case invited them, all of whom now faced voters rather than state legislators, to play to the grandstands. The concluding chapter traces the fate of the FCPA, as federal campaign finance legislation mattered only in Senate hearings and then only through the 1920s.

In 1935, Spencer Ervin subtitled his book on Ford and Newberry *The Famous Senate Election Contest*. Fame proved fleeting. Unlike, for example, the Teapot Dome scandal, this case provided neither a neat morality tale nor a symbol for the period. Yet the case deserves new attention. My purpose is not to excavate a tale of the evil power of money in politics or to condemn the hypocrisy of campaign finance reform, although readers can find evidence for both. It is to examine how politicians found their footing in a new electoral environment and created modern campaigns. Most of all, it is to pry apart two persistent strains in American political culture—suspicion of money in politics and suspicion of politics itself. For insurgent Republicans and Democrats, the investigations were one way of returning justice and purity to politics that had been corrupted and confused by money and party loyalty. For regular Republicans, the investigations violated a different sense of justice, one connected to the rule of law. And they described the investigatory fury as just politics—mere politics that covered mundane motives with a scrim of principle. The controversy may no longer be famous, but it outlines classic appeals to cynicism and principle in American politics and the blurry lines between the two.

2

Detroit

No one was as convinced of the genius of Henry Ford as Henry Ford. His spectacular success proved just how right his gut instincts were. A farmer's son with a love for machinery, a grudge against horses, and a few winters' worth of formal education, Ford walked to Detroit in 1879. The series of jobs that followed gave him experience with engines, which fascinated him. He worked on experimental cars in his spare time; after a few failed ventures, he built a company that sold more cars than all of his American rivals. When other makers seemed incapable of building a car priced within reach of most Americans, in 1908 Ford introduced the Model T. With it he changed both the industry and American society. Ford rapidly became a legend, the everyman industrialist who made everyman's car. Unpretentious, plainspoken, and full of praise for rural life, he seemed to embody the values of an America of a simpler time, even as he equally symbolized the modern consumer culture and cult of celebrity. With a sophisticated sense of public relations, Ford marketed himself as a regular guy unconcerned about wealth and its trappings, since the image helped sell cars. Mail poured in from fans around the world. Ford was the most famous man in America, surpassing even his idol, Thomas Edison.[1]

The man was much more complicated than the legend. Fifty-five years old in 1918, he was tall, lean, and fit, with sharp features and gray eyes that flashed from kindly to cold to completely distracted within a second. Even those who worked closely with Ford believed they understood him only until he proved them wrong.

For all his wealth and celebrity, his resentments ran deep and his suspicions bordered on paranoia. He retained the countryside's abiding hostility to the upper crust and especially "Wall Street," bankers, and stockholders, whom he sometimes referred to as Jews. And having perfected the automobile and its assembly, he cast about for new projects, succumbing to the tempting idea that accomplishment in one area brought expertise in all. Those ventures included politics. There, Ford's legend and the complications underneath it made high elected office well within reach—and a dangerous prospect.

No legend trailed Truman Newberry. Outside of the tight circle of family and equally well-off friends, only devotees of the society pages would have even heard of him. Between rounds of golf, sailing, and social obligations, he attended to his varied businesses. In finding new ventures for investment, Newberry followed Henry B. Joy, his brother-in-law and millionaire son of a railroad executive. One initiative was purchasing Packard, which became a maker of luxury cars with the speed, style, and comfort to suit passengers on their way to the club. Another project, the Michigan Naval Brigade, combined a love for the water with worries about America's ability to defend itself. On an inspection tour of the brigade, Theodore Roosevelt, then assistant secretary of the navy, met Newberry and saw potential and too much of himself in the rich, well-educated Detroiter. Newberry never forgot the meeting and would follow nearly anywhere TR led. That included the Spanish-American War, in which Newberry's naval service included just enough danger to be memorable without undo unpleasantness. TR also provided political inspiration, although Newberry clung to the gentleman's aversion to the professional politician that TR overcame. Neither reform issues nor Republican Party politics inspired much passion in Newberry. He would be pulled into public life, an uncomfortable place for a private man, out of duty and a touch of vanity.

Newberry and Ford had this in common: both were rich and were part of an industry that was changing Detroit and the nation. There it stopped. They occupied different Detroits. Ford scorned the city Newberry inhabited, the city of private clubs, golf, charitable institutions, and pleasant small talk. That elite matched Ford's pointed effort to separate himself from them with their own bemused (or horrified) contempt. There things might have rested, with both sides counting slights and slinging insults, a gossipy topic at the

Detroit Club and an occasional news story. But the paths Ford and Newberry took through progressive politics and World War I turned private barbs into increasingly public fights.

When Elihu and Rhoda Phelps Newberry brought their five-year-old son, John Staughton, to Michigan in the 1830s, Detroit was a town of about 5,000 inhabitants, in what people then considered the West. John lived to see Detroit become a regional commercial center, where makers of railroad cars, carriages, cigars, and packaged seeds set up shop and investors in timber and iron ore became rich. Like many among the tens of thousands with the "Michigan fever" in the great land boom of the 1830s, the Newberrys came from New York State, which in turn was a stop on the way west out of the New England states. In 1802, Elihu's father, Amasa, a captain in the Continental army, gave up trying to support his ten children on a worn-out farm in Windsor, Connecticut, where the Newberry family had settled in the 1630s. All but one of Amasa's children scattered from their new home in Oneida County, New York. Six of Amasa's sons went to Michigan. Elihu settled in Romeo, where he farmed and ran a store; two sons died exploring northern Michigan. Henry, Oliver, and especially Walter had an eye for new transportation technology and the land that transportation links would make valuable. First investing in steamships, then railroads, and, for Walter, Chicago real estate, the brothers prospered, Walter hugely so.[2]

John did not see an inheritance from Walter's holdings in his lifetime. He amassed a fortune anyway. Graduating at the top of his class at the University of Michigan, he briefly tried engineering before turning to the law, building a reputation in the Great Lakes region in an admiralty practice. Real wealth, however, arrived through his connection with James McMillan, the son of a Canadian railroad owner. John abandoned his legal practice in 1863 and won a contract for building railroad cars for the Union army. With the considerable boost from wartime business, the Michigan Car Company, with Newberry as president and McMillan as treasurer, thrived. It was just the beginning of a lucrative partnership. Together, the two men's holdings were varied and vast, including interests in banking, street railways, seeds, timber, iron, and smelting (a town in Michigan's Upper Peninsula took its name from Newberry, with the major streets named after his children). McMillan's holdings, both with Newberry and with a web of associates and family members, made him "the most influential businessman in late nineteenth-century Detroit."[3]

Newberry's business interests traced the main lines of Michigan's and Detroit's economic advance. The Erie Canal, steamships, plank roads, and railroads made it possible to develop the products of the state's farms, mines, and factories and to get them to markets in the East. Those same resources created a diverse industrial base in Detroit. What once were immense stands of white pine left Saginaw as lumber for the East; copper and iron ore finds built boomtowns in the Upper Peninsula; hardwoods became furniture in Grand Rapids; and wheat, dairy, fruit, and vegetables fed the nearby and more distant cities. Taking advantage of the resources near at hand, Detroit's factories turned out heat and cook stoves, carriages, railroad cars, ships, shoes, cigars, and packaged seeds, while the city remained a regional transportation and banking hub. Detroit may not have provided the wealth that John Newberry's uncle Walter found in Chicago, but his fortune grew with the expanding city.[4]

Between 1860 and 1880, Detroit's population more than doubled. The effects of the New England and New York migration were still evident, but immigrants, chiefly Canadian, Irish, and German, joined them and a small (under 3 percent) African American population. By the 1890s, Polish and eastern European immigrants looked for work in the city's factories. And in those factories worker discontent with wages, hours, and working conditions inspired organization and strikes. The most spectacular of these was in 1886. Some factory owners agreed to workers' demand for a nine-hour day. But when the Michigan Car Works fired a Knights of Labor organizer and laid off 125 men on May 3, thousands of workers from a wide range of industries struck. A few firms settled with the strikers. Even Michigan Car offered a nine-hour day, although tied to a wage reduction. The strike dragged on, ending only when the company brought in strikebreakers. The moment of widespread worker cooperation faded, and unions would butt up against a strongly open-shop town until the 1930s.[5]

Labor unrest and a population more diverse than the old crowd of Yankees and Yorkers challenged the standing political as well as industrial arrangements. True to his New England roots, John S. Newberry joined the Republican Party after the collapse of the Whigs. Led by Zachariah Chandler, a New Hampshire transplant deeply opposed to slavery, Republicans dominated the state after the birth of the party in 1854, when it won the governor's office and a majority in the state legislature. Newberry served as provost marshal in Detroit during the war, overseeing two drafts and one draft riot that targeted the small black population. He remained active enough in the party to run for a House seat against a Democratic incumbent (and Civil War general) in 1878. The *Detroit Free Press,* then a Democratic Party organ, described Newberry as rich and respected but cold, a man with "fewer warm personal friends than any respectable citizen his age in the community." He won, according to the *Free Press,* because of a "lavish expenditure of money," along with divisions among Democrats. In a Congress with a Democratic majority and Greenback party freshmen pushing hard for inflationary policies, he opposed anything more radical than matching the gold and silver held by the Treasury with circulating notes. The pace of work—or lack of work—in the days when a small number of House members could stop everything with a filibuster or by refusing to answer a quorum call had to frustrate a businessman accustomed to doing things. He refused the offer to run for reelection, believing that he had been shut out of patronage decisions by the state's two Republican senators, and therefore denied the chance to reform the Detroit customs house. That decision doomed any further political career as far as Detroit Republicans were concerned, although there were rumors that Newberry wanted to run for the Senate and was under consideration as secretary of the navy in 1880.[6]

James McMillan proved to be far more politically ambitious and skilled than his business partner. McMillan gradually took control of the party after Chandler's death in 1879, positioning it in support of economic protection and business. Deft, judicious, and willing to invest some of his money in the party (he kept it financially afloat on a number of occasions), McMillan was an "easy boss," neatly coordinating federal patronage and the concerns of regional factions and economic interests. He, not Newberry, went to the Senate. Still, a thread of antimonopoly sentiment had long run through Michigan politics, and when coupled with demographic and economic upheaval, Republican control of the state cracked. While Michigan remained a Republican state in presidential elections, the party lost the races for governor in 1882 and 1884, as the Greenback and Prohibition Party votes tipped the elections to a Democrat. Michigan Republicans owed what unity they mustered through the 1890s to McMillan. He knew when to bend in order not to break the party. It was clear that Hazen Pingree, the popular reform mayor of Detroit, was the party's best hope for winning the governor's race in 1896 and bringing in a full Republican vote for presidential candidate William McKinley. McMillan disliked and distrusted Pingree's populism, but he approved Pingree's nomination. McMillan held control until his death in 1902.[7]

Newberry's alliance with McMillan went beyond business and politics: Newberry had at least one close personal friend. They built fine Italianate brick mansions near each other on Detroit's fashionable East Jefferson Avenue, the elite neighborhood since the 1850s, close to downtown and the two men's offices and businesses. It was also close to the river, where they docked their steam-powered yacht, the *Truant,* so they had easy access by water to their Grosse Pointe cottages. Built in 1875, the same year as the East Jefferson Avenue houses, "Lake Terrace," the twin three-story houses, were at the early edge of a building boom in summer homes for Detroit's new industrial and banking elite. Newberry and McMillan also teamed up on charities, founding, for example, the Grace Homeopathic Hospital.[8]

Truman Handy Newberry, born November 5, 1864, was the second son of John's second marriage. His first, to Harriet Newell Robinson in 1856, ended with her death ten days after the birth of their son, named Harrie in her memory. John met Helen P. Handy, daughter of a Cleveland banking magnate, on a business trip, and they married in 1859. John and Helen's first son died at birth. Truman was next, followed by John S. Jr. and Helen.[9]

Truman recalled a childhood that revolved around the Jefferson Avenue Presbyterian Church, where his father led the singing. There was sailing on the *Truant,* and plays and skits performed by those on board. There was a succession of private boarding schools, first a military academy outside Detroit and then a French-language school in New York. He continued his studies at Yale's Sheffield Scientific School. Both Newberry sons focused on science and engineering in college, as their father had, in preparation for business careers. Truman remembered Yale as "a very happy experience." He met his "best friend for life," Charles MacAvoy, and joined a fraternity and the Republican club. He kept score for the baseball team.[10]

At a Yale football game, Truman met his future wife, Harriet Barnes (known in the family as Violet, her middle name), whose father headed the American Book Company in New York. They married in February 1888. The Newberry family was a tight clan that moved as a pack. Consider the new couple's wedding trip. The first stop was Montreal, but upon learning of the death of Violet's grandfather they went to Brooklyn for the funeral. In the aftermath of the Great Blizzard of 1888, they boarded an ocean liner for Europe that carried only twenty-five passengers, nine of whom were with the Newberry party. Truman's mother and sister and their maid, and three friends (including a McMillan) and their maid, joined the couple. When they reached Paris, the bride's father and mother, Harrie Newberry and his family, and Truman's brother John met them. Decades later, Newberry related nothing about the trip itself except the list of travelers and the complaint that he "had all the cares of the finances and the bookkeeping for the party, but the courier that we had gave some help in that respect."[11]

Newberry had some practice watching the family finances. He had taken responsibility for the family's holdings the year before, when John S. Newberry died. He may have, as a *New York Times* obituary claimed, begun his "career in overalls," learning the railroad business from the bottom up, but the apprenticeship was short. Harrie, who had also taken his place in one of his father's businesses, was bypassed, and the twenty-two-year-old Truman assumed control of most of his father's firms (his brother John also had been placed in one), the investment portfolio, and a protracted tussle over Walter Newberry's estate. The John S. Newberry fortune alone was considerable—an estate of roughly $4.25 million, of which $500,000 went to various charities. "My mother's wisdom was great," Newberry wrote, "for from the day of her husband's death . . . she treated me as head of the family and accorded me judgment, respect and consideration. She let me conduct affairs which she said later always proved correct."[12]

Newberry had reason to look back upon his stewardship of the family's resources without being able to suppress an uncharacteristic boast. While no visionary, he did well, expanding the Newberry investments in new, profitable ventures, such as beet sugar, Michigan Bell Telephone, and Parke, Davis and Company pharmaceuticals, while modernizing the operations of Detroit Steel and Spring. He sat on the boards of two banks, a New York insurance company, a shipping firm, and various manufacturers.

In 1902, Newberry and others in the city's elite circle crammed the equipment of the Warren, Ohio, Packard Electric Company into nine freight cars and hauled to Detroit what became the Packard Motor Car Company. Henry Joy and Newberry were impressed with the car after seeing one perform in New York. When Joy searched for partners for the Packard venture, he did not have to look much beyond his brother-in-law Newberry and other members of the Yondotega Club, the most exclusive of the half dozen Detroit clubs Newberry and his friends organized and led. The company built one of the era's premier luxury cars. Packard positioned itself, according to its early promotional literature, as "a gentleman's car, built by gentlemen." Packard built cars for presidents, movie stars, royalty, and, closer to home, people like Newberry and his friends, a tight-knit, provincial group linked by club memberships, intermarriage, and business partnerships. "Ask the Man Who Owns One," Packard's long-running slogan implored, inviting prospective buyers to learn about the company's technological innovations and quality from its quality owners. Soon Joy was general manager and president, and James Packard was on the sidelines. The energetic and charismatic Joy used his position at Packard as platform for pronouncements on tariffs (high was good), prohibition, military preparedness, and good roads (including making a cross-country drive to promote the Lincoln Highway), when he was not following his interests in radio and aviation. Newberry, a board member, once urged the directors to try to market a less expensive car in the interest of sales and profits but otherwise contentedly handed the lead to Joy.[13]

Newberry lived larger than his father had. By the early twentieth century, industry and an exploding working-class population drew closer to East Jefferson. The city's recently minted fortunes built new houses in the Boston-Edison development or in the suburbs. The sons of what now seemed like old money moved to Grosse Pointe. Newberry stayed on in the city longer than many of his peers, but in the 1910s he built "Drybrook," a Georgian-style limestone and brick mansion in Grosse Pointe Farms. Built for entertaining on a grand scale, its music room (with a pipe organ) extended into outdoor space large enough for the Detroit Symphony. Keeping friends and family close, Henry Joy, Truman's brother-in-law as of 1892, built his own estate nearby. They also bought summer cottages at Watch Hill, Rhode Island. When traveling on business, Newberry used his memberships in the Chicago Club, "which included in its membership many of my classmates and Chicago friends," and, in New York, the University Club, the Yacht Club, the Union Club, the St. Anthony Club, and the Recess Club. His family merited mention in the New York Times society pages, noting their arrival at Watch Hill, his daughter Carol's debut into society, and the exploits of his twin sons, Phelps and Barnes.[14]

While surely a member of what historian Michael McGerr called the "upper ten," Newberry avoided the ostentation and temptation to flaunt middle-class moral codes that made the very rich a target for progressives. In Newberry's circle, good people did not throw ostentatious costume parties or get divorced. Violet Newberry was active in the thoroughly middle-class temperance campaign and a needlework guild that directed its work at charity. Truman appeared every inch an Edwardian gentleman, someone who would have left a seat on a *Titanic* lifeboat for a woman or child. No leader or innovator, he was a nice man with the manners and sense of obligation that spoke of good breeding. John S. Newberry would not have been ashamed of his sober and responsible son.[15]

Ford was a leader and an innovator. Looking back, those who knew him as a boy saw the marks of his latter success, even if his beginnings were not nearly as auspicious as Newberry's. Born in 1863, Henry was the second son (the first died in infancy) of William and Mary Ford. William had arrived in the United States in 1847, a twenty-one-year-old fleeing poverty and famine in Ireland with his parents and six brothers and sisters. Two of his uncles had migrated thirty years earlier. The Fords settled near them, in Springfield Township (later Dearborn). With the generous help of Henry Maybury, William Ford's father bought an eighty-acre farm. When he prepared to retire, William and one of his brothers each purchased a half. William prospered, eventually expanding his forty acres to more than 200. Feeling secure enough to start a family, in 1861 he married Mary Litogot O'Hern, the adopted daughter of a well-off farmer in Dearborn.[16]

Henry would be followed by five brothers and sisters, and he especially was raised with a gentle hand. He had slack the other children did not enjoy—sleeping in, staying up late tinkering with watches, and disappearing before finishing onerous farm chores. The one stroke of tragedy was his mother's death when Henry was thirteen. If some of the lightness and spirit left the family with her, Henry's status in the household as a special child remained. His love and intuitive understanding of machines attached itself especially to self-propelled vehicles, such as a steam-powered cart he saw on a trip to Detroit with his father. Machines far outstripped his interest in formal education, which began with McGuffey readers and, apart from some business and mechanical drawing courses, ended with them.

At age fifteen, Henry walked to Detroit to continue his mechanical education. Staying with relatives, he first found work at McMillan and Newberry's Michigan Car Company. He was fired six days later. But using his father's connections, he quickly found a new job, and better ones followed. What mattered more were off-hours (and work hours) experimenting with engines. Ford returned to the farm twice, but in 1891 he moved to Detroit for good. He brought his wife, Clara Jane Bryant, whom he had met at a dance in Dearborn and married three years later, in 1888. Their only child, a son, Edsel, was born in 1893, while Ford worked for Detroit Edison. The young family lived in a rented house with a workshop near the plant.

Even as a teenager without a record of success, Ford had a magical charm—a charisma that sprang from his fierce belief in his ideas—that persuaded friends to work for free, carrying out his plans. "I never saw him make anything," one of the men who helped Ford recalled. "He was always doing the directing." Ford, along with scores of Detroit machinists, bicycle enthusiasts, and engineers (the city's railcar and stove industries meant that there was a lot of skill hanging around in the city), set his sights on building a motorized carriage. He succeeded in 1896. After busting an opening large enough for the 500-pound carriage on bicycle wheels to exit the workshop, Ford took a short drive around Detroit. He was not the first to devise a working internal combustion engine. He was not even the first in Detroit. What mattered was that the contraption was a beginning for better designs.[17]

It was promising enough to attract the attention of a tony group of investors, including Democratic mayor William C. Maybury (a relative of the financial benefactor of Ford's grandfather) and men associated with some of Detroit's major businesses. But with little to show for their (less than magnificent) stake—one truck and no profits—Detroit Automobile Company dissolved in 1901. A few members of the group still believed, and financed a new venture, the Henry Ford Company. Ford, more interested in building a car that would break speed records than one that would make money for the stockholders, frustrated his backers. Ford resigned in 1902, vowing to "never again" be bound to other men's ideas, and carrying with him his name, $900, and his race car design.[18]

With two failed businesses behind him, Ford for this third try turned to investors well below the thin air that Newberry, Joy, and the McMillan families breathed. Alex Malcomson, a coal dealer, and his relatives and business acquaintances held the largest stake. The most consequential stockholders were the Dodge brothers, Horace and John, who took 10 percent of the company in exchange for parts and a loan, and James Couzens, who acted as the general manager of Malcomson's company. He would later do the same, still without title, for Ford. This time, Ford called the shots. When Malcomson urged Ford to follow the successful Model A and Model B with more expensive and luxurious cars, Ford forced him out.

In 1908, Ford introduced the Model T. Before the T, driving was more a rich man's recreation than ordinary transportation. Powerful and stylish cars had not displaced the horse: something had to pull them out of the ditches of the largely dirt and stone roads of America. With its high wheelbase, the Model T could handle rutted roads and with accessories even could be pressed into service in plowing and providing power to farms. It was cheap, simple, and durable. Offering features associated with far more expensive cars, the Model T was within reach of the middle class, and soon enough farmers and the working class. Squeezing every possible efficiency out of mass production, Ford dropped the price of the Model T from its $850 debut to $250 in 1927, when it was discontinued. (By contrast, a hand-built Packard cost more than $4,000.) Ford cut prices even when the demand for the car outstripped supply. His Highland Park factory attracted rivals eager to adopt Ford's methods as well as tourists who marveled at the choreography of men and machines. The "Tin Lizzie," easily repaired by anyone with a modicum of mechanical skill, made the automobile an essential part of American life.[19]

The Model T would have made Ford rich and famous. But his successful attack on an automobile consortium that claimed to hold the patent on the internal combustion engine moved him toward stardom—an industrialist who would fight monopoly in the interest of consumers. At issue was a patent for gasoline engines filed in 1879 by George B. Selden, an attorney and inventor, and the Electric Vehicle Company. A group of companies formed the Association of Licensed Automobile Manufacturers (ALAM), which struck a deal with Selden. Members paid a royalty of 1.25 percent for every car sold, with the money divided among Selden, the Electric

Vehicle Company, and ALAM. The association, in turn, had the power to admit—and therefore to reject—new members. Led by Packard and Olds, the ALAM discovered few newcomers that met their high standards. The ALAM sought to bring order to a chaotic industry and to maintain prices, not to welcome new competition.[20]

Ford knew he had no chance. Besides, the whole patent idea just seemed wrong: What had Selden or the Electric Vehicle Company ever built or sold? So Ford braced for the inevitable suit. The ALAM brought it in 1904, and for more than seven years, from the Models A and B through the wildly successful launch of the Model T, it moved through the courts. Newberry's brother-in-law and Packard president Henry Joy was especially adamant that ALAM pursue Ford. Both sides also fought in the court of public opinion, lobbing full-page ads at each other. The ALAM warned of the consequences of buying or selling unlicensed cars. Ford ads, prepared by Couzens, declared, "While I am at the head of the Ford Motor Company, there will be no price that would induce me to permit my name" to be added to the list of ALAM members. Ford won that battle. Eventually standing nearly alone against the industry, Ford seemed to be fighting the auto "trust" that blocked competition and jacked up prices. Ford, according to the *Detroit Free Press*, "presents a spectacle to win the applause of all men with red blood; for the world loves a fighting man, and needs him, too, if we are to go forward." A federal district court in New York decided in favor of ALAM. On appeal, however, Ford won on every point.[21]

The case was dry and technical. But Ford emerged from the suit as the consumer's hero against the trusts at a time when antimonopoly feelings ran strong. He became famous not only as a manufacturer of a popular car but as an industrialist who cared more about people than profits. His victory, too, perhaps gave him too much confidence in the courts as an effective advertising venue for Henry Ford.

The Selden suit doomed the already unlikely prospect of Ford being welcomed into Detroit's elite circles. That group congregated in the city's exclusive clubs and built and supported hospitals, charities, and cultural institutions, adding a symphony to the existing art institute, announcing Detroit's arrival as a major city. Attempts to involve Ford and Couzens in Detroit's charitable endeavors ended in frustration on both sides. Ford did not believe in charity—it destroyed self-reliance—but he was generous when he retained control. When he found himself heading a fund-raising drive for a hospital, the project lagged. Ford did not hang around the Yondotega Club asking rich men for subscriptions. To avoid embarrassment, he paid for the hospital himself; members of his family populated the board. As the benefactor of Henry Ford Hospital, he instituted a low fee schedule that promptly annoyed doctors. Funding hospitals was no different than building cars: Ford either controlled everything or did nothing at all.[22]

Ford and Couzens built substantial homes in the Boston-Edison district, part of which Newberry had sold to developers. But Ford's house soon seemed a bit small and closed in. Clara and Henry considered Grosse Pointe, but instead they built a fifty-six-room mansion on the Rouge River. The limestone house had its own power plant and 1,300 acres for gardening, walks, and bird-watching. There were no snooty neighbors to disturb the Fords.[23]

If the Selden case was Ford's first bow as a figure who was more than a mere automaker, Newberry's entrance into public life was less dramatic and more ambiguous. The jovial Newberry would have remained a fixture in Detroit boardrooms, devoted to family and his friends and associates at the Yondotega Club, if not for his naval service in the Spanish-American War. Preparation began in 1893 with the formation of the Michigan Naval Brigade, with Newberry, Joy, and other elite Detroiters urging the state legislature to establish the reserve. Like similar units in other states, it was the naval version of the National Guard, inspired by the idea that the U.S. Navy was so pathetic that state volunteer groups had to fill the gaping holes in the nation's defenses. The units trained in the summers, first with antiquated cutters and steamers, and then, with the intervention of Michigan senator Julius Burrows and assistant secretary of the navy, Theodore Roosevelt, the less outdated wooden-hulled *Yantic*, which first saw service in the Civil War. Under the direction of Commander Gilbert Wilkes, who had actual naval experience, the reserve trained for a few weeks each summer. The cruise always included a stop at Mackinac Island, by then a well-known resort. There was more fun than privation for the young scions of Detroit. On the 1895 cruise, Newberry led the crew in singing pirate songs. Detroit mayor Hazen Pingree wondered why the state spent money on the "champagne reserves." He suggested giving those men "Gatling guns to protect

Grosse Pointe Farms from the rest of the country with its common herd," which he thought was their real worry.[24]

The ever-aggressive assistant secretary of the navy, angling for war with Spain over Cuba and despairing that it might never come, inspected the Michigan reserves in 1897. TR saw more potential than Pingree had, describing the Detroit unit as having the efficiency and professionalism of a regular naval unit, and "worthy of the gratitude . . . of every patriotic citizen." The regular and reserve units such as Michigan's protected Americans adequately, "provided only that in time of peace, the people are not misled by the sinister folly of demagogues or the timidity and selfishness of those too short-sighted to look ahead, into preparations for war." Newberry joined the cheers for Roosevelt's red-meat speech. He had the chance to extend his meeting with Roosevelt, since after returning to Detroit from Chicago, TR hitched a ride on Newberry's yacht to Buffalo, the next inspection stop.[25]

TR soon got his wish for war and went to Cuba with his own regiment, the Rough Riders, a mix of college men and cowboys. Newberry went, too, blockading ports rather than charging up hills. When the reserves were called, the Michigan unit could send only 155 men, and Lieutenant Newberry, acting commander in the absence of Wilkes, winnowed down the unit on the basis of "good physique and health and intelligence," as well as time in service. Newberry's friends who had been with the brigade from the beginning—many of them club men—made the cut. Those going to Norfolk, Virginia, included Cyrus Lothrop, Strathearn Hendrie, Henry Joy, Edwin Denby, J. Walter Drake, and John S. Newberry Jr., along with forty-six students and faculty from the University of Michigan.[26]

Their ship, the converted freighter *Yosemite*, saw two notable bits of action. The first was a controversial incident of inaction. Ordered to intercept a Spanish freighter loaded with provisions, the captain of the *Yosemite*, William H. Emory, did not move from his cabin after the men on watch sighted their prey and, according to Henry Joy, repeatedly relayed the location of the target. Gilbert Wilkes, the officer on watch duty, shouldered the blame for the *Yosemite's* failure. The next assignment brought more danger and glory. The *Yosemite* replaced the *St. Paul*, a regular navy steel-hulled cruiser, which was low on coal and had sustained some damage while blockading the port at San Juan. The *Yosemite*, an unarmored ship, was left to patrol the harbor alone until a heavier vessel could replace it. The port was well defended by the big guns at Morro Castle, overlooking the bay, two cruisers, a gunboat, and the torpedo boat that had damaged the *St. Paul.* The *Yosemite* pursued merchant ships by day and maneuvered out of the way of danger at night. But one night, the *Yosemite* took on a steamer that charged for the cover of the guns at Morro Castle. The *Yosemite* gave chase, damaging the steamer but drawing fire from the shore batteries. Shells hit close enough to spray the decks. The two Spanish cruisers and torpedo boat joined the battle. Lacking a better option, the *Yosemite* attacked, damaging one of the cruisers, before the Spanish ships withdrew. The *Yosemite* continued its lone blockade for another three weeks.[27]

The war linked Newberry to TR and pushed Newberry into his half-hearted political career. Newberry's introduction to politics happened when he was twenty-one. He and Cyrus Lothrop decided to "take on civic work," so they asked the boss of the Fifth Ward how they could be helpful. The "Irishman by the name of O'Shea" made them election inspectors. Leaving no cliché behind, sure enough, Newberry recalled seeing someone stuffing ballot boxes. He ran off to warn O'Shea. "'Never mind, my boy, we aren't going to use that ballot box, the one we are going to use is fixed up under the table,'" said O'Shea, at least in Newberry's recollection. His day as an election inspector "put an end to my aspirations in local politics," a corrupt endeavor unfit for the upright and well-bred. What interests he had were progressive, despite the old family ties and current friendships with the McMillan circle. "I'd sooner see almost anyone elected senator other than Burrows," he told a reporter in 1899. He broke from the conservative wing of the party also by favoring new railroad taxes and other measures supported by Governor Pingree. He wondered loudly enough about a run for Congress in 1904 to gain newspaper attention. According to Newberry (and a newspaper reporter), Roosevelt urged Newberry to get in. When Newberry explained that his district was unlikely to send a Republican to Congress, Roosevelt brought him up short. "'Truman, it is the things in this life that are so hard to do that are worth doing,'" Roosevelt said. "'Anyone can do the easy things.'" The remark "greatly influenced my whole life," Newberry claimed.[28]

Heeding Roosevelt's counsel, Newberry ran. Sort of. Edwin Denby, Newberry's shipmate and friend (and future secretary of the navy), had already announced his candidacy. When Newberry returned in September from his summer vacation and confirmed that he was running, it was not clear why he was exerting himself. Asked about revisions to Michigan's primary election laws, Newberry boldly claimed that he favored reform "so that it would be more practical. The principal is all right and it requires only experience to show us just how the statute ought to be amended." A supporter claimed that Newberry would run as someone who understood industry, which was, of course, important in the district. Aside from backing the removal of tariff barriers with Canada, he offered little discussion of national issues. The primary election against Denby was "not one in which such matters are involved," he claimed. The choice for voters, he joked, was between "a fat lawyer" and "a fat businessman." When his district picked the lawyer, Newberry did not seem heartbroken. "'They have elected a good man,'" he said, and promised his support. The *Detroit Free Press* chalked up Denby's victory to the 300 "personal friends, former college friends, and athletes who worked like beavers" for him. Newberry men thought it had more to do with nasty infighting among factional leaders in the district. One side backed Newberry; the other, including James O. Murfin, supported Denby.[29]

It was a small world. Murfin managed Denby's campaign and would be Newberry's Michigan attorney in the legal battles following the 1918 election. Newberry claimed he told TR one reason he had not gotten involved in politics was that electing a Republican in Detroit was impossible. But Denby won the November election in John S. Newberry's old district, beating Democratic incumbent Alfred Lucking. A longtime party activist and a law partner of former mayor Maybury, Lucking went on to handle legal matters for Henry Ford and his company, including the 1918 election contest.[30]

Newberry reflected TR's military if not insurgent spirit, and as president, Roosevelt kept Newberry in public life. In 1905, Newberry became assistant secretary of the navy. "Do not care what your title is as you have the work to do," Roosevelt told Newberry. "You will have the Secretaryship a little later." Because secretaries of the navy came and went under Roosevelt, who no doubt believed that job was his too, the assistant secretary did have work to do. The navy was in the midst of a period of reform, modernization, and expansion, and managing that fell to Newberry. Newberry gained the gratitude of sailors by relaxing the rules that had put a crimp into shore leave at a few ports and reorganized office and port operations. He managed the logistical details of the voyage of Roosevelt's Great White Fleet. He took charge of a particularly ticklish reorientation of promotion criteria and the transport of a dry dock halfway around the world. A "rotund, jolly fellow, highly educated and with polished manners," according to a *Washington Post* profile, Newberry brought business efficiency to his department, approaching it as if it were a "railroad or a big department store." With no patience for "cliques," he gained the trust of officers and became more popular with them than the secretary.[31]

While Newberry mediated between Roosevelt's ambitions and the navy bureaucracy, he and his family were a hit in Washington society. Purchasing a house on Sixteenth Street, they entertained frequently and graciously. The Newberrys in turn made the rounds of Washington receptions, dinners, balls, and charitable events. Their daughter, Carol, made her debut in society in 1907 and christened the USS *Michigan* in 1908. The Newberry teenage twin sons managed to find trouble, with TR's son Archie needing medical care after a roller-skating accident.[32]

Newberry did become secretary, Roosevelt's sixth in his seven-year presidency, but not until December 1908, at the end of Roosevelt's term. Newberry wanted to stay on, but Roosevelt's successor, William Howard Taft, offered him an ambassadorship instead. He declined the chance to move to Russia. Rumors circulated that he might run for the Republican Senate nomination against Burrows (as the "barrel," that is, the big-money, candidate in one account). But returning with his family to Detroit, he turned his attention back to his firms and investments and to building his new houses. Washington society shed a little tear to see the Newberrys leave.[33]

Roosevelt gave his chosen successor some space and with Archie left for Africa on an extended hunting and specimen-gathering trip. The insurgent spirit in the Republican Party and in the country at large did not sail away with him. The 1910 congressional elections, in which Republican regulars ran poorly against progressive Democrats and Republicans, demonstrated dissatisfaction. TR listened intently to grumbling about Taft's unpopularity and stand-pat tendencies while still in Africa. Upon his return, his broad hints of his own unhappiness with the president widened into an open break.[34]

Newberry was among the industrialists and friends who helped pay for Roosevelt's safari (Andrew Carnegie was the primary donor). Newberry also joined the pilgrimage to Roosevelt's Oyster Bay house in February, as friends pleaded with Roosevelt to challenge Taft for the Republican nomination. The *Detroit Free Press* described him as the leader of the effort to organize a slate of delegates for Roosevelt from Wayne County (Detroit). But politicking could wait. After the meeting with Roosevelt, he sailed with the family to Bermuda, for a vacation where his daughter Carol would meet and announce her engagement to a British army officer.[35]

When Newberry returned in March, he met with Roosevelt's national organizers in Chicago, where he would learn about his role in the campaign for the GOP nomination. Back in February, a group of Roosevelt boosters in Washington had set up a committee that included Newberry. Edwin Sims, a federal district attorney in Chicago during the Roosevelt administration, prodded Michigan governor Chase Osborn to ensure that Newberry was included in the Chicago group. Newberry was ready to do whatever asked. "I believe they gave me some kind of title," he said, "but really I can't remember what it was." Newberry followed Roosevelt because of his character rather than issues. The colonel was "a big man" who was "espousing a cause." "Unless one has been intimately associated with him he has no knowledge of the breadth of the man." He would chair the administrative committee of the National Roosevelt Committee, finding office space and overseeing fund-raising.[36]

It is unlikely he found many contributions at the Yondotega Club or many people to join him in working for Roosevelt among his usual circle of Detroit friends. Roosevelt was scary to them, in contrast to the steady Taft. Head shaking turned into hostility after TR's speech in Columbus, Ohio, in late February. Adding something new to what otherwise sounded like progressivism circa 1906, Roosevelt proposed the recall of judges, so that the judiciary might be in better tune with the people's wishes. For some Republicans, the judiciary was all that remained to protect the country from the madness overtaking the executive and legislative branches. Henry Joy would soon be stumping for price maintenance agreements—which progressives considered illegal price-fixing. Newberry, for once outside of his tight circle of friends, funded Roosevelt's Wayne County and Michigan effort. If he was to help nominate Roosevelt, he would have to learn to work with grubby pols, not gentlemen.[37]

There was considerable rancor in many state Republican conventions as they picked delegates for the national convention. In Michigan all hell broke loose. In February, the state central committee named Newberry the Bay City convention's temporary chairman. Bitterly divided county meetings gave a taste of what to expect at the April convention. Some counties, including Wayne, sent dueling slates of delegates and allegations of fraud for the state committee to sort out. Frank Knox, a Roosevelt man and former Rough Rider, chaired the state central committee, but the party secretary, Paul King, was for Taft, as was a majority of the committee. King and his men took control. On the day before the convention opened, the central committee voted to remove Newberry as the temporary chairman and to seat Taft delegates in disputed cases. Knox, who had deliberately absented himself from the meeting, argued that the decisions were not binding, since they had been made without the chairman, but King acted within the rules. The central committee soon replaced Knox with Alex Groesbeck, a Taft supporter.[38]

The state militia and local police were on hand for the opening of the convention. Members of disputed delegations who supported Taft got red credentials cards, while Roosevelt men had white ones. Those with white cards could not be seated; few managed even to enter the hall. It was bedlam. "Policemen in full uniform and with clubs tried to maintain a semblance of order. Police with clubs knocked men off the platform," wrote a reporter for a Grand Rapids newspaper. In the hall, "nearly 1000 delegates fought and screamed. . . . In through the transom over the doors men tried to force their way in, only to be knocked back by sergeants-at-arms." Some Roosevelt men carried both white and red cards; they, together with unchallenged TR delegates, fought with Taft men. When a Roosevelt man catapulted from the press table to the stage, a Taft supporter shoved him back into the reporters. No one could hear a thing. Outside it was worse, as "nearly 500 men, in whose faces the doors had been closed, fought and yelled and sought means of gaining entrance." Some tried climbing in through transoms and back windows. The Roosevelt forces inside the hall finally walked out before the roll call, shouting and jeering as they went. Indiana senator Albert Beveridge, who was scheduled to address the convention, gave up.[39]

The Roosevelt delegates met in a rump convention, bellowing about how they had been robbed. Newberry chose not to chair the meeting. It settled on its own set of delegates, including Governor Osborn, who would go to Chicago along with the delegates chosen in the regular meeting. Everything would get sorted out at the national convention in Chicago. Paul King got a note of thanks and a photograph from Taft in gratitude for King's good work.[40]

King, who would later manage campaigns for Newberry and others, had a treasure to add to his scrapbook. Roosevelt himself moved on to the next primaries and convention fights. For his supporters in Michigan, there was nothing to do but to point fingers and concoct face-saving explanations for what went wrong. Knox had worried about whether Newberry was up to the job from the start. Before the convention he urged Roosevelt to "send Newberry [a] strong message to stiffen him up for a bitter fight . . . we cannot lose if he stands up to it." Roosevelt obliged, calling on Newberry to be a man. "Do not let them run over you," he wrote. "Stand absolutely stiff and do not give them an inch. They are a thoroughly corrupt gang and any sign of conciliation is accepted as weakness." Newberry reported to TR that he had been unseated and that everyone was "fighting mad and are going through for a touchdown without flinching." What play Roosevelt's managers wanted to execute is not clear. Newberry might have asserted his right to the temporary chairmanship—after all, he had been duly elected in February. If that was the plan, he did not follow through. It might have been simply to challenge the whole convention as illegal, since Knox did not participate in the organizational meeting before the convention. If so, neither Newberry nor Knox seemed to know who was supposed to bring the challenge and when it would happen. They exchanged nasty letters. Newberry implied that Knox high-handedly put a challenge in motion without explaining to him what, if anything, was done, and Knox claimed that Newberry simply disappeared without taking care of the challenge. Years later, Knox still "despised" Newberry, who "quit like a yellow dog in Michigan in 1912 and did more than anyone else to precipitate the riot which ensured and which resulted in a divided delegation." Osborn thought Knox had poisoned the situation before the convention with an impolitic letter. Beveridge suggested that nothing except having a Roosevelt man serve as sergeant at arms could have prevented the fiasco.[41]

The *Detroit Free Press,* no friend of Roosevelt's in 1912, saw plenty of incompetence in TR's entire Michigan team. Once the committee without Knox removed Newberry as temporary chairman and Newberry did not assert his right to the post, there was no strategy that had a chance of working. Evasion was not a strong strategy. Even if Newberry had insisted on his place as temporary chair, the Taft side still likely had the votes. The national convention seated the regular Michigan delegates, as it did with most other disputed state delegations. With that, Taft won the Republican nomination. Knox bolted with Roosevelt for a third party. Osborn kept changing his mind. Newberry's resting place is not certain. Detroit newspapers suggested that he was "hesitant" about bolting. Newberry offered no public statement. When nagged, he repeated that he was "not going to think about politics for several weeks." He wrote to TR after the election, restating his admiration for Roosevelt's character and fight for "great principles," pledging his "loyalty to the cause we both worked for," and taking some credit for TR's carrying Michigan in the general election.[42]

Newberry missed his daughter's wedding to attend the Republican National Convention. The groom was not the man who dazzled her in Bermuda ("a fine specimen of the British army officer," in Newberry's estimation) but the son of a Detroit railroad executive. After 800 invitations went out to what promised to be a grand social event, the bride broke her engagement and announced she would marry someone else in a small, sudden ceremony. With what, for Newberry, were risks and public embarrassment in both politics and family life, 1912 was a tough, altogether uncharacteristic year.[43]

Still, there was one moment that was classic. Amid the shouting and pushing at the Michigan convention, Newberry stood in a doorway across the street, watching. In the midst of the melee he reverted to his habit of observation over action. Newberry's passivity recalled his college days, when he "generally took part in any election, always on the winning side. I was never a candidate for any office." The square, solid block of a man watching is the one who emerges from his correspondence—proper, restrained, polite, and indistinct. In contrast to his hero, the irrepressibly alive TR, Newberry seemed almost an observer of his own life. Just as he surveyed the chaos in 1912, he would watch his own Senate campaign unfold, as many of the same people involved in the convention—King, Osborn, and Groesbeck—took action. When controversy came, his distance and passivity and his family's loyalty to him were his defense. Only people who did not know him found it hard to believe.[44]

Ford may not have noticed the implosion of the Republican Party in Michigan. He probably did not vote in the November election. He had his mind on business, but as the decade wore on, much more. With the much less publicized work of James Couzens, Ford expanded his reputation as a businessman who was not like the rest, whose aim was "to do as much good as we can, everywhere, for everybody concerned."[45]

Even when he was the wealthiest man in the country, Ford considered people like Newberry to be rich. He saw himself as a workingman. "Every manufacturer should be able to go into the shop and with his own hands make the thing that he wants to manufacture," he argued. "If he cannot do this . . . [h]is workingmen are the real manufacturers, and he is but a parasite that lives upon them." He considered stockholders to be a greater menace than manufacturers who could not make anything themselves. Ford and Couzens had been developing a grand plan for a factory complex at the Rouge River, south of Detroit. Most everything necessary for building the Model T, from glass to steel, would be made on-site in state-of-the-art plants, and the shallow, muddy Rouge would get a port capable of docking iron ore shipments carried by a Ford fleet. To help finance the Rouge plant, Ford cut off dividends to the remaining handful of stockholders. Aghast at a highly profitable company ignoring the stockholders' interests, John and Horace Dodge sued Ford in 1916. They liked the dividend income, which they had sunk into their own car company, and believed they were owed something for the risks and thin rewards in the early years. The suit was about the value of the company (which Ford downplayed) and also about power. Did Ford get to do what he pleased, or did the stockholders, even a minority group, have a say in the company's direction? Ford lost the first round. On appeal, he won the right to pursue the Rouge project as he saw fit, but he still owed the stockholders a more than $20 million payment. To eliminate the possibility that meddlesome, bloodsucking stockholders could get between him and his vision, Ford bought out the stockholders, who thought it wise to get out in the face of rumors that Ford was prepared to abandon the company. By 1920, Ford had consolidated all aspects of the firm within the Ford Motor.Company of Delaware. Ford family members held all of the stock.[46]

Bankers loomed over even stockholders in Ford's hierarchy of evil, and he avoided them except when necessary. His aversion was more like fear than merely the countryside's loathing of predatory banks. He packed a gun and kept armed bodyguards nearby, in the event that Wall Street tried to take him out. At some point—it is hard to say when with Ford, since we have little to work with other than the recollections of those who worked with him—bankers occasionally became "German-Jewish bankers," responsible for war and assorted troubles worldwide. "The international Jewish interests play behind the scenes and carry on different activities," recalled Ernst Liebold, Ford's secretary, by way of explaining Ford's views. "Mr. Ford's definition of Wall Street was the Jewish interests" that pushed for war because it would mean profits.[47]

None of this was public yet. What was, captured in newsreels and endless newspaper stories, was the humble genius of Dearborn, Michigan. Ford's affection for the outdoors and a lost rural America inspired him to re-create a nineteenth-century village in Dearborn; for a time he encouraged his workers to buy and work plots of land. Exercise would be good for them, just as it was for him. Ford walked for miles in the woods and challenged visitors to high-kicking contests, his shoe whizzing by their ears. With an eye toward publicity as well as recreation, Ford joined Thomas Edison, Harvey Firestone, and the naturalist John Burroughs in what became an annual summer jaunt. The camping trips of the "vagabonds" were "as private and secluded as a Hollywood opening," according to Charles Sorenson, a Ford confidant. Reporters and still and newsreel photographers recorded hikes, wood-chopping contests (Burroughs was the champ), and homey stories of Ford repairing busted cars that their caravan happened upon. Ford stories sold newspapers, so even editors who disliked providing free advertising for Ford could not help but publish the tales.[48]

Convinced that with the Model T he had perfected the automobile, Ford drifted toward other projects, which he approached with the same cocksure attitude. "The confidence born in him of success along one line never forsakes him when he enters other spheres of thought and action," observed Samuel S. Marquis, an Episcopal priest who briefly worked for Ford. Surrounded by sycophants in his immediate circle, Ford was beginning to develop a reputation as a crank or worse outside of it. He had views on health and diet—sometimes weeds were in and meat was out. Ford asserted that no one who worked for him could smoke or drink alcohol. The Model T and the Fordson tractor had demonstrated the superiority of machines over horses. Next in line were cows, "the crudest machine in the world." Ford expected to cut out the offensive, inefficient middleman by taking "the same cereals that cows eat and mak[ing] them into milk that is superior to the natural article and much cleaner." Ford believed in reincarnation; some of his flashes of insight, he believed, came from being open to the wisdom of previous lives.[49]

Except to dairy farmers, such ideas were the harmless quirks of a great man who made an affordable car and instituted humane hiring policies. Ford employed disabled workers—some 1,700 on the eve of World War I—as well as thousands of men with medical conditions that other employers might have rejected. At the war's end, Ford found work for thousands of disabled veterans. The company also hired ex-convicts. All of this made for publicity that burnished Ford's reputation as an unusual industrialist—an individualist who treated workers as individuals rather than as categories. Ford's workforce also included a much higher percentage of black workers than was the norm in the industry, although this fact did not get the same play in the white press.[50]

The most sensational move came in 1914 with the announcement of the Five Dollar Day for eight hours of work, "the greatest revolution in the matter of rewards for its workers ever known to the industrial world," according to the press release. The Ford legend grew: here was an industrialist who actually shared his profits with his workers. The plan also aimed to solve a series of problems. Despite the expansion of the workforce and refinements to the assembly line, productivity had not increased nearly as much as Ford might have anticipated. Perhaps if the firm paid attention to the workers' lives outside of the factory, their attention to their tasks might improve. Couzens thought wage incentives would cut costs. The prospect of better pay might reduce absenteeism and employee turnover, which had been as high as 370 percent. The Five Dollar Day scale also provided the opportunity to revamp the factory's chaotic wage scales. Ford added philosophy to Couzens's bottom line: if workers were able to afford the products they made, everyone would benefit. Capitalism would unite everyone as consumers rather than divide people into classes. After putting in eight hours' labor, workers would have both the time and the means to consume goods, in turn benefiting manufacturers. Even better, the Five Dollar Day was a stick in the eye of Wall Street and other industrialists. Detroit manufacturers seethed about the potentially ruinous wage. With all the publicity generated by the Five Dollar Day, the firm was able to pull the ads that had made the man and his company known around the world.[51]

To ensure that the workers' money would not be wasted (perhaps the most stinging curse in the Ford lexicon), the premium wage went to those whom Ford deemed worthy—married men of good habits, single men over twenty-one who had established savings accounts, and those who had been with the firm with an unblemished record for at least six months. The Sociological Department checked into the merits of workers' home lives and habits, providing suggestions for improvement, such as moving into better housing, saving money, and spending evenings at home. "A worker is only put on the list of profit-sharers after he has been carefully looked up, and the company is satisfied he will not debauch the additional money he receives," the company explained to the workers. The restrictions meant that perhaps 40 percent of Ford workers earned less than five dollars, although with a good record in time served, even less than model employees shared in the profit-sharing plan on a sliding scale. A larger percentage of workers gradually qualified, but soon, inflation narrowed the gap between the standard wage, climbing at Ford and its competitors, and the full profit-sharing reward. Even when the Five Dollar Day became the Six and then the Seven, the incentive for good behavior was never as great as it had been in 1914. There was no public relations rollout, but interest in workers' lives also faded. By 1920, the Sociological Department was no more, and its replacement, the Service Department, focused more on spying on potential union organizers than on social uplift.[52]

After war broke out in Europe in 1914, Ford's views on world affairs became as well-known as the company's compensation policies. He spoke out against war and against American preparedness toward the possibility that it too would be drawn into the conflict. "I hate war," he said, "because war is murder, desolation, and destruction." When German U-boats sank the *Lusitania* in 1915, Ford was quoted as saying, "Well, they were fools to go on that boat, because they were warned." He was willing to back up his views with cash: "I have prospered much and I am ready to give much to end this constant, wasteful 'preparation.'" The opportunity came in November 1915. Rosika Schwimmer, a Hungarian writer and activist in various progressive causes, and Louis P. Lochner, former secretary of the International Federation of Students, read about Ford's pacifist commitments and came to call at his Dearborn home. Both had been busy lining up progressive luminaries, among them Jane Addams of Chicago's Hull House and David Starr Jordan, president of Stanford University, for a plan to end the war. They favored "continuous mediation," which required representatives of neutral nations to keep devising peace proposals until they hit on one acceptable to the warring powers. Ford took the proposal to President Wilson, who after trying and failing to avoid meeting with the automaker, argued that he could not commit to any single plan.[53]

Dismissing Wilson as "a small man," Ford bankrolled the "Peace Ship," *Oscar II,* which set sail with much fanfare from New York. Many big names, including Jane Addams, William Jennings Bryan, and John Dewey, skipped the trip. But with Ford, Schwimmer, and other delegates along with students and reporters aboard, the ship headed to Oslo, Norway, where the delegation would meet with its European counterparts and try to construct the peace. From the start, press coverage was tough. A bit more vicious than most, the *Baltimore Sun* opined that "if a brutal German submarine should sink her nothing would be lost." Diplomats saw little reason to take the amateur negotiations seriously. Reporters on board added to a ship-of-fools story line with dispatches about the "squirrel food" delegates. Ford took sick in Oslo and returned to Dearborn. Ford's commitment did not slacken; he purchased newspaper space for advertisements opposing preparedness.[54]

Where Ford's pacifist convictions came from is hard to say, which is true of all his views about anything outside of machines. The writing attributed to him was the product of trusted ghosts. When his fame and fortune grew, Ford usually gave statements only to dependably sympathetic reporters, and even then often with a trusted employee nearby to translate his ideas. His opposition to American involvement in a European war did not set him apart from a great many Americans who saw fighting among decadent imperial powers as none of their business. Yet, sentiment in favor of preparedness was growing, pushed forward by such popular figures as Theodore Roosevelt. America could not afford isolation from the world, especially when its now close ally, Great Britain, and other democracies were at war against the evil Hun. As the war settled into a bloody stalemate, the preparedness debate became more urgent. Ford's statements on war and peace cost him Couzens, his top manager, a Canadian by birth, whose talents were at least as responsible as Ford's for the company's success.[55]

In 1916, Woodrow Wilson was the closest thing to a peace candidate for the presidency. (As a write-in candidate, Ford beat favorite son Senator William Alden Smith, fresh off his fame in the *Titanic* investigation, in a nonbinding

Michigan presidential primary.) While Ford never had much use for politics or politicians, he decided to back Wilson's bid for reelection. He was even persuaded to give generously, but it was not like Ford to simply contribute to a campaign fund put at the disposal of politicians. His $58,800 contribution bought a last-minute advertising onslaught in California and a handful of other states. Produced and placed by Ford's staff, the ads urged citizens to follow Ford and "guard against Wall Street influence again securing control of our government" and to vote for Wilson because he had not "plunged the country into war for profit."[56]

Ford's views had earned him the enmity of those who had backed preparedness. Churning slowly though preliminary motions was Ford's $1 million libel suit against the *Chicago Tribune*. In 1916 the newspaper ran an editorial calling him an "ignorant idealist" and "an anarchistic enemy of the nation" because of an erroneous report from a company treasurer that Ford was denying support to National Guard troops in his employ called for duty along the Mexican border. If Ford saw in the Detroit elite's support for preparedness the "pathetic sight" of plutocrats aiming to "convert their factories into workshops for making shot and shell for destroying mankind," *Detroit Saturday Night,* a publication favored by the Detroit elite, described the Peace Ship as "a humiliation to his city and his country." Henry Joy stumped for preparedness almost as soon as war broke out. He condemned "the loud-mouthed bleaters for peace at any price" and answered Ford's 1915 peace statement with an argument centered on Ford's naive views of human nature and world affairs. As the Wilson administration appeared to be acting too slowly against German attacks on neutral shipping that killed Americans, Joy sent letters to Packard agents about his growing shame in America's inaction. "Babbling boobs continue to babble of peace and neutrality when there is neither," he said, as the letter generated follow-up news interviews. Crazy Henry was now a threat to America's self-worth.[57]

When President Wilson asked Congress to declare war against Germany in 1917, Ford put aside his pronouncements about preparedness and peace and offered his factories for whatever the military needed. "Perhaps militarism can be crushed only with militarism," he said. "In that case I am in on it to the finish." With his usual public relations flair, he vowed that he would refuse profits. If Wilson had not kept the United States out of the war, Ford made sure his son, Edsel, stayed out of uniform. He arranged a deferment, claiming that the twenty-four-year-old who became the company secretary two years earlier was an essential war worker. He privately mused that if his son went to war, "some among them would have seen to it that he did not come back"[58]

Ford was an unguided missile in public life, and in later years his anti-Semitic rants, use of union-busting thugs, and possible Nazi sympathies destroyed his carefully crafted reputation. But in 1918, he remained a formidable public figure. He was the worst kind of opponent—with buckets of public goodwill and even more cash and fame; he was also litigious, a touch paranoid, and convinced that a man of the people like himself could never really be wrong.

3

Laws and Effects

The Ford-Newberry controversy was personal, but it was possible because of early twentieth-century election laws and the expectations for politics and politicians that arose with them. Primary elections and the direct election of senators obliged candidates to spend money, while campaign finance reform ostensibly limited expenditures. In the classic telling, these laws were the product of a Progressive Era reaction against machine politics, of middle-class outrage against corruption and bad government. Disgusted with how politicians did the bidding of their big business cronies, Americans demanded a government honest enough to be entrusted with the expanded responsibilities necessary in an urban, industrial society. Government needed to be more accountable too, which meant new rules that took from the parties and gave to the people the power to pick who would govern.

Legislatures passed the new laws, covering how parties, candidates, and voters went about their business, with much sputtering about corruption, money in politics, and democracy in peril. But outsiders were not alone in sensing that the rules that seemed adequate for Lincoln, Garfield, and Cleveland were not working. Party leaders calculated that government regulation of elections could enhance their control over internal factions, unflattering news stories, and third-party challenges. Partisan ends might be served alongside of progressive pieties. Democrats and insurgent Republicans hoped the direct election of senators and campaign finance reform would improve their prospects for election and cause the regular Republican fund-raising machinery to creak at least a little.

The new regime in practice pleased neither reformers nor crafty politicians. If the new rules slightly weakened the parties, partisanship sailed forward unobstructed. Campaign costs rose. Advertising and public relations, hardly forces designed to provide citizens with the tools to rationally weigh men and measures, gained influence, along with independent but still partisan press. Electoral scandals, which sold newspapers and could tip the balance of power in Washington, motivated reform and drove investigations of candidates who might have violated standards of political decency. Where morality ended and politics began in politicians' scrutinizing of their own was difficult to pick out.

A 1920 *New York Times* story described what seemed to be a paradoxical turn in American election campaigns. Why, since "open and flagrant 'vote buying' is no longer in evidence" and state governments had "taken over so many of the expenses which formerly fell upon political organizations," were campaigns more expensive than in the "sordid" days of ward heelers and hired "repeaters"? The author blamed "the professional campaigner, amiable, energetic, a political profiteer, whose emergence marks the change in the politics of the United States." Unlike old-time politicians, these men had no personal acquaintance with the voters they tried to persuade, and they did not pinch pennies. Their job was to spend all the money that could be raised, not to maintain an organization. They approached their work as pseudo-businessmen, leasing office space and machines, hiring clerks, buying advertising, distributing literature, and paying workers to gin up voter enthusiasm. Their "new methods" made for national campaigns that the author imagined would soon cost $30 million. The story did not condemn such huge budgets as a peril to democracy. The spending was not corrupt. It was wasted. It clogged the newspapers with boring, amateurish advertising and constituents' mailboxes with reams of useless literature. The "golden stream" of massive campaign contributions found its "final resting place in the sand."[1]

The author was nearly half right. Campaign costs had been rising steadily. Some of the spending was silly, but that was true of campaigns from the very first. By the 1910s, national campaigns and reasonably extensive state and big-city contests hired "publicity men," typically former newspapermen who coordinated advertising and produced and distributed flyers, buttons, and posters, and scheduled events and speeches. The breakthrough year for publicity men in politics was 1916, when across the country billboards advertising Woodrow Wilson proclaimed, "He Kept Us Out of War." Wilson's Committee on Public Information boosting America's involvement once the United States entered World War I relied on the public relations expertise of former muckraking journalist George Creel. A generation of public relations men got their start working under Creel. As the advertising profession grew in size, sophistication, and self-consciousness in the 1920s, the men who handled campaign publicity grew along with it.[2]

Candidates and their managers had not suddenly turned stupid or trendy. They hired publicity specialists and their staffs because the old-school methods were either unavailable or ineffectual. Progressive Era election laws had changed how campaigns were conducted. The new men helped candidates find their way through a thicket of rules without the familiar marker of tight party control over elections and with new paths opened by commercial advertising and publicity. They were the products of reform.

The list of innovations is long and touched on how citizens participated in their government and what they ought to be thinking about when doing so. Primary elections replaced party conventions as the device of choice for picking nominees. Federal civil service laws gained strength and scope. The secret ballot printed by state governments replaced tickets provided by the parties, cast in public. The direct election of senators removed that function from state legislatures. The initiative and referendum allowed direct citizen access to lawmaking. State laws required in-person voter registration well before election days. State and federal laws aimed to limit the influence of money in politics by publicizing its sources or regulating spending. Other reforms changed the makeup of the electorate. Woman suffrage (by constitutional amendment in 1919) doubled the number of eligible voters. Disfranchisement measures passed by southern legislatures and written into state constitutions drastically minimized the African American electorate in those states where violence and laws enacted in the late nineteenth century had not already done the job.[3]

Reformers who advocated these measures argued that the new rules would elevate politics by loosening the grip of parties on elections, diminishing fraud, and reducing the power of wealth. Progressives were hardly of one mind about the specific reforms the nation required. On any single issue they offered different solutions and at times found among their allies socialists, conservative business interests, immigrant workers, and machine politicians. But whatever their causes, reformers agreed that the changes they demanded, their rendition of the public good, could not happen without dismantling nineteenth-century political institutions. Reclaiming the integrity of the ballot and the election machinery was essential in order to serve their vision of the public interest and responsible citizenship, one in which voters made deliberate choices after taking the measure of the issues and candidates.[4]

A good forty years of scholarship warns against taking such arguments at face value. The laws wounded the parties, but not mortally. In fact, there were some advantages for parties and candidates. Leaving the ballot printing and distributing business to the states gave the parties a smaller printing bill and better control over the party vote absent the mischief that local workers sometimes caused. Third-party threats diminished. State legislators, most of them good Democrats or Republicans, made access to a place on the ballot difficult for minor parties by requiring them, but not the major parties, to demonstrate sufficient support among the electorate. In the South, candidates and parties no longer had to stir themselves to buy the votes of blacks and poor whites or to cheat those voters of their rights. Parties, which had operated without much if anything in the way of formal rules, now adopted them and welcomed governmental regulation.[5]

Something like the reformers-against-the-machine story happened with the adoption of the direct primary in Wisconsin and New York. But that story obscures politicians' much longer period of experimentation with direct primaries. Historian John F. Reynolds and political scientist Alan Ware point out that the breakdown of the convention system, felt most acutely in the cities, set politicians to cast about for an alternative. The fraying of the convention system had a number of sources. Reynolds describes the rise of "hustling" candidates, who appealed directly to voters and were not willing to wait their turns in conventions. Party organization men cared about winning but also about keeping the peace among their varied constituencies, which meant balanced tickets and rewards for service. Pushy candidates punctured both the chance of consensus and smoothly running conventions in which men graciously accepted the party honors bestowed by their peers. Fistfights between candidates' friends during conventions and loud protests of fraud from the losers of contested nominations did not enhance a party's chances in a general election. Ware traces the evolution of nominating systems, from caucuses and conventions through the direct primaries in some rural areas, the implementation of primaries in the South, and the adoption of the system in cities and states. An expanded population made conventions seem narrow and unrepresentative; candidates' increasing spending before conventions seemed to stink of fraud; delegates broke pledges; and party rules proved too weak to settle disputes arising in conventions. Cities such as Cleveland experimented with primary elections in the 1890s as a solution to the problems that conventions could not contain.[6]

Party leaders in urban districts pushed primary elections forward. Rural politicians feared that their candidates would not stand a chance against city candidates in statewide races. Wisconsin, where Robert La Follette fought party regulars for the direct primary, was both exceptional and fairly late in adopting this reform. Elsewhere, party leaders hoped the direct primary would strengthen their organizations by diminishing internal battles and enhancing the legitimacy of their nominees. After all, some reasoned, the Australian ballot—printed by states and listing candidates by office and party—had done just that.[7]

Voters, contrary to reformers' wishes, greeted most primary elections with yawns: turnout tended to be low, reflecting a lack of public information and interest in the candidates. But changes in both the rules and voter attitudes meant that the parties could not simply carry on as usual. The fights over nominations that party operatives used to have in convention hotel suites now took place in public. In contested primaries managers competed for the services of party workers, and through the 1930s there were a lot of meaningful primaries. This was especially true in the South; in the North, the smaller number of tough primaries often involved rival Republican factions. Candidates vied for the attention of increasingly independent voters who split their tickets between the parties and confined their attention to the personalities at the top, when they bothered (or were able) to register and vote at all. The slippage of party loyalty among voters can be overstated. Many voters learned that they *should* vote for the man and not the party—not a hard lesson, since the idea of party had been a tough sell in the nineteenth century and the sale had never been fully consummated. Even if lofty expectations proved naive, reform of electoral politics had changed how the parties functioned.[8]

A more gradual transformation in the media, newspapers especially, also amplified the changes in campaign styles. While the party press that depended on government patronage began a long descent in the 1830s, most nineteenth-century newspapers had party ties and gave their candidates publicity and support as a normal part of their work. By the 1880s, city newspapers fattened on commercial advertising revenue, and politicians needed the press more than the press needed the parties. Unable to assume prominent coverage of their every wise utterance (political coverage competed with gruesome murders, sports, comic strips, and the scandal of the week), candidates and parties bought ads, with their pitches and photographs set alongside those of Camel cigarettes and specials on pork chops at Rury's Grocery. By the 1910s and 1920s, political ads were a newspaper staple in cities and the country alike during the weeks before an election.[9]

An independent press did not mean a nonpartisan one. Even as newspapers drew readers with racy scandals, crime, stunts, and sports coverage, many editors made their views clear in political stories and editorials. Indeed, some owners and editors exercised their clout as would-be kingmakers and candidates for office themselves. Without competition from radio or television, it was the place to go for news. It was the place where product advertisers connected with customers. It was where people searching for houses, apartments, rooms, and jobs found notices. Editors often still had a partisan slant and were now freer to exercise it, as they, perhaps more than the parties or candidates, shaped public opinion. The newspaper empire of William Randolph Hearst, covering many of the nation's biggest markets, took on the role of protector of the people's interest against the plutocrats. Hearst's platform was not sturdy enough to make him president or governor of New York or mayor of New York City, but he was elected twice to Congress. Hearst was a fierce enemy or ally, and politicians in cities without one of his papers dreaded the prospect of getting one. "Colonel" Robert McCormick's Republican but antimachine *Tribune* jousted with Hearst's *Examiner* in Chicago. J. R. Knowland and the Chandler family's influence on conservative politics in California stretched into the 1950s. Elsewhere the Booth and Scripps chains were important in their communities. The newspaper business was viciously competitive, but one with influence that politicians courted.[10]

Politicians responded to the new political environment by spending money. By the early twentieth century, things the parties once had controlled in-house—a party press and a ready workforce—now often had to be purchased. Candidates running in primaries were on their own. In 1920, a full-page ad in the *New York Times* cost $1,539 and in the *Chicago Tribune* $1,708. Newspapers with smaller circulations charged less for the space, but they often charged more for political ads than they did for the notices of their regular retail customers. Campaign ads, after all, were seasonal rather than regular buys, and political managers paid for good placement. Campaigns also produced boilerplate "news" stories for rural weeklies. Primary candidates and parties in general elections purchased billboard advertising, buttons, lithographs, and posters in addition to the standard campaign literature mailed to voters. Advertising totaled between 25 and 50 percent of campaign budgets by the standard estimate, depending on the expense of the market and the need of the candidate to introduce his name, face, and message to voters. Speakers also needed to be paid and organized; now their function was not so much to rally the faithful as to generate publicity and news coverage.[11]

The next largest expense was running campaign headquarters. Here a candidate could count on spending between 15 and 20 percent of his budget. This item included rents for buildings and equipment and telephone and telegraph services. The rest went to aid other political organizations (state party committees sometimes sent funds to county organizations) and election day expenses. Voters sometimes needed rides to the polls (some states prohibited that expense); poll watchers and challengers had to be paid to be alert to their parties' interests (about $15 per day); and runners and door knockers were sent to remind voters of their duty. In the 1923 mayoral election in Philadelphia, the cost per ward for such items ranged between $270 and $2,740 (there were forty-eight wards); the price per assembly district paid by Tammany Hall in New York was $4,000. Even campaigns free from ordinary corruption could cost quite a lot.[12]

Rising campaign costs hit Democrats and Republicans alike. And while primary elections had been a bipartisan innovation, the direct election of senators and campaign finance reform were partisan. Insurgent Republicans and Democrats promoted these reforms because they might help to defeat the regular Republicans. Scandal and congressional investigations were both cause and consequence of reform in an atmosphere that brought out the partisan long knives.

The election of senators by state legislatures, a constitutional requirement, not an unregulated practice like convention nominations, was limping into the early twentieth century. Like convention nominations, this method of election groaned under the weight of ambition and new demands. Hustling candidates balked at doing the gracious thing by accepting disappointment and waiting their turn. State legislatures deadlocked. Between 1891 and 1905, fourteen seats remained unfilled for at least one state legislative session because of unresolved fights in statehouses. Some states, especially in the South and Midwest, began to approximate direct elections, generally offering a popular vote for the office that was advisory to the legislatures. By 1912, more than half of the states used some form of popular selection for Senate races. These elections were not binding. Sometimes they just gave bickering state legislators more talking points. The math mattered: Was a representative obliged to follow his district's preference, or to ratify the statewide vote?[13]

Charges of corruption and the generally bad reputation of the Senate as a "millionaires' club" made matters worse. Two senators, John H. Mitchell of Oregon and Joseph Burton of Kansas, were convicted of trading favors for financial kickbacks. Mitchell appealed but died in 1905 before his case was heard. Burton's 1906 conviction sent him to jail. William Randolph Hearst added *Cosmopolitan* magazine to his stable of publications in 1905. Inspired by the Mitchell and Burton cases, he commissioned novelist David Graham Phillips to write a series of articles on the perfidies of the upper house. Later published as *The Treason of the Senate*, it condemned the collusion between senators and the railroads, Wall Street, and big business. Senators may not have been wealthy when taking office but too often grabbed the chance for the good life available by striking deals with the corporate powers that really ran the country. Phillips and other critics of the Senate imagined a corrupt web of influence when a simpler explanation would have done the job. Old-guard Republicans, many in office since the 1880s, believed that legislation that helped business helped the nation. With or without the writers Theodore Roosevelt called "muckrakers," their days were numbered, defeated by a newly energetic Democratic Party, insurgent Republicans, or old age and death.[14]

Seating challenges advanced both the immediate purposes of the Democratic and insurgent Republican coalition and the case for the direct election of senators. Over the sessions in 1910 and 1911, the Privileges and Elections Committee took aim—or chose not to consider—a series of elections that taken together illustrated the difficulties state legislatures had in electing senators, the partisan and factional interest in devising new rules, and the role of the press in generating outrage.

The most spectacular seating challenge involved Republican William Lorimer, the "Blond Boss" of Chicago, elected to seven terms in the House from normally Democratic districts. Born in Manchester, England, in 1861, he moved with his parents to the United States in 1866, settling in Chicago in 1870. Lorimer's father, a Scottish Presbyterian minister, died when William was ten, and the eldest of six children dropped any effort at formal education in order to support the family. In Chicago's West End ethnic neighborhoods, Lorimer distributed newspapers, shined shoes, and hauled coal. He also worked in the packinghouses and as a streetcar conductor. Through those jobs, the boy made friends ("Hinky Dink" Kenna and "Bathhouse" John Coughlin among them), some of whom later became his political lieutenants and business associates. He determined he was a Republican, but without any special attraction to the party's issues and history, and with hostility toward some of its tendencies, such as temperance. His Republicanism began and ended with the observation that the party held power nationally often enough to mean patronage that was useful in building a local organization. His ties to Democrats remained deep. He converted to Catholicism upon his marriage to an Irish Catholic woman, which did not hurt his appeal among that traditionally Democratic group, and he kept up friendships throughout the city's varied ethnic working-class neighborhoods.[15]

Lorimer, self-educated, ambitious for a political career, but located in a Democratic district, began his rise with his 1885 election to the party county committee. Betting right on a mayoral candidate, he moved into a patronage-rich city office. From there, he weaved through the city's bewildering factions and alliances made and broken, a force in the Republican Party. Caring far more about the health of his own organization than about national politics, he cut deals among other city and state politicians, Democrats and

Republicans alike, with the flow of patronage foremost in his calculations. Lorimer ducked or opposed causes that appealed to a reform segment of the party—temperance, overly Protestant public education reforms, and primary elections. They threatened the continued support of his working-class base and his ability to trade support and patronage with Democrats. His trimming on issues, deals with Democrats, and profits turned from his political contacts won Lorimer enemies in the press, beginning in the 1880s with the Republican *Chicago Tribune,* then under the control of Joseph Medill. In Lorimer's heyday as a state and city Republican boss in the 1890s, he could count on critical coverage in most of Chicago's newspapers, including ones that ordinarily supported his party.

The criticism cooled with Lorimer's service in the House, where he tended to the interests of his district. Lorimer represented the big meatpackers in working out the details of the Meat Inspection Act (while also taking credit for protecting consumers in his campaign literature). He nurtured a waterways project that would connect Chicago to the Gulf of Mexico via the Mississippi and Illinois rivers. An influential member with good relationships with the leadership, he might have happily remained in the House, while he watched his private fortune grow. But the inability of the state legislature to fill a Senate seat that came open in 1908 brought Lorimer a promotion, and then his exit from public life.

Illinois was among the states that offered voters the chance to indicate their preference for Senate seats. The winner, with 43 percent of the vote, was Albert Hopkins, likely a comfortable fit with the Republican regulars on the need to protect American industry with high tariffs. He was the candidate of the "federal" faction—the men who enjoyed federal patronage appointments in Illinois. His margin was not large enough to overcome opposition from both Lorimer and Governor Charles Deneen. That the two agreed was man-bites-dog news. Once allies, they had become implacable rivals for power in the state party, with Deneen attempting to channel the reform element. Like much in Illinois politics, the matter of electing a senator had more to do with which faction would benefit than with politics or programs. So, if not Hopkins, who? The legislature deadlocked. Lawmakers got punchy enough to vote for a clerk and a bald man in the gallery. In Washington, Republicans worried about votes for a tariff bill and wished Illinois could get on with it and appoint a Republican. The clerk or the bald man would do if he would

vote with the regulars on the tariff. Conferences between Lorimer and Deneen settled nothing. Deneen considered running but feared losing clout in
the state. Lorimer turned down the suggestion that he offer himself as a candidate at different points as vote after vote failed to produce a winner. When
Hopkins fell short again on the ninety-fourth ballot, Lorimer's name went
forward. With support from Democrats (and the opposition of Deneen's
men), he won the seat.

Lorimer's victory lap was short. A Democratic legislator peddled a story
to the *Chicago Tribune* that detailed how he had received $1,000 for his vote,
and claimed that other Democrats were in on the "jackpot" collected and
spent by friends of Lorimer. After additional investigation, the *Tribune* made
it the front-page story—the entire front page. The sports page was undis-
turbed—a Cubs loss to the Cardinals got space—but the Lorimer revelations
pushed other news items back to page four. Permutations of the story made
the front page for weeks. Denials followed, as did a state investigation. A few
more Democrats admitted being paid for their votes, but not by Lorimer. The
hearings did not uncover a direct link to Lorimer, but they revealed much
that stank. In late December 1910, a majority of the Privileges and Elections
Committee cleared Lorimer, citing a lack of evidence of his participation in
bribery, and the majority report carried in a floor vote. The Chicago press, especially the *Tribune,* kept the story alive and Lorimer's name associated with
vote buying and big corporate contributions that made the purchases possible. Even smaller interests, such as Illinois River fishermen who said they
had been contributing to a Republican slush fund for years, had their day in
the mud. A measure of how damaged Lorimer had become was Theodore
Roosevelt's 1910 refusal to speak at a Chicago club meeting unless Lorimer
was disinvited.[16]

New evidence—or rumor—of a corporate slush fund was enough for
La Follette to insist on a new investigation of Lorimer's election. The tim-
ing was right: 1910 was a bad year for Republicans, regulars especially. The
Republican Party lost twelve seats and was barely able to organize for the
session. A Senate energized by a reform-minded freshman class (twenty new
members were sworn in by May 1911) heard the testimony, with Lorimer sitting through the entire proceeding. Many of those freshmen had replaced
old-guard members who had voted for Lorimer's seating in the last hearing. Lorimer defended himself with gusto, denouncing the sinister "trust

press" that had unfairly targeted him and detailing the motives of each of the Democratic state legislators who had voted for him. His fourteen-hour speech had turns of bathos, too, in the story of his childhood and rise from poverty. There never was evidence, historian Joel Tarr suggests, of Lorimer's involvement in a scheme to buy a Senate seat. Major Republican donors had collected a tidy fund for the 1908 elections, but the Illinois situation was too tangled for their tastes. He was guilty of being an unashamed machine politi-cian at a time when that political type had fallen into bad odor. If he did not handle the "jackpot," he was too close to those who did reward legislators, even if they got money for something other than the Lorimer vote. He was also a regular Republican who had little political support to fall back on. A "boss" who commanded only the fragment of a machine, his was a high-wire act, depending on shifting factions based on patronage and personality among Illinois Republicans and Democrats willing to make deals. The Sen-ate, convinced that there were more than enough tainted votes to have denied Lorimer the majority he needed in the state legislature, removed him by a vote of 55 to 28.[17]

While the second Lorimer investigation was going forward, the Privileges and Elections Committee of the same Congress considered the fate of Isaac Stephenson of Wisconsin. Stephenson, in his eighties as the Senate weighed his right to a seat, joined the Republican Party soon after its founding and served three terms in the House in the 1880s. Business concerned him even more than politics: a Wisconsinite since the state's pioneer days, he made a fortune in lumber, with holdings throughout the Great Lakes region. He used some of his wealth to support worthy candidates, among them Robert La Follette for governor and then senator. That support went as far as the pur-chase of a Milwaukee newspaper to guarantee La Follette positive coverage in the state's largest city. When the state legislature needed to fill an unexpired Senate term in 1907, Stephenson won, in recognition of his long service to the party, and with the grudging gratitude of La Follette and opposition of some of his acolytes.[18]

La Follette and his organization expected Stephenson to welcome this bit of recognition and return to Wisconsin to spend time with his grandchil-dren. But spry and healthy, Stephenson decided that he would like to serve a full term. La Follette and his organization had other worthy supporters of the senior senator in mind, and they opposed Stephenson in the state's primary.

Stephenson wanted to win. He spent nearly $110,000 for advertising, publicity, and organization. The sum dwarfed his competitors' expenditures, but he had nothing like the La Follette machine on the ground working for his candidacy. He won, and the state legislature ratified his election, after delays created by La Follette men walking out of the chamber in order to prevent quorums. He took his seat in March 1909.[19]

Two years later, with a new Wisconsin legislature stocked with additional La Follette loyalists, a state investigation charged that Stephenson had won his seat through corrupt practices. The allegations would become familiar to Newberry a decade later. The money Stephenson spent on the primary—reported as state law required—was excessive, although neither state nor federal laws limited spending at the time of that election. It bought newspaper support, workers, and perhaps voters. Surely, the La Follette faction reasoned, campaign contributions from Stephenson to statehouse hopefuls counted as bribes just as certainly as wads of cash handed to legislators in a hotel room.

The Senate agreed to investigate the claims in August 1911. Testifying before the Privileges and Elections Committee, Stephenson's manager, who had once worked for La Follette, claimed that the sum spent in the primary was necessary given the extent and activity of La Follette's organization. It furnished things—campaign workers, advertising, office space, and flyers—permitted by Wisconsin law. The state senator who brought the charges admitted that he had no direct evidence of corruption in the Stephenson campaign. "I always assume a thing is reliable until it is proven otherwise," he said by way of explaining why he had little more than Democratic stump speeches and editorials in anti-Stephenson newspapers to ground the charges of corruption and bribery.[20]

By a 9 to 5 vote, the committee affirmed Stephenson's right to his seat. The division was not along party lines. The majority included two Democrats, one of them, Ohio freshman Atlee Pomerene, on the progressive end of the party. The majority nonetheless worried about the size of Stephenson's spending, calling it a "violation of the fundamental principles underlying our system of government." The minority report accepted the rumors of corruption as fact. Insurgent Republicans and progressive Democrats put the burden of proof on Stephenson. He had not demonstrated the absence of corruption, and they were "unable to comprehend" how such a large sum could be spent "and not be tainted by corrupt methods and practices." William Kenyon, one of the freshmen who finally arrived when a deadlock in the Iowa legislature broke in April, helped lead the Republican anti-Stephenson forces. He warned senators that any one of them could be next. "If a man can be sent here by money, others can be defeated by money, and there are men in this chamber who know what it means to have the purses of great interests opened to defeat them," he said. Stephenson's expulsion would teach the rich that "the people, not money, are going to rule in this country."[21]

Lorimer, whose expulsion vote was still pending, sat near Stephenson, listening with interest while the elderly, bearded lumber magnate dabbed his eyes with a handkerchief, stung by hearing how he had brought democracy low. The attempt to remove him involved many of the same people, as well as arguments, that would be important in the Newberry case. Freshman senator James A. Reed, a former Kansas City prosecutor, "the supreme artist in assault," was especially brutal. Stephenson did not have to violate any laws in order to be disqualified for the Senate, Reed argued. The "revelry of crime and corruption" that passed for an election in Wisconsin "brought the Senate and the prison too close together for comfort or respectability." The money spent was an "appeal to cupidity not to reason" that endangered the Senate and the idea of free elections. Stephenson must go.[22]

When the full Senate vote finally came, opponents of Stephenson were nowhere close to the two-thirds majority necessary to remove a sitting senator, with forty in favor of retention and thirty-four against. Pomerene, who would guide the effort to unseat Newberry, took the floor in favor of seating Stephenson as the speechmaking wound down. There was no law in effect dealing with campaign spending when Stephenson ran for the Senate. Some senators found condemning Stephenson's campaign for breaking a law that did not exist to be unfair. For others, the case was simply unpersuasive. Yes, $107,000 was a lot of money, but no one offered clear evidence that it bought anything illegal. Besides, the eighty-three-year-old probably had "but a few more days and he must pass on," so he should be allowed to do so with his good name intact. He lived out his term—and long enough after to write a get-even autobiography.[23]

The work of the Privileges and Elections Committee of the Sixty-Second Congress had more on its plate than the Lorimer and Stephenson cases. Reed urged the committee to investigate newly reelected senator Henry A. Du Pont, claiming that both of the Delaware millionaire's elections had been tainted. Repeating allegations generated by a Judiciary Committee confirmation hearing for a federal marshal, Reed claimed that at least $60,000 went to buy votes ($10 for whites and $5 for blacks) for Du Pont. "In view of these startling and appalling disclosures," Reed contended, the Senate had no choice but to follow its "plain course of duty." Reed had to find satisfaction in giving a speech, and the *Chicago Tribune*, which gleefully had run with the story ("Du Pont May Lose His Senate Seat"), had to be content with Lorimer's ejection. The committee let the matter slide. It publicly slapped down the West Virginia governor's challenge to the seating of Clarence W. Watson for an unexpired term and William E. Chilton for a full term. Rumors of bribery and vague charges were not enough to stir the weary committee to action.[24]

That the West Virginia cases disappeared without a sound other than groans of exasperation had as much to do with politics as with the merits. Some of the facts of the West Virginia elections resembled those of others that seemed to imperil the Republic. Watson, head of the Consolidated Coal Company, the state's largest employer, was, like Stephenson, very, very rich. The governor was a progressive who advanced the full good-government agenda and went beyond it in his relative willingness to defend African Americans' rights. The charges against the winning senators included vote buying, which had so roused Reed in Du Pont's case and most of the Senate in Lorimer's. The elections were tight and controversial, and, as in Wisconsin, a faction of the state legislature made itself absent in order to prevent a quorum. But it mattered that Chilton and Watson were Democrats. Insurgent Republicans and Democrats propelled seating controversies, and none of them could find the outrage or the hearty spirit of adventure required for delving into the murk of West Virginia politics.[25]

The Democrats and a sizable Republican faction had the means and motive to chase down allegations of corruption, but even so, removing a member was hard. Despite the potential gains for the group, to vote for expulsion many Senators needed more than the sorts of stories that losers floated after nearly every campaign. What measured up as convincing evidence varied. A few senators found nearly any story about a regular Republican believable on its face. No senator defended bribery, and most found the prospect of spending or raising big campaign budgets uncomfortable, if not immoral. The Senate's standards of evidence fell below those demanded in the courts, but usually above the low bar of simple politics. Lorimer proved to be the exception, not the template for future action.

The facts of these seating cases also demonstrated that the election of senators by legislatures brought no end of trouble. Preference primaries in the states had made the process of electing senators worse, not better. They added a plotline to what was already a factional melodrama in state legislatures. And senators could imagine that legislative elections were corruption magnets. The Senate fights strengthened the case for cutting out the middleman and passing a constitutional amendment providing for the direct election of senators.

A cause of nineteenth-century third parties, direct elections fit within the let-the-people-decide ethos of the early twentieth century. As a growing number of states adopted a version of direct election, the House passed an amendment with the necessary two-thirds majority five times between 1893 and 1902. While the second investigation of Lorimer went forward, the Senate came within four votes of passing the amendment early in 1911. A special session found the votes in June 1911. After reconciling the House and Senate versions, the amendment went to the states, and it went into effect with the elections of 1914.[26]

Passage took more than the ripening of a democratic impulse. It took having enough Democrats in the Senate who, with insurgent Republicans, consistently supported the amendment. In the South, where preference primaries for Senate candidates began, direct election could solve the problem of deadlocked legislatures, which especially bedeviled those states. For urban Democrats in the North, direct election might overcome apportionment in state legislatures skewed toward rural areas (and Republicans) that hurt their candidates. Insurgent Republicans, many of them products of some variety of direct election, touted the need to trust the people over corrupt or corruptible state legislatures. Regular Republicans could only talk about the wisdom of the framers in creating a body that moved slowly and deliberately and try to divide Democratic support by adding federal control of elections, the South's great fear, to the amendment. That tactic stalled but failed to stop the amendment. The Democrats' success in the states against a divided Republican Party in 1912 ensured speedy ratification.[27]

In more optimistic (or fanciful) moments, supporters of primary elections and the direct election of senators argued that these reforms would drive down the cost of elections. How could it be otherwise, without candidates trying to buy convention delegates or legislatures? Lorimer's fund, word was, reached $100,000. But the Stephenson campaign showed how spectacularly wrong such speculation was. His manager told the Privileges and Elections Committee that if he had done his job thoroughly, he would have spent $200,000 to organize all of Wisconsin's counties to match La Follette's presence in the state. If the $107,000 Stephenson spent seemed shocking, learning that the manager had cut corners in hiring workers might have caused the committee to consider what it took to challenge an entrenched organization. To win a primary in California against any sort of opposition, according to Senator Frank Flint, would cost at least $57,000 in 1910, more than the $45,000 a senator then earned over a six-year term. He retired rather than face the fund-raising or financial hit.[28]

That was a reality that Congress seemed to ignore. As lawmakers took the first steps toward direct election and investigated Lorimer and Stephenson, it went after the costs of elections through campaign finance reform laws. This was perhaps an effort to contain runaway costs. But it was also the Democratic and insurgent Republican coalition's effort to trim the power of the regular Republican organization. In doing so, Congress coupled unrealistic expectations for spending with provisions that were more loophole than barrier.

Big campaign budgets had few defenders in Congress or anywhere else. The indictments tended to coast on the standing suspicion that all those dollars were up to no good, so much so that it did not seem necessary to explain what exactly was wrong. Two themes can be teased out. Most commonly, reformers cared about the sources of money and its misuse. Contributions cloaked in secrecy could hide a private, nefarious agenda. The purpose of publicity was "to secure the freedom of elections from improper influences," according to Perry Belmont, head of the National Publicity Bill Organization and brother of August Belmont, the financial angel of the nineteenth-century democracy, and himself a former congressman and fund-raiser. Big money implied bribery. It could buy legislators, either directly through a crude tit-for-tat agreement or, more subtly, through concurrence that did not need words. It could buy voters, along with newspaper editors and campaign workers. A smaller number of reformers added the second argument. Money in politics was evil, period, whatever its sources and uses. Even if campaign funds purchased innocuous things—posters, flyers, and ads that got a candidate's views in front of voters—costly elections endangered democracy. Only the rich or those with rich friends could run for office if spending were unlimited. Candidates with the best, most expensive propaganda (not yet a bad word), not the best men, would have the edge. Money corrupted public life by making it harder for the truly meritorious and the public interest to succeed.[29]

Civil service laws had already cut into some sources of party workers and funds. At the national level and in some states, the potential for patronage jobs available for loyal party workers had diminished after the 1880s. The practice of dunning public employees for the good of their parties had begun to fall away, at least in filling the coffers of the national party organizations. New legislation went after the sources of funds that had replaced party assessments. The first round attacked corporate contributions, the mainstay of party fund-raisers in the 1890s. The Tillman Act (1907) made it "unlawful for any national bank, or any corporation organized by authority of any laws of Congress, to make a money contribution in connection with any election to any political office." Corporations or their officers or board members found to violate the law were subject to fines and up to one year in prison.[30]

The bill emerged out of scandal—or, more precisely, a long-running effort came to fruition after revelations of how corporations contributed generously to Republican campaigns. In the 1904 presidential campaign, Democrats made much of corporate contributions to President Theodore Roosevelt, although the charges did not help the doomed Alton B. Parker. An investigation of the life insurance industry in New York headed by Charles Evans Hughes, however, added the disturbing news that George W. Perkins, TR's campaign manager, a vice president of New York Life, and partner in the J. P. Morgan investment bank, deposited nearly $50,000 in the account of the Republican National Committee in 1904. Worse, such contributions had been standard practice since 1896. Roosevelt got in front of the growing scandal by urging Congress to pass legislation banning corporate contributions. The Senate resuscitated a bill proposed by William Eaton Chandler in 1900. A radical Republican in the Reconstruction years, Chandler had served as secretary of the Republican National Committee in 1868. He knew firsthand how fund-raising had changed from the days of assessments on public employees, the grudging gifts of a handful of financial angels, and states slow to ante up their share of the campaign bill. A lame duck who blamed his defeat on the New Hampshire railroads, he drafted a bill that went nowhere. But he found an unusual partner in "Pitchfork" Ben Tillman of South Carolina, a former Confederate who had joined the terror campaign against the Republican and African American political organizations that Chandler had tried to support with cash. Tillman kept the bill afloat. The version that passed, supported by President Roosevelt, trimmed the original. It did not touch contributions of state-chartered corporations. It did not require the parties to disclose the sources of their funds, although the RNC (Republican National Committee) and DNC (Democratic National Committee) voluntarily released financial records for the 1908 presidential election. The Tillman Act prevented contributions to campaigns using "other people's money"—that of stockholders. Otherwise the fund-raiser's burden—finding large contributions from wealthy partisans—was undisturbed. There is record of only one violation that was prosecuted: a gift from the United States Brewers' Association to a House candidate.[31]

In 1910, the same reform-minded Congress that had revamped House procedures and scrutinized the credentials of the insufficiently insurgent or Democratic filled in what reformers saw as the gaps left by the Tillman Act. The 1910 Federal Corrupt Practices Act provided for publicity. It required every House candidate and "political committee" to report the sources of their contributions. In the House, the 1910 bill's supporters expected no real debate and quickly doused the few quibbles that emerged. James R. Mann, a Cook County, Illinois, Republican and rising star, worried that the bill had not clearly defined "political committee," fearing the language would encompass good groups, like labor unions. The proposal's supporters dismissed his arguments as a "bogy to frighten members into voting against the bill." What criticism emerged had to do with the bill not going far enough. It was less a debate than a riot of pious expression on the House floor. The bill "will render impossible that debauchery of the electorate, which has so frequently thwarted the popular will. . . . Extravagant campaign contributions, which exceed in quantity what is necessary, and only what is necessary, to meet the legitimate expenses of a campaign, have degenerated into a moral, a social, and a political evil." The measure would "dissolve this corrupt alliance between business and politics." Campaign finance reform was nonpartisan goodness itself, involving "the moral rectitude of the nation." "Every man who genuinely believes in the purity of the ballot and the integrity of the right of franchise should, in the interest of honesty, justice, and fair play, unhesitatingly give his earnest support to this measure," assured New York congressman Michael Conry.[32]

The Senate took its time in getting to the bill. Perry Belmont, whose organization lobbied for the bill, suspected the regular Republicans would let it die. But the FCPA made it out of the upper house with one change, the elimination of a requirement that political committees file reports on contributions before as well as after elections. It cruised through at the end of the session with President William Howard Taft's support after more pressing matters such as the tariff and a railroad bill received attention.[33]

Energized by a majority that signaled popular demand for reform and reports of big spending campaigns, Congress amended the FCPA in 1911. The House brought back the preelection reporting requirements. The Senate had bigger ambitions. In this version both House and Senate candidates had to disclose contributions before and after elections. With Lorimer in mind, disclosure also covered elections of senators by state legislatures even when a candidate emerged late in the process. And it applied to primaries, special elections, and conventions. Reed of Missouri added a late flourish: candidates for the House and Senate could not spend more than $5,000 or $10,000, respectively, unless state laws specified a smaller amount.[34]

This bill went further than anyone imagined, as Democrats and regular Republicans bid up the provisions intending to highlight the other side's hypocrisy. Regular Republicans insisted on disclosure of contributions and spending limits for primary as well as general elections, a provision southern Democrats were sure to reject. The spending caps attacked wealthy Republican candidates, a dare to the regulars to vote against the bill. But the 1911 amendments were adopted unanimously by the House and passed the Senate with only seven no votes. They came from southern Democrats, who faced plenty of primary but no general election threats and who smelled an opening to the dreaded federal control over state elections. They argued that federal control over state primary elections was unconstitutional. The law passed in the same session in which the Senate failed to gain the two-thirds majority for direct election. Democrats proposed further amendments, most seriously in 1916. Senator Robert Latham Owen of Oklahoma, a Virginia native whose hostility toward Wall Street arose perhaps from his father's railroad that went under in the depression of the 1870s, offered an amendment that extended the FCPA's spending limits to political commit- tees. His own situation, Owen claimed, pointed up the need for broader regulations: the "lumber trust" spent $40,000 trying to defeat him because he voted to expel Lorimer. But this was a presidential election year. The bill disappeared in fist-waving accusations of corrupt contributions in the past and plots to steal the upcoming election. Codified and slightly modified in 1925 and 1926, the Corrupt Practices Act was the basic campaign finance law until the 1970s.[35]

For all the fearsome speeches about defending democracy from money's evil effects, the FCPA did not regulate much. A scholarly consensus developed al- most as soon as the legislation left the printers that campaign finance reform had minimal effect on campaigns. The law permitted standard campaign ex- penditures. Travel; stationery and postage; distributing letters, circulars, and posters; and telephone and telegraph charges were among the items that did not count toward the spending limit. And the spending caps applied to can- didates, not to committees formed to advance their campaigns. The clerk of the House and secretary of the Senate, patronage appointees of the majority party, did not make it easy to use the reports. The curious souls who sought out the reports (including charitable fund-raisers seeking prospects) before they were destroyed to make room for new files found papers filled out with a whimsical understanding of bookkeeping.[36]

If the FCPA did not really regulate spending, its political advantages were easy to spot. Congressional Democrats hoped spending limits might weaken the Republicans' traditional fund-raising advantages by curbing the spending of rich candidates and putting a scare into some of the party's deep pockets. Capitalizing on voters' suspicion of money in politics, an opponent's spend- ing could be made a campaign issue. The greatest benefits naturally enough flowed to those comfortably in power, not those banging on the doors to get in. Spending limits, if obeyed, helped incumbents who enjoyed name recognition and the perks of office. Those familiar with the rules knew how to spend the money necessary for a campaign without violating the letter of the law. And, depending on the political environment and the level of spending, Congress, as judge of its own members, could still remove a senator or representative. A conviction in court was not necessary, since each house enforced its norms as it saw them through investigation, censure, and expulsion.

So although violations of the FCPA threatened jail time and fines, aggrieved losers usually took their cases to Congress, not to the courts. Seating challenges now added charges of excessive spending to classic illegal campaign shenanigans. The Democratic House in 1912 enthusiastically tried out the new tool, perhaps in payback for Republican investigations of allegedly illegally won Democratic seats in the late nineteenth century. The House declared a Pennsylvania seat vacant, since it appeared that both candidates in the 1910 election had bribed voters and spent too much. The House awarded Democrat Patrick Gill the seat Republican Theron Catlin had won in 1912, declaring that Catlin won because of illegal spending. Catlin's father had made a fortune in the tobacco business and allegedly spent more than $10,000 in his son's campaign against the incumbent Gill. Catlin claimed he spent $550, or $100 less than the limit on candidates in Missouri, and knew nothing about his father's activities. The House Elections Committee searched for fraud, chasing after Catlin's sister so that she could be subpoenaed to testify about whether a dinner party she threw for fifteen bricklayers was a payoff for union support. Fraud should have been easy to find in St. Louis, but the committee uncovered little substantial evidence. In a disappointment to Washington society, where the tall, good-looking bachelor was a hit, Catlin lost his seat anyway, amid "wild enthusiasm" on the Democratic side of the aisle. Eight Democrats, however, balked at giving Gill, the loser on election day, the seat.[37]

Some cases included violations of state statutes. All but four states—Illinois, Mississippi, Rhode Island, and Tennessee—had some sort of campaign finance legislation on the books by the time of the second FCPA of 1926. Thirty-six states regulated how much candidates and/or party committees could spend on campaigns, either setting a fixed sum or using a formula based on the number of voters in the last election. Many states extended reporting requirements to groups other than party committees and the candidates' own committees. States also prohibited the use of funds for a wide variety of items—Arizona prohibited using money in an election for anything other than "holding public meetings to discuss public questions and to print and circulate handbills and papers." Some states regulated what campaign workers could do (prohibiting, for example, rides to the polls) and when they could do it (preventing paid workers from "electioneering" on the day of the election). Both Nebraska and Massachusetts targeted contributions rather than spending, capping donations at $1,000.[38]

Candidates could spend lavishly without violating state or federal laws. Federal candidates rarely indicated that they had spent anything more than a nominal sum. Campaign committees raised and spent the necessary funds. Accuracy was uncommon. In the 1920s, a state officer who processed the paperwork told a researcher that the laws were "worse than dead letters because they make perjurers out of every one who files a statement." Even if caught violating spending rules or filing provisions, congressmen did not necessarily merit expulsion. In 1910, incumbent congressman George C. Sturgiss did not challenge the election of William G. Brown Jr., a member of a West Virginia political family, although Brown's expenses ($3,017.30 reported) ran over the state limit of $893. Nor did Congress question the election. The Senate could have contested the elections of both Democrats and Republicans charged with excessive spending in their 1914 races. The targets included Pennsylvania boss Boise Penrose, who, according to A. Mitchell Palmer, the defeated candidate, spent $1 million in the campaign. No investigations followed.[39]

While Congress chose to act—or not—in cases of potential fraud or excessive spending, in 1915 the Department of Justice became curious about state and local elections in Republican strongholds. Attorney General Thomas Watt Gregory ordered investigations in Pennsylvania, Illinois, and Indiana. The Pennsylvania case netted the one and only conviction, that of the Brewers' Association, under the Tillman Act. The Illinois probe had symbolism attached to it, as it covered the district of the former infamous Speaker of the House, Joseph Cannon. Special Assistant Frank C. Dailey handled the prosecution in Terre Haute, Indiana, himself. A grand jury indicted 114 local officials and Republican Party activists on charges of mail fraud and intimidation. That he wrung guilty pleas from a large number and won the convictions of others made him someone to watch in Indiana Democratic political circles. Henry Ford's legal team would remember his success and look to this proven winner to prosecute Newberry.[40]

Although finance cases were difficult to prosecute, there was a law on the books, vague on what it prohibited but politically potent. It expressed a preference for low-budget campaigns even as costs were rising. And they would continue to increase, since campaigns in the first decades of the twentieth century were caught between modern commercial methods and old-fashioned ward politics. The political context made the circumstances of an election a compelling scandal or a snore. William E. Chilton threatened to unleash shocking revelations in his challenge of Howard Sutherland's victory in their 1916 Senate race in West Virginia. Sutherland had spent more than permitted under state law, Chilton alleged, and Sutherland's campaign was guilty of a variety of corrupt practices, including transporting blacks from other states to vote in West Virginia. Charges about "colonization" also rang through Indiana, where Democrats, including John Worth Kern, a progressive who had championed the direct election of senators and taken a lead in the Lorimer case, lost to regular Republicans.[41]

Senator Reed and the Department of Justice attempted to put back some of what voters had undone. Reed tried to stop James E. Watson of Indiana from being sworn in, with his election instead going straight to the Privileges and Elections Committee. That move failed, and Watson, along with the class that dropped the Democratic majority from sixteen to four, took his seat. His case, along with Chilton's and that of his Indiana colleague, Harry New, had been the focus of Department of Justice attention before the election. The department announced an "in no way political" investigation of frauds in the 1916 elections, with agents working in Indiana and West Virginia, as well as Michigan, Minnesota, Ohio, New York, and Illinois. All but Ohio, where Pomerene won a second term, and Illinois, where there was no Senate race, had elected or reelected Republicans. The effort netted a congressman, Orrin D. Bleakley, a western Pennsylvania banker who had, in a stunt, flown to Washington for the swearing-in ceremony. His plea of no contest to spending more than $5,000, followed by his resignation, helped the Democrats organize the House, although they still needed independents to get to a majority. Elsewhere the probes fizzled, like those in the Senate.[42]

There was enough static in the air, however, to have warned Newberry and his manager of potential trouble. The strict letter of the FCPA did not forbid extensive spending, except by candidates themselves. But in the right partisan circumstances, those who opposed large campaign budgets on principle could find allies among those who could muster outrage if it suited. What the FCPA allowed was not necessarily what the Senate would permit.

4

Michigan

For months, the Michigan primary looked like a game that might never begin. Players, backups, spectators, and coaches milled around the sidelines, with no one certain of who would take the field or for which side. When it was finally sorted out, the results were odd indeed: a nominal Republican running as a Democrat and Republican, a Democrat in the race because of Republican support, two Republicans with Progressive credentials, and a retiring incumbent who kept hinting that he had second thoughts about stepping down after all. Both sides pulled out every available trick in the general election. Before voters had their say, a president and ex-presidents intervened; lawyers and detectives combed the state in search of the faintest rumors of corruption; and federal investigations amplified the rumors. Voters had to sift through a great deal of advertising, mudslinging, and real and feigned shock at campaign spending.

A freakish set of national and local circumstances created the frenzy. The Wilson administration and the Republican National Committee (RNC) strained to turn voters' attention to the national and international implications of the Senate elections, especially the proposed League of Nations. If, in some states, voters attended to the concrete and local—the prices of corn, wheat, and hogs—Wilson's choice of Ford put national questions at the center in Michigan. Voters had the chance to weigh in twice, since the state's Progressive Era election laws allowed candidates to run for nomination under as many parties as they wished in primary elections, an opportunity that suited Ford's above-the-fray political image. The state also limited candidates' campaign expenditures at an even more miserly rate than did the federal laws. Spending limits were easy enough to dodge—every campaign simply set up a committee that handled contributions and spending. But "excessive" spending of the Newberry campaign became one of the election's story lines, brought to public attention by rival candidates, the press, and the federal Department of Justice.

The campaign included little direct discussion of the great national questions. Ford and the spending of the Newberry campaign, the two big issues, stood in for them. To listen to the charges hurled back and forth, the future of democracy and world peace hung in the balance in the form of the Newberry campaign's profligacy, Ford's pacifist history, his son Edsel's draft exemption, and the Wilson administration's meddling in Michigan politics. Neither Ford nor Newberry made campaign appearances. Swept along by harsh partisanship and the playing-for-keeps approach of everyone involved, Newberry seemed clueless and Ford careless about what was being done for them. Gradually, they came to believe what their publicists wrote, sure of their own virtue and their opponent's viciousness.

The election brought forward the conflict between Progressive Era laws that limited campaign expenditures and replaced party conventions with primary elections. This would be clear in hindsight. A more pressing set of questions demanded attention in 1918. Were the Newberry campaign's expenditures illegal? Were they corrupt, even if they were legal? Were they necessary, given Ford's fame and the high stakes of the election? When Michigan voters had their chance to answer the questions, they elected Newberry, barely, despite the whiff of scandal. Ford, with the help of Wilson's Department of Justice, would see to it that the answers ultimately would not rest with them.

State politics and election laws, products of the mid-nineteenth-century antislavery controversy and Progressive Era reform, provided the context for this strange election. Michigan had been a normally Republican state since the birth of the party in 1854, when it won the governor's office and a majority in the state legislature. By the 1880s, Republican control had weakened. While James McMillan's tact usually managed the egos and demands of striving politicians, it failed to patch the deep cracks in the Republican coalition. Populism made little headway in the state, but many voters had grown restless with a party leadership focused on satisfying the desires of the state's major economic players. Some Republican politicians responded. Detroit's mayor, Hazen S. Pingree, did battle with the streetcar and utility franchises and responded with some sympathy to labor unrest and the plight of the poor and unemployed during the depression of the 1890s. Pingree's battle against the streetcar franchise owners—wealthy, solidly Republican Detroit families— earned him McMillan's hostility. But his reform reputation made him governor in 1897. McMillan still controlled enough of the legislature to block some of Pingree's agenda, but it was clear to a growing faction of Republicans that the party had to do more than merely deliver for the state's elite. McMillan had trouble enough keeping the party both together and regular. After his death in 1902, no one else came close.[1]

Progressivism intensified and complicated Republican factionalism. Some fights pitted insurgents and regulars, but far more than that, they involved sharp-elbowed men, all positioned as reformers, maneuvering for influence. In 1907, the last Senate contest decided in the legislature, the seat went to William Alden Smith, a Republican unaffiliated with the remnants of the McMillan clan, after the defeat of two candidates favored by the group. Even when the old McMillan loyalists got their man, their control was weak. Fred Warner, whom they had selected for governor, turned out to be a reformer in office. He served three terms before Chase Osborn, a progressive who endorsed Pingree's agenda with greater pugnaciousness than even Pingree managed, replaced him in Lansing. Divisions between the Roosevelt and Taft men opened the way for a Democratic governor in 1912 and again in 1914, but Republicans had not simply divided into two. Alex Groesbeck was for Taft in 1912 but thereafter presented himself as a man above faction. Osborn bounced between Roosevelt and Wilson in 1912. Progressivism had cachet in Michigan—it was one of the six states that went for Roosevelt in 1912. What it meant was anyone's guess. Nearly every candidate marched near, if not under, its banner, even as they tried to shove each other out of line.[2]

The direct primary, passed in 1909, turned Republican family quarrels into public brawls. Democrats did not have to settle for cheering from the sidelines. Michigan's law allowed voters to choose the party for which they wanted to cast a ballot on the day of the primary election. Democrats rarely had competitive primaries, so they could meddle without consequences to their own tickets. Republicans, for example, charged that Democrats had raided their 1914 gubernatorial primary in order to support Osborn, the more divisive and weaker candidate, over Groesbeck. Republicans tried a few different schemes to keep Democrats out of their primaries, but in a normally one-party state, nothing worked. As a last-ditch expedient, they occasionally sponsored dummy candidates in Democratic primaries to keep Democrats from crossing over.[3]

Republicans contemplating the 1918 Senate race could be certain only of a primary fight. The sitting senator, William Alden Smith, whose fame and reputation for independence were burnished in the investigation he led into the *Titanic* disaster, announced in March that he would not run again. Even with only rumors in hand, potential competitors with serious resumes were weighing their chances. Among the names mentioned were a sitting congressman, former governor Warner, and Detroit police commissioner and former Ford executive Couzens, who was quickly building a reputation for political independence and administrative talent. Future senator Arthur Vandenberg, editor of the *Grand Rapids Herald*, Smith's newspaper, considered a run as the natural heir to and protégé of Smith. Rumors had John Dodge, friendly with Ford despite the suit over dividends and never fully welcomed into Grosse Pointe society, considering his chances.[4]

One candidate was certain. Former governor Chase Osborn, naturalist and explorer in the TR mold, who made his fame as owner of the *Sault Ste. Marie News* and his fortune in iron ore and timber, staked out the progressive vote. Born in Indiana in 1860, he set off at the age of seventeen, making his way to the Soo after stints in the newspaper business in Milwaukee and Florence, Wisconsin. He soon turned to politics and made enough friends in the Republican Party to be appointed to the state railroad and fish and game commissions. "Strapping [and] muscular," with a reputation for impulsiveness (Osborn saw it as an admirable willingness to respond to new facts), he ran unsuccessfully for Congress in 1896 and governor in 1900, before winning in 1910. He had significant strengths as a Senate candidate in 1918, including a statewide network that grew out of his earlier campaigns, wide and deep press contacts courtesy of his newspaper career, and a considerable reputation as an eloquent and tireless public speaker who talked "like a gatling gun." Yet he had lost elections, most recently in 1914, and had created enemies as well as friends. He was a free spirit who separated from his big-game-hunting wife in 1923, legally adopted his thirty-seven-year-old secretary in 1931, and annulled the adoption in order to marry her two days before his death in 1949. He once said of himself that "he was charged with being erratic, not a few called him crazy, and everybody agreed to the fact that he would not stand hitched."[5]

And then there was Newberry. As early as August 1917, Governor Albert E. Sleeper and his staff, who styled themselves as moderate progressives, had fingered Newberry as the ideal candidate: a Detroiter (the city had not been honored with a seat in the Senate recently) with TR connections and past and current military service, an obvious plus in a wartime election. Sleeper backed off on an endorsement given the knot of potential candidates, but his staffers pressed on. One of them, Menominee publisher Roger M. Andrews, urged Newberry to run in order to "give us a real man in the senate . . . whose Americanism is unquestioned" and whose "Roosevelt ideals" were solid. Burt D. Cady, Sleeper's pick to head the state party committee, thought Newberry was a winner: "With the Metropolitan Dailies behind you and no other candidate from Wayne County [Detroit], with the assistance you can secure in the Upper Peninsula and what we can do for you in the Thumb together with the important support that I know we can get throughout the entire state, . . . you would be elected as United States Senator from Michigan."[6]

Newberry was characteristically interested but cautious. From his naval post in New York, he sounded out newspaper reporters about the political situation in Michigan. Frederick Cody, a glad-handing, garrulous lobbyist for the American Book Company (controlled by Newberry's wife and brother-in-law), AT&T, and other firms, shuttled between New York and Detroit, tracking the interest in Newberry's candidacy. By mid-February, Newberry had decided to run, so long as his campaign committee understood that he would remain in New York for the duration of the war. A committee formed to organize a campaign, chaired by Allen A. Templeton, a business associate, with Frank W. Blair, president of the Union Trust Company, serving as treasurer.[7]

Like the other candidates and potential candidates, Newberry would need to build an organization out of party activists willing to support his run in the primary. Unlike Osborn or, potentially, Warner, he lacked statewide political contacts. Outside of the Upper Peninsula, where John S. Newberry and McMillan had invested heavily in iron, lumber, and railroads, and among

the elite in Detroit and those who followed their exploits, Newberry was unknown. He rejected doing the obvious things—speaking and appearances—
that would have built name recognition and political friendships. Still,
without an obvious front-runner, his chances were as good as the rest with
skillful management and the application of enough cash.[8]

Paul H. King was the right man to make the most of a blank-slate candidacy.
The forty-year-old King had been around politics since he was a boy who
helped support his family by working as a page in the Minnesota and Michigan state legislatures. His father, a physician who, like "the prospector who is
always about to strike some Eldorado just ahead of him," dragged his family
around the Midwest in search of the perfect opportunity that never appeared.
King's earnings had helped the family make ends meet from the time he was
a ten-year-old newsboy. After his father's death, the boy's jobs kept the family
together. With a combination of hard work, discretion, competence, and a
knack for networking, King began to climb. His first political position came
as a result of a typing job for a Populist Minnesota legislator, whom he had
met while working as a janitor and typist in a law office. King moved with his
new patron to the legislature, where his contacts widened. An ailing grand-
mother brought the Kings to Michigan, where he finished high school. There
King flourished, advancing from a page to the clerk of the Michigan House,
while studying law in his spare time.[9]

King's diligence, connections, and attention to detail made him a formidable political organizer. He managed the Townsend Senate campaign in
1909 and became secretary of the Republican State Central Committee in
1910. He was setting up a legal practice (with a specialty in bankruptcy) but
took time away in 1917 to head the Michigan Red Cross Fund, the type of
job that was a finishing school for future public relations and fund-raising
professionals. He managed to build wide friendships while racking up no
enemies. In anticipation of Newberry's meeting with King, Blair described
him as "one of Michigan's cleverest politicians." He knew everybody in
state politics and was "politically honest, that is, he will faithfully fulfill
any promise he makes." King insisted on meeting with Newberry, since he
had helped lock Newberry out of the 1912 Republican state convention. The
meeting went well enough for King to sign on to the Newberry for Senate
Committee without pay.[10]

Newberry imagined that he was hiring a man who would run a high-minded, gentlemanly campaign that would not discomfit anyone at the Yondotega Club. The campaign would have to proceed without platforms or policy statements, since as long as he was in military service, Newberry was not free to offer them. In his correspondence with George Miller, head of the Washington bureau of the Democratic-leaning, progressive *Detroit News*, Newberry thought through what he might say if he could speak. "I have considered long, sincerely and searchingly, my all too few qualifications," he wrote, and made a Boy Scout's list: "loyalty, education, experience, a desire to serve and help others, honest, sincere, sober," with no motives beyond service to "my Country and my State." Newberry agreed with Miller that the changes the war brought required new ideas, but he stopped short of agreeing with Miller's sense that both wartime experience and the likely demands of returning veterans would mean either revolution or wise policies that went well beyond anything Progressives had imagined. Newberry suspected after the war "radical" changes, including "the readjustment of compensation for labor of all kinds; equalization of burden of taxation by existing or greater super taxes on incomes, and a revolution in our inheritance tax laws," were certain, with the only struggle being how to make such measures "fair." He favored "Unionism" but not the closed shop, and "hope[d] that Government will so arrange its taxes that every dollar made by an individual or corporation" in war profits would be whisked away in taxes. He supported women's suffrage, regretting only that it remained too easy for immigrants to gain the vote. Miller thought Newberry's wealth and refusal to clearly tell voters what he believed about looming national issues weakened his candidacy; his exchange of letters with Newberry did not change his mind.[11]

Ironically, Newberry's opinions on money and politics echoed those of reformers. "No one is more opposed than I to any improper or even questionable use of money," he assured Miller, "and not one cent will be spent by me or in my behalf with my knowledge and consent, that cannot be published to the world, and this keystone principle of my candidacy I wrote out and delivered months ago to those concerned." He had instructed Templeton to go to Fred Smith, who controlled the family's accounts and who would mind "the money matters referred to and such others as may hereafter arise." Smith knew that "I believe the proper use of money in political campaigns is confined to all matters of publicity and the payment for time and expenses of any man who is legitimately devoting himself to any political cause." Suspecting that King took on the campaign with his "political future" in mind, Newberry hoped that "the lawful expenses connected with publicity and service . . . be entirely in [Templeton's] sole control" as "the only man in my acquaintance whom I want to handle this matter." Even publicity disturbed Newberry. "As I always hate to see my name in print, I will be as glad as you are that the question of further publicity will be seriously considered by you and Mr. King," he told Templeton in March. "I am sure from what you write me, that your ideas and mine will exactly coincide on the proper, sincere, clean methods that both Mr. King and yourself, and myself, and in fact all of my friends, stand for."[12]

Newberry attended to the legal as well as moral side of campaign finance. In May, Smith consulted an attorney at Newberry's suggestion for an interpretation of the 1913 Michigan statute. The law limited candidates' spending to 25 percent of the salary of the office, although there were no limits on what committees could spend. It described permissible expenses, which included the travel, advertising, and office support required for modern campaigns. It also publicized contributions, prohibited corporate giving, and prevented charities from soliciting candidates (churches and other organizations otherwise hoped that running for election would put candidates in a generous mood). The law allowed for the sort of campaign that would keep Newberry's name in the newspaper.[13]

Templeton checked on the progress of the campaign, but it was King's show. "I considered myself a free agent, a free lance, to do just as I felt should be done in the management of that campaign," he later said. This was the way he ran campaigns—even the far more experienced Townsend did what he was told in his 1916 campaign, speaking when and where King determined, with voters invited by personal letters to hear him. For Newberry's race, King traveled the state, perfecting an organization that reached down to the election district in every county but Chippewa, Osborn's base. Following the pattern of Red Cross fund drives, he divided the state into territories and assigned each region (and a number of economic and ethnic groups) a "field man." Those men in turn identified county and district leaders, who distributed literature and organized meetings, and prepared daily reports for King. By April, according to a friend of Newberry's, King was "on the jump" and had "secured the best people in the state" to work for the campaign. King kept a sizable clerical staff in Detroit busy, sending cards to Republicans (purchasing the lists from county clerks) and keeping track of the payments owed to the workforce. He arranged for the production and screening of a short film on military recruitment, *Our Navy*, in which Newberry appeared. While King had "inserted an occasional advertisement in some newspapers" for Townsend, the Newberry campaign featured "a series of advertisements in all the newspapers," with many of the ads depicting the "Commander" in uniform, sometimes flanked by his uniformed sons.[14]

King frequently updated Newberry by letter and telephone, supplemented by a few meetings in New York. How much Newberry understood of the detailed missives is unclear. At times he offered his concern about such things as the labor vote in Detroit, and he responded as best he could to King's requests for letters on issues that went to field men. Mostly he was not a font of suggestions. He replied to a long letter on conditions in the Upper Peninsula, saying that he "filed away in my mind" the names King mentioned "and only hope that I can remember the various individuals if I ever have the good luck to meet them." Newberry read through reports on four counties "in order to get some hazy vision of the really tremendous travel and effort that you are putting into this campaign. I never can half thank you for what you are doing for me personally, and the party should thank you for really awakening the interest of the leading men of the various portions of our state in our state's representation in Congress." With no statewide political experience, Newberry sat slack-jawed at King's grasp of Michigan politics and gratified by the (mostly) good news he heard.[15]

What King built for Newberry was neither inexpensive nor reticent. He never wrote a word, at least a surviving one, about the cost of his publicity and organizational feats. So when King mentioned that the state president of the Brotherhood of Engineers and Firemen would "devot[e] a month of his time to visiting the various locals and interesting the boys in our cause," he did not say that he added another man to the payroll, joining field men, publicity specialists, clerks, stenographers, and local organizers. The campaign also covered everyone's expenses. When he first met with Newberry, King guessed that a campaign might cost as much as $50,000, or $30,000 more than the campaign of the better-known Townsend. King was off by more than $120,000. What Newberry knew about any of it would become the legal—and criminal—question.[16]

With the ads, mailings, and organizers, it did not take long for Osborn to pick up on how expensive the Newberry campaign was becoming. "Mr. Newberry is spraying or smudging Michigan with money," he wrote to a Chicago news-paperman in early June. "They have undertaken to buy every newspaper in Michigan." A Detroit newspaper editor who supported Osborn hoped that taking a Newberry ad would not give Osborn the wrong idea. "You have got to do business and I hope you will get all the advertising Mr. Newberry can do under the law," Osborn responded. Osborn, a rich man himself, focused on his own fund-raising. Publicity alone would run up to $15,000. Osborn counted on John C. Shaffer, owner of the *Chicago Evening Post*, and John F. Dodge to raise the money. Meanwhile, one of his managers worked for the endorsement of former governor Warner and Lieutenant Governor Dickin-son and encouraged those who angled to get Senator Smith back in the race, on the theory that Smith would divide Newberry's support.[17]

Both Newberry's and Osborn's managers reported that the other side was making little headway, perhaps because neither side had gained much press or public attention. According to an Osborn aide, things were locked up in June. "We have the Dry vote, the Labor vote, and the middle class manufacturing and business vote pretty well in hand," he reported. Osborn's intelligence in the field reported what the former governor already believed: Newberry's support was "manufactured" and amounted to nothing but a "fife and drum" campaign. With King's reports of steady progress and solid organization in hand, Newberry blew off the idea of Smith reentering the race. "As you know our friend, Chase, is a good deal of a spellbinder, and if two spellbinders were working on the same number of impressionable listeners, they would prob-ably split the vote," he reasoned. Still, it remained a race without real issues or buzz. King admitted that "it has been really tremendously hard to get people worked up to the point of even talking about it, let alone working."[18]

That is, until Ford entered the race. King later claimed that his organiza-tion spent so heavily not just because it could but because he suspected Ford would run. He began tracking rumors in the early spring; by early April he had concluded that the Booth family, owners of the *Detroit News*, among other papers, was behind Ford's potential candidacy. King's intelligence was good. In April, the discussions among Democrats about getting Ford into the race had advanced far enough for Josephus Daniels, Wilson's secretary of the navy, to investigate the prospect. "'It's a cinch,'" said a Detroit Democrat, Daniels recalled. "'He would get the nomination of both Republicans and Democrats in the primary. He could be elected, and his desire for peace and his admiration of Wilson would give the President a Senator who would stand by the League of Nations and his other policies. . . . We will elect him, if Wilson can induce him to run.'" And so Daniels made it happen.[19]

On June 12, a Democratic conference announced that the party would back Ford, "although he is not within our fold," and urged that the Republicans do the same. Ford went to Washington a day later. When Daniels failed to persuade Ford, it was Wilson's turn to try. "'Mr. Ford, I feel that it is your patriotic duty to come to the Senate from Michigan,'" said Wilson, Daniels recalled. "'We must carry on to both victories—an end of fighting to be followed by a war-less world.'" Ford succumbed, and issued a statement that characteristically focused attention on himself in the guise of selflessness:

The president has asked me to become a candidate for United States Senator from Michigan. I know nothing whatever about parties or party machinery, and I am not at all concerned about which ticket I am nominated on. They can put my name on all the tickets if they want to. I will not spend a cent nor make a single move to get into the Senate. Nor will I have a campaign organization, nor pay any campaign bills. . . . I do not care anything about parties or politics or politicians. I would not walk across the street to be elected president of the United States, and I certainly would not make a public speech for the purpose of getting the nomination or to be elected.[20]

To promise that he would not bother with speechmaking was not saying much: the excruciatingly shy Ford never spoke in public. Ford's friend Thomas Edison wondered why Ford wanted to be a senator. "You can't speak. You wouldn't say a damn word. You'd be mum." Ford planned ahead. He asked Daniels, "'What does a Senator have to do?'" and got Daniels's assurance that he would only have to be in Washington "when questions of major importance are under consideration." As senator, Ford would not have to worry about speaking and committee meetings, since "I will move my whole force down there." Surrounded by his "whole organization," Ford would "serve the people of the United States, and the people of the world." Ford overcame his misgivings in order to "work with the President with everything I possess first to win the war and then to help the Government develop ways of insuring us against future wars."[21]

King thought Ford's entry had "inject[ed] some ginger into the campaign" and expected Osborn to "wield his battle-axe." Osborn, with his "good temperament for a row," did not disappoint. What he told King privately—that Ford was "a liar, a horse-thief and a murderer" and that Wilson, "the war lord of the country," could not "come into Michigan and tell the Republican Party who to nominate for the United States Senate"—he embellished on the campaign trail. "Ford doesn't believe in the American flag and says he won't fly it after the war. He admits he hasn't voted but twice in twenty years, and he knows nothing of history, affairs of state, or anything to qualify him for office," Osborn proclaimed at a campaign stop. At another event, he decried the "intriguing Democrats who would capitalize politically on [Ford's] notoriety and at the same time get their hungry hooks into his fleshpots." He lampooned Ford's pledge to bring his team to Washington and linked it to Ford's limitations:

His "whole force" is needed right where it is now. . . . Mr. Ford does not think or act for himself. His statements are made for him by his secretaries and attorneys. He was a rubber stamp in the crazy Germanized peace ship adventure; he is a rubber stamp Senatorial candidate, and if elected to the United States Senate he will be a rubber stamp Senator. The only thing he is sure of politically is that he voted and spent thousands of dollars for Woodrow Wilson.

This was a start, and Osborn had more in reserve, including Edsel Ford's draft deferment and opposition research that dug up complaints of former Ford employees and a potential example of tax evasion.[22]

With no opponent in the Democratic primary, Ford seemed to be the man to beat on the Republican side as well. There was an effort in May to place Ford in nomination on the Republican ticket, following talk among Democrats about Ford receiving the nominations of both parties. As soon as he announced his candidacy, he picked up the support of some prominent Republicans. Alex Groesbeck, the state attorney general, argued that the nation's need for war production made putting Ford in the Senate "a patriotic thing to do." Former governor Warner urged both parties to "work with the national administration," since partisan bickering would prolong the war. Ford, "the greatest constructive force in America," would be an asset in the Senate at a time when industry was a matter of national security. A Grand Rapids Republican glumly reported to Newberry in July that the State Central Committee agreed "there was practically no chance for any one as against Ford" and that it had deadlocked on which opponent had the best of these slim chances. Rumors flew about party leaders searching for a dark horse candidate to replace both Osborn and Newberry. Remembering his defeat in 1914, Osborn warned of "old republican intriguers that developed a dishonest and disgraceful vote swapping league between republicans and democrats in Detroit . . . [who are] endeavoring to sell out the party to the democrats" and Ford.[23]

In the interest of the party and patriotism, either Osborn or Newberry should exit the race. But which one? Osborn told King soon after Ford announced that "the thing for Newberry to do is to get out of the race and let me beat Ford," to which King replied, "Why don't you get out and let us beat him?"[24]

In early July, a supporter advised Osborn not to "waste much time or effort on Ford. Your job is to beat Newberry. Let him or his machine fight Ford." Osborn, who saw nothing but an empty uniform in Newberry's candidacy, instead continued to attack Ford, while cautiously exploring how to get Newberry to quit the race. "I have already prevented many newspapers from attacking him for the bold and criminal use of money that his managers and agents are engaged in," he wrote to John C. Shaffer. "If he doesn't get out he is apt to be blown out by the press of events . . . and the results will be embarrassing and humiliating and even may be disgraceful and criminal." He alerted RNC chairman Will Hays of the looming problem, hoping Hays would nudge Newberry out of the race. He enlisted influential supporters such as Dodge and William H. Field, vice president of the *Chicago Tribune*, and Senator Albert J. Beveridge to do the same. Republicans in Michigan needed to unite around "the strongest man," Beveridge wrote, touting Osborn as "*the* man" who is a "*fighter*, is rich . . . and honest."[25]

Ordinarily a national party chairman would avoid poking around an intraparty fight, if anyone bothered to ask him to do it. But this was not a normal off-year election, and Hays was an unusual party chairman. Tiny (five feet, four inches, 120 pounds) and a bundle of energy, Hays was a successful corporate lawyer in Indiana who had involved himself deeply in party affairs (his fame would come later as president of the Motion Picture Producers and Distributors of America, where he oversaw making Hollywood moral). As

chairman of the Indiana GOP, he remained pointedly neutral in party conflicts and focused on strengthening the organization. He followed the same
general policy when he took on the national chairmanship. He was a dervish,
bringing together the principals involved in the party's factions and lining up
speaking engagements across the country. Hays, not one of the ex-presidents
or a current senator or congressman, was the spokesman of the party out of
power. The spacious permanent RNC offices in Washington symbolized the
new prominence of the national party under Hays. He attended to substance
as well as form, and by May 1918, he designed a national theme for the year's
House and Senate races. The Michigan primary race mattered to Hays, who
surely did not want Wilson determining a Republican Senate nomination
and potentially spoiling his strategy for 1918.[26]

Both Newberry and Osborn believed it also mattered to Roosevelt, who
despised Ford's pacifism. Given the Colonel's popularity in Michigan, his endorsement could settle everything. From nearly the point that Osborn and
Newberry announced their candidacies, their supporters intimated that their
man had the ex-president's blessing. TR kept his preferences to himself. "I
am not interfering in any shape or way in any local contest," he reminded
one of Osborn's newspaperman friends. "The first protest made to me was by
Mr. Newberry's friends, who asserted that it was being reported everywhere
that I was supporting Governor Osborn. You now tell me that the same statement is being made by Mr. Osborn's friends, namely, that I am supporting
Mr. Newberry. There is not and has not been a particle of foundation for
either complaint." With Ford capable of winning the Republican primary,
the demand for TR's intervention mounted. Newberry appealed to Roosevelt
to "give your advice to Osborn and to me . . . to eliminate one of us and you
could then tell the truth about Ford without violating your wise rule to keep
out of primary contests." Newberry added flattery and urgency to his plea,
claiming that "only you, and you alone, can solve for the best interests of your
Country, our Army and Navy, and our Allies" the Michigan problem, which
risked "the sinister menace of Ford."[27]

Osborn might have expected Roosevelt to shun Newberry as he once
did Lorimer, while Newberry anticipated TR would back the man with the
best chance of beating a loathsome alternative. But TR was not interested.
His thoughts focused on the war and its aftermath and the fate of his sons.
Two had been wounded in battle; Quentin, the youngest, was shot down and

killed in France in July. He was tired and in pain. Roosevelt tossed the problem back to Hays, promising to be at his service if Hays would "be reasonably
clear as to what ought to be done." Osborn believed that he earned the right
to run by pummeling Ford, and Newberry believed reports that put him well
ahead of Osborn. Neither man budged, each convinced he had TR's silent
blessing.[28]

The campaign solidified in the first week of August, as Michigan melted in a
lethal heat wave that brought temperatures of 116 degrees. The news spread
that Democrat James W. Helme, state food commissioner, had made his
long-rumored filing to run for the Senate. "The autocracy has selected a candidate for United States Senator for both parties," he declared. "I have seen
an expert ride two horses at a circus, but he would not have attempted to ride
the donkey and the elephant at the same time." The Helme candidacy sprang
from two sources: disgruntled Democrats, including Helme, who favored
a reform-minded Democratic gubernatorial candidate and wanted to keep
Democrats in their own primary for him, and Republicans nervous about
Democratic crossover voting. In July, a subordinate of Helme's had contacted
the treasurer of the Republican State Committee and later met with King.
Helme turned down his subordinate's requests a number of times but finally
agreed to run so long as it was "no trouble or expense" to him. Newberry
campaign workers gathered the signatures to get him on the ballot and sup-
plied some $300 for promoting the "One Hundred Per-cent Democratic
Senatorial Committee." Helme said he knew nothing of the Newberry connection until after the campaign.[29]

Helme's candidacy relieved some of the pressure on the Republican ticket.
It was perhaps not unrelated that the newspaper attack on the Newberry
campaign opened on August 2. Editorials in the *Escanaba Journal* lamented
that Newberry's "money campaign . . . will create a condition which must
inevitably mean the debauchery of Michigan politics." A few days later, the
Charlotte Republican followed the lead of the Upper Peninsula newspaper.
Osborn's manager gathered rumors that the Newberry campaign had spent
as much as half a million dollars, convincing him that Newberry "must be
blown out, bag and baggage." He sent a copy of the editorials to Hays but advised Osborn to "hit this crew a punch yourself . . . in time enough so that we
can get it in every weekly in the State as well as every daily." Osborn held off

such a direct attack, but his manager sounded out contacts to get a statement denouncing Newberry from the lieutenant governor, Luren D. Dickinson.[30]

Other Michigan Republicans picked up the slack. Arthur Vandenberg, editor of the *Grand Rapids Herald*, wrote to Newberry on August 8. The editorials peddled gossip, "but gossip, in this instance, is too wide-spread to be longer ignored. It charges you and your associates with the expenditure of money running into six figures. . . . Such a situation must be intolerable for you, if these reports are false, as it is intolerable for the state, if the reports are true." On August 17, the paper published an editorial denouncing the committee's spending. A few days later, Dickinson came through with an open letter published in the *Detroit News*. He cited the campaign advertising, organization, and cars as evidence for the "conservative estimates" of spending that ranged "everywhere from $250,000 to $500,000," numbers drawn from Osborn's manager. "In case you get the most votes," Dickinson cautioned, "you must expect to have the election ballot contested" and "every church and moral organization to work until election night to keep our fair state from the baneful influences" of money in politics.[31]

Once again, the Michigan primary landed on Hays's doorstep. Newberry assured him that "whatever expenses have been incurred for advertising and publicity" were handled by a committee, "and I had their assurance long ago that all their financial transactions would be a matter of record and in every way conform to the spirit and letter of the statutes." Hays called Osborn to arrange a meeting in New York involving Hays, Osborn, and Newberry, asking that Osborn not "make any statement as to Newberry's expenditures until I have talked to him." Newberry, summering in Watch Hill, ducked the meeting. While explaining to Hays that he did not know that Osborn had traveled to New York, he told King that he had "no desire to meet [Osborn], as I am under the impression that an interview would have been devoid of any useful result." Still, Newberry fretted. Could King give his "cold conservative opinion" about whether Newberry's candidacy was sinking?[32]

King was unruffled. The "attitude of Groesbeck representing Ford and Vandenberg representing Osborn [is] neither surprising nor disconcerting," he assured Newberry. "They are licked and know it. Simply squealing now." In the narrow sense of winning the Republican nomination, King was right: on August 27, Newberry got 114,963 votes to 71,800 for Ford and 47,029 for Osborn. But King, the organizational wizard, missed the bigger picture. Vandenberg would support Newberry in the general election only because the alternative reeked. A campaign finance moralist, he saw the "extravagant political expenditures to be a vital menace to the future of Republican institutions. It makes no difference to me that the money in a campaign may be spent 'legally' and for 'legitimate' ends, as permitted by loose law. If the money expended amounts to an extravagant sum, the net result is undemocratic and, therefore, un-American." Newberry's responses—that the attacks were just politics ("I see by the papers that the expected 'mustard gas attack' by Osborne [sic] has been delivered through Dickinson, the Lieutenant Governor"), that he personally opposed large spending ("under no circumstances would I knowingly be a party to any scandal . . . such as you fear will be brought upon our State"), and that the committee's spending was within the law ("I know they have nothing to hide and are proud of everything they have done") and necessary to fight "capitalized pacifism"—did not answer the moral objections.[33]

Osborn wondered whether he should have gone after Newberry. "The facts are frittering into the public mind now perhaps not fast enough," he wrote to a supporter as election day approached. Still, the spending of the Newberry campaign had received a lot of attention—the Osborn campaign had used the press to make that certain. Newberry won anyway. King had lined up the regular Republicans behind Newberry and convinced most of the rest that Newberry was the only choice if Ford was to be defeated in the primary. The chairman of the state party claimed that his polling indicated that Newberry was ahead 2 to 1 in August, which "probably explained why Hays is so slow on the trigger in this matter, and probably T.R. also." The underwhelming endorsement of the *Detroit Free Press* captured the sense of Newberry as the best of a bad lot. While "Mr. Newberry will not be a spectacular senator," at least "he never has fitted out a peace ship" and would not embarrass the state with "any weird oratorical display."[34]

With their work over, King and his staff emptied their Ford Building offices, discarding what overnight had become worthless detritus—correspondence, reports, pay stubs, clippings. As was the custom, the state Republican Party, not Newberry's own organization, would handle the general election. The state GOP moved into the same downtown Detroit space that the Newberry committee had used, with King staying on as a consultant and Hannibal

A. Hopkins remaining as publicity director. There was one last task: preparing the committee's final financial report in compliance with state law. Newberry had already filed his personal statements, which declared no contributions from him or to him and no spending. The committee, however, spent $176,568.08, with all but $28,707.92 going to advertising and publicity. Contributions totaled $178,856, of which about 88 percent came from family and close friends: $99,900 from Newberry's brother, $25,000 from his wife's brother, $25,000 from Henry B. Joy, his brother-in-law and partner in Packard, $10,000 from his sister, and the remaining large sums from a college friend (Frederick Brooks, of Brooks Brothers) and a family friend (Lyman D. Smith, a New York stockbroker). When late receipts of about $12,000 came in after the close of the campaign, Andrew H. Green, an anti-Ford Democrat and shipmate of Newberry's on the *Yosemite,* covered the shortfall. Now there were real numbers to which to attach outrage.[35]

The general election campaign accentuated the negative, hammering on two issues: the Newberry campaign's spending and Ford's pacifist history. The candidates, silent and invisible, watched as the parties, their supporters, surrogates, and the press spun the election into a judgment on democracy and patriotism. Three federal investigations intensified the hysterical charges and countercharges, while demonstrating that the election mattered to national leaders perhaps more than it did to Michigan voters.

The $178,856 sum anchored the negative attacks of Ford's and the Democratic Party's campaign. They depicted Newberry as everything Progressives distrusted about wealth: a bloated millionaire, spending a pile of his inherited fortune buying an election and hiding behind his uniform in a cushy navy desk job. Newberry's campaign film reappeared as the perfect summary of what a fake he was. Shot in a New York City park in front of a wooden replica of a navy ship, here was a man who played a hero in his own movie. The *Detroit News,* which had not been breathing fire about Newberry during the primaries, now gave Newberry's spending its undivided scorn. A story claimed that workers concluded that "if an unknown millionaire can boost himself into the United States Senate by hiring a herd of county politicians and conducting an advertising campaign, there is no chance in this country for a poor man." Newberry found the stories, editorials, and cartoons alarming enough to explore retaining "for me personally the best available lawyer," a "good fighter," to "protect my interests in every way involving newspaper attacks."[36]

Even the Ford campaign's positive messages drew contrasts with its opposition. Newspaper ads, a pamphlet printed in four languages, and booklets reminded voters about the Five Dollar Day, the Henry Ford Hospital, the automaker's efforts to Americanize immigrants (through the now largely defunct Sociological Department), and his efforts to both end war and win the Great War. "He is doing more to help win the war than any other individual citizen of the United States," claimed an ad that ran a few days before the election. Not only had he amassed the greatest "CLEAN FORTUNE IN THE WORLD," but he also gave "employment to cripples" and "turned all his industries over to the Government with their 46,000 men, WITHOUT ONE CENT OF PROFIT TO HIMSELF." In contrast to Newberry, "now a candidate solely because of an unlawful expenditure of vast sums of money," Ford "refuses to spend one cent to win the Senatorship."[37]

That was not quite true. How much Ford spent, however, is impossible to say. This was the sort of project Ford handled with cash. E. G. Pipp, in 1918 a Ford confidant and managing editor of the *Detroit News*, later claimed that Ford's dealer network and employees helped with the campaign. Under Pipp's direction Ford's firm produced all but one of the glossy pamphlets and brochures (one running sixteen pages) the campaign produced. There were billboards and posters featuring Ford. The printing bill for one pamphlet was $16,000, with the cost covered by a $20,000 contribution to the Democratic State Central Committee. Perhaps Pipp wrote "Why Henry Ford Wants to Be Senator," credited to Ford in the September 1918 issue of *World's Work*. Not that Ford needed the publicity: Ford short films, friendly press outside of his political ventures, and automobile advertising made it redundant.[38]

Making sure that Ford's candidacy was not just in the hands of the fates and the perhaps not especially skilled Democratic State Central Committee, Alfred Lucking, Ford's personal attorney and former congressman, organized the Non-Partisan Ford for Senate club. Certain that Ford should not "take any chances of defeat by Newberry, but should give all the assistance you can without it being known," Harvey Firestone, Ford's tire supplier and friend, stepped in to provide direction and financial help. "Knowing how you like to receive information through unusual channels," Firestone sent a report from Bernard M. Robinson, an attorney with Firestone's Akron, Ohio, tire company. Traveling the state undercover, with a letter "introducing me as of Indiana, sent in 'national interest' to survey the Michigan situation," Robinson "investigated carefully and . . . found that the Newberry primary charges are established irrefutably." The "vicious" Newberry spending and "the magnificent war record of Ford" needed to be brought before Michigan voters more effectively than the Democratic Party had managed.[39]

Newberry's campaign had the support of the far more numerous Republican-leaning newspapers. In the general election, the *Free Press* focused on the presumptuousness of Democrats in Washington trying to shape Michigan's representation and implying that Republicans were not patriots. If Josephus Daniels (and others) belittled Newberry's current military service, the *Free Press* gave space to the response of the state Republican Party chairman. Newberry had asked to be sent overseas; his sons and son-in-law were serving as well; and Packard, not Ford, was "building more airplane motors and more trucks than any other concern in the world." Even newspapers that had supported Osborn in the primary endorsed Newberry, if only because "Michigan is not looking for men of Ford's brand of statesmanship" and a sure vote for the League of Nations. For the most pointed attacks on Ford the places to look were *Detroit Saturday Night*, heavily supported by the Dodge brothers, who were suing Ford, and the *Chicago Tribune*, still defending itself against Ford's libel charge.[40]

Hopkins, the publicity director, mailed "a blinger" of an anti-Ford editorial from the *Tribune* to Newberry, noting that "of course nothing of this kind should ever emanate from our committee, and to our everlasting credit, we did not throw a bit of mud or mention Mr. Ford or his son throughout the primary campaign." They did not have to, since Osborn had taken care of the attack, and the Edsel Ford deferment matter was obvious from the beginning. In June, Osborn heard that Detroiters "have been talking about nothing else but Edsel," with the chatter focusing on how "it was bad enough for Alfred Lucking to go to Wilson for Edsel anyway; it's worse when Wilson asks Henry Ford to leave his job as a munitions maker when he tells Edsel he can continue to 'make munitions.'" The *Free Press* published a letter written by James O. Murfin, chairman of the Selective Service Board of Appeals for Detroit, deriding Edsel's exemption. The political problem of Edsel's status as an essential war worker expanded in the general election.[41]

Campaign ephemera put the matter bluntly. According to Ford's secretary, Ernest Liebold, a bumper sticker that read, "My Son Is Not a Slacker," especially enraged Ford. Perhaps that was because he did not see the window placards with a large gold star. "Henry Ford has nothing like this in his window," it read. One Republican county chairman thought it was especially effective, since (echoing the best advertising wisdom) it "tells a whole story in itself. . . . It is lambasting Edsel without mentioning his name." Ford might also have missed a card that read, "His Country Needs Edsel Ford. Where Is He?" and asked voters "to send the fighting father of fighting sons . . . to represent a fighting State in the United States Senate" by making a cross under the picture of Abraham Lincoln on their ballots. Newberry privately winced at the "sickening exhibition" of his sons being used in campaign fodder, but he stopped neither that nor the attacks on Edsel.[42]

Belatedly, Woodrow Wilson recognized the Edsel problem. In the judgment of Daniel C. Roper, the Internal Revenue commissioner, "Mr. Ford can not be elected to the United States Senate from Michigan so long as his son occupies the status of an exempt man and two sons of Mr. Newberry are in the military branch of government." He advised finding a way to "place [Edsel] into a position of military or naval responsibility." Wilson agreed, but Ford tackled the problem on his own. He devoted most of a campaign letter to Edsel, both attacking critics and defending the deferment. "The full responsibility for his absence from the firing line in France rests with me. He has wanted to go from the day we declared war, and he wants to go now." If Edsel had to go, "he will be found at the front fighting, and will not be found sticking his spurs into a mahogany desk at Washington."[43]

That Wilson tried to fix the Edsel mess showed how much this campaign mattered to national politicians. In October, Wilson asked Americans to vote for Democrats if they "approved of my leadership and wish me to continue to be your unembarrassed spokesman in affairs at home and abroad." Daniels advised Michigan voters to elect Ford because "in war he knows how to produce weapons to win peace, and in the problems to be settled after the war his practical judgment as Senator would be of the highest value." Hays jumped on Wilson's appeal as evidence of his persistent confusion of healthy debate with disloyalty. He directed advertising wizard Albert Lasker's national campaign countering Wilson that brought together ex-presidents (and adversaries) Roosevelt and Taft. Full-page ads courtesy of Lasker, tailored for Michigan, reproduced a letter from Theodore Roosevelt:

The failure of Mr. Ford's son to go into the army at this time, and the approval by the father of the son's refusal, represent exactly what might be expected from the moral disintegration inevitably produced by such pacifist propaganda. . . . If there should be at any time in the future a Hindoo Senate, and it should choose, in a spirit of cosmopolitanism, to admit outsiders, there is no reason why Mr. Ford should not aspire to membership therein; but he would be signally out of place in the American Senate so long as that body is dominated by men who zealously believe in the American ideal.[44]

The ads had to speak for themselves, since even surrogates were silenced at the height of the fall campaign. The influenza epidemic in Michigan began with a few cases in September. It reached its deadly peak in mid-October, when the governor issued a ban on public meetings. The number of new cases grew nonetheless; sixty-seven people died in Detroit in a single day in the last week of October. What was left were press coverage and a series of federal investigations that reinforced the campaigns' attacks and generated material for new stories.[45]

The first came in the middle of September, when Senator Atlee Pomerene, Democrat of Ohio and chairman of the Privileges and Elections Committee, presented a resolution for the investigation of the Newberry primary campaign expenditures, as well as of other campaigns rumored to have hefty expenditures. Michigan's senior senator, Charles E. Townsend, condemned the resolution as extending "a political scheme that originated in the White House" that began with tapping Ford as a candidate. The committee voted 10 to 1 to delay action on the resolution until after the general election, leaving for then the question of whether this Senate had the authority to pass judgment on the composition of the next Senate.[46]

While Pomerene readied his resolution, the Department of Justice was looking into the Newberry campaign. In July, William G. Simpson, an engineer with Timken Detroit Axle, asked John E. Kinnane, the U.S. attorney for Michigan's Eastern District, to investigate the Newberry spending, complaining that the governor had "refuse[d] to act." The wheels moved slowly, perhaps because Simpson's request fell outside of the expected channels.

Simpson also addressed his request to the U.S. secretary of state, confusing the state and federal functions attached to the office, and ran for the 1916 Republican presidential nomination in Michigan ("I am my own bandwagon," he said). But by September, the Department of Justice was intensely interested. Attorney General Gregory demanded to know whether a grand jury was in session "and if not how soon it can be summoned." The Newberry case was now important enough to replace Kinnane ("not regarded as a very strong man") with a special prosecutor, S. R. Rush, whose experience stretched back to the 1890s, and additional investigators.[47]

Rush and his team determined that the prosecutable offense was making false statements—that Newberry committed perjury when he signed the statement required by the FCPA that described his spending. The trial would go to New York City, since Newberry prepared the statement while he was stationed there. On October 4, the news broke that Judge Learned Hand of the Southern District of New York had seated a grand jury to investigate the Newberry primary campaign. Most of the Newberry campaign team, the losing candidates other than Ford, and the major donors were called to appear before what Newberry supporters saw as a "Tammany jury and an Alabama judge." The state party chair pestered Senator Townsend to counteract this "dirty political move," by arranging for speeches on the Senate floor "so we can have at least a quarter of a million" distributed in Michigan. Everyone answered the grand jury's questions except Blair, Templeton, and Thomas P. Phillips, an assistant publicity director. Their lawyer wanted to make the point that the New York court did not have jurisdiction over an alleged crime committed in Michigan. What might have been good lawyering was bad politics. Michigan's representative to the RNC warned Newberry that "the average person at once assumes that the failure to testify was because they did not want to incriminate themselves, or because they were trying to shield you." But a Tammany jury was unimpressed by a campaign finance case: on October 29, it failed to return an indictment by a vote of 16 to 1.[48]

The Democrats were not finished. Signaling an aggressive use of executive power, Attorney General Thomas Watt Gregory issued a circular to all agents of the Bureau of Investigation urging investigation of potential violations of the FCPA. The Democratic National Committee (DNC) followed up with instructions to national committeemen and state chairmen to "gather and submit" information about "the improper or excessive use of campaign funds." In October, Congress gave investigators a new tool in the Gerry Act, which criminalized offering money for anything in an election. Investigators crawled through the northern and western states—Connecticut, New Hampshire, upstate New York, Illinois, Colorado, New Mexico, and California. They watched polling places for violations, with their eyes focused by local Democratic leaders. They stuck around in some states to follow up rumors of potentially actionable improprieties. This was perhaps the most intensive examination of election practices until the Voting Rights Act of 1965, and it both avoided the South and paid special attention to African American and immigrant neighborhoods in the search for corruption.[49]

What federal agents failed to find, Colorado Democrat Charles Thomas attempted to have the tax man remove after the fact. Goaded by Wilbur Marsh, the DNC treasurer, Thomas inserted a provision in a 1919 revenue bill that would have taxed the excess of political contributions over $500 at the rate of 100 percent and made the tax retroactive to the 1918 campaign. The DNC chairman imagined "our friend Hays [at the RNC] would have to re-arrange his whole program" if the measure passed. It failed, largely because of the retroactive feature.[50]

In November, it was Ford's turn to cry foul. In May 1917, Charles Evans Hughes, Wilson's Republican opponent in 1916, became chairman of an investigation of airplane production under wartime contracts. It seemed like a good idea: Hughes had given a strong speech praising Wilson as a war leader; his appointment struck a soothing bipartisan note; and the former Supreme Court justice's reputation as a zealous investigator went back more than a decade. In late October, Hughes delivered the report to the attorney general, and it made the front pages on November 1. Most of the Hughes report focused on classic instances of waste, fraud, and abuse, but it also dealt with the question of disloyalty among German workers at Ford and elsewhere. Although "nothing conclusive" turned up on the loyalties of Ford's director of the drafting department, Carl Emde, "the advisability of removing him from his position of strategic importance was clear to some of the most important men in management." Because Henry had blocked "the proposed removal," the report concluded that "there has been a laxity at the Ford plant with respect to those of German sympathies which is not at all compatible with the interests of the Government."[51]

The *New York Times* praised the "comprehensive" report, written "without the slightest tinge of partisanship." It did not look that way in Detroit. Jay Hayden of the *Detroit News* saw a purely partisan document, in which Hughes targeted Emde from among the "thousands of Ford employees in an effort to prove that Mr. Ford was over considerate of men of German name and birth." The newspaper published Ford's defense of company policy and of Emde, who had worked at Ford for a dozen years. On November 3, two days before the election, the Republican State Central Committee printed a full-page ad in the *Detroit Free Press* insinuating that Ford gave safe harbor to employees whose allegiance to the United States was questionable.[52]

It is of course impossible to know the effect on voters of this bitter eleventh-hour controversy—or of the campaign ad promise of a "FORD FACTORY IN ADRIAN" that urged "as an appreciation for putting Adrian on the Ford map" a "VOTE FOR FORD TOMORROW!" Michiganders had other things to worry about—rising prices, the progress of Allied troops, and caring for the sick and burying the thousands of flu victims. This much was clear. The election was a squeaker. Newberry defeated Ford by a margin of just over 8,500 out of more than 430,000 votes cast. Turnout was low, about one-third lower than in 1916. Newberry's candidacy, a product of divisions among Michigan Republicans, had deepened those fissures. Department of Justice prosecutors had not given up on the case, convinced that a new hearing in Michigan would defeat the "subterfuge" of the men involved in the Newberry campaign. And while Ford may not have been willing to walk across the street to become president, he was anxious to spend considerable effort ensuring that Truman Newberry would not sit in the Senate. He was "so angry that he can talk of nothing else," according to Horace Dodge's friends. In Robinson, Ford had an investigator on the ground assembling evidence of perfidy in the Newberry campaign. "Put a gang on 'em," Ford said, certain that an investigation would uncover the fraud that explained his defeat. In Lucking, a former congressman, he had an attorney who knew Washington. And in the Senate he had allies, who for their own reasons were as mad about Newberry's victory as he was.[53]

The young Truman and
John S. Newberry (Courtesy
of the Detroit Public Library)

A "Vagabonds" camping trip: Thomas Edison, John Burroughs, Henry Ford,
and Harvey Firestone. (Courtesy of the Benson Ford Research Library)

Front page of a Henry Ford for Senator campaign pamphlet (Courtesy of the Benson Ford Research Library)

A Newberry newspaper advertisement, in context [Marshall, Michigan] (*Evening Chronicle*, July 26, 1918)

Newberry and sons (*Grand Traverse Press*, July 12, 1918)

Committee on Elections of the Senate engaged in the counting of the Ford-Newberry vote. Tellers in the foreground of the picture are Senators Walter E. Edge of New Jersey and Selden P. Spencer of Missouri (Courtesy of the Library of Congress)

Senators James A. Reed, left, and Thomas Walsh (Courtesy of the Library of Congress)

Truman Newberry, with Phelps and Barnes, at the Capitol after the Senate vote. (Detroit News photo, in author's possession)

Violet and Truman Newberry, December 1921. (Detroit News photo, in author's possession)

Senator Charles E. Townsend of Michigan (Courtesy of the Library
of Congress)

THE
SEARCHLIGHT
REGISTERED U.S. PATENT OFFICE

To Advance Democracy by Enabling the People to Know and Apply the Truth
about Congress and All Other Departments of their Government at Washington.

| January 31, 1922 | Washington, D. C. | 20c a Copy |

NEWBERRYISM MEANS DEATH TO DEMOCRACY

The Shameful Story of How The Senate "Saved" Newberry
and "Disgraced" Itself—All About The Humiliating Amendment of "Conviction and Acquittal" Willis—Big Moments in
The Dramatic Debate—Portions of the Great Speeches

Seats Are For Sale Says The Senate

A Summarized Story Of The Scandal

A New Kind of Roll Call—
Newberryism Reduced To Individual Senators
Showing Where Each One Stood

| Volume VI | Copyrighted 1922, by The Searchlight Publishing Company | Number 8 |

The Searchlight, distributed by Ford and Lucking for 1922 Senate elections.

Men removing ballot boxes from the William S. Vare–William B. Wilson
Pennsylvania state election from truck at the Capitol, Washington, D.C.
(Courtesy of the Library of Congress)

5

Washington

Four days after the election, as news of the Armistice brought revelers thronging into the streets, Newberry continued to sort through a gratifyingly deep stack of congratulatory messages. He looked forward to his release from naval service (and feared that if it did not happen soon, the Wilson administration might have him sent abroad) and mulled over how to prepare for his new job. He thought he should begin by making "a real personal acquaintance in every county, which I know will take two or three months of hard travel, but . . . I shall not hesitate at anything in the way of work or inconvenience in order to have the people know I want to be called their friend, and I do not want to be known as a politician." Many Senate races in 1918 had been as tight as Newberry's, turning in some places as much on the domestic impact of wartime policies, such as controls on wheat prices, as on foreign policy. The Democrats lost seven seats, giving the Republicans forty-nine and the Democrats forty-seven. Wilson's bid for a friendly Congress had failed.[1]

It was a Senate in flux, where old institutional patterns were gone but new ones had yet to take shape. Progressive politics had toppled the cozy, predictable turn-of-the-century club. In old days the "big four"—Nelson Aldrich, John C. Spooner, William B. Allison, and Orville H. Platt—ran the Senate in the interests of high tariffs and business stability, presiding over colleagues who had joined the club as reward for years of party service. Progressive Republicans, first a handful but eventually a separate caucus, chafed under the regulars' control of choice committee assignments and chairmanships. By

1912, the "big four" were gone; Democrats had reduced the Republican majority; many states, mostly in the West and Midwest, had moved toward the de facto direct elections of senators even before the Seventeenth Amendment; and service in the Senate was a career choice, not a pat on the back for sturdy partisans. In the Wilson years, Democrats briefly gained a majority, and by both partisan and policy inclination they were reliable progressive votes. Progressive Republicans, a loose confederation of westerners and midwesterners, joined the Democrats on issues that touched on corporate power and regional interests. In 1918, they numbered about a dozen, joined on some issues by a half dozen others. This time they voted with the regulars to organize the Senate in exchange for some committee chairmanships (the progressives' attempt to deny Pennsylvania boss Boise Penrose a chairmanship failed). In a Senate with a bare Republican majority, they held the balance of power, and their regularity could not be taken for granted. Neither could collegiality, given unsettled old scores and new conflicts now aired in popular elections.[2]

The big issues of postwar reconstruction awaited this fractious Senate. The League of Nations was one important item on the agenda, but more diffuse issues would define what became of the progressive or liberal impulse. Newberry never did make a full statewide lap. He would spend his time in the Senate as the subject of a debate about one of those issues, campaign finance, that was also about partisanship, the rule of law, and liberal democracy—about justice in politics.

Before they could organize the Senate, the apparent election day Republican majority had to survive under-the-radar legal investigations. Immediately after the election, Department of Justice agents looked for violations in fairly close races Republicans had won. They tracked rumors that Indians and blacks who voted for Lawrence Phipps of Colorado expected and received payment. Greater effort went into Missouri, where Selden Spencer solidly defeated Joseph "Holy Joe" Folk, a down-the-line Wilson Democrat and sitting governor. Investigators followed up the stories told by Folk and others about abnormally high turnout in some districts and free beer on election day. A St. Louis Democrat said that an investigation was a waste of time, since "there was no trick in beating Folk in a straight way." Wilson's popularity especially among German Americans had ebbed, and Folk's position on prohibition annoyed many Democrats. According to one uncooperative Democratic leader, the minor irregularities that likely happened (this was Missouri, after all) were not enough to explain Spencer's win. The Bureau of Investigation agent replied that the fact of "irregularities that violated federal law," not their magnitude, was at issue, but no indictment followed. The election of George Moses in New Hampshire seemed more promising from a prosecutor's point of view. Working with leads provided by the chair of the Democratic state committee, investigators combed the state to pick up evidence that Republicans had violated the month-old Gerry Act by purchasing votes, liquor, and newspaper editors. They gathered enough stories from people who heard about such things to bring the case before a grand jury. When it did not indict Moses, the agents sent the allegations on to the Senate Privileges and Elections Committee, as the chair of the state party requested. The partnership between the DNC and the Department of Justice had come up empty.[3]

If not for Ford, perhaps the Newberry election would have fallen into the same uneasy sleep, with a failed indictment followed by an unproductive search for fraud. But Ernest Liebold, Ford's secretary, had misread his boss's intentions when he issued a statement on November 7, saying then that "we believe that the campaign has been clean, as campaigns go, and therefore are willing to abide by the return sheets." A week later Ford's new edict promised to contest the election for the edification of the nation, to show "how our elections are manipulated by the moneyed interests." "Wall Street influences," he charged, "admit spending $176,000 to get the nomination for their man, and how much was actually spent in the election to secure that Senatorial seat, goodness only knows." Alfred Lucking's Ford-for-Senate club filed a Senate contest the same day, alleging excessive spending to the tune of $500,000, illegal payoffs, and 10,000 votes for Ford counted for Newberry by corrupt Republican election officials. Hannibal Hopkins, the publicity director, advised Newberry not to worry, since all the departing Sixty-Fifth Congress could do was "act mean, cut up dog and make it unpleasant for us." He was sworn in with the rest of his class in March 1919. But while this demand for an investigation expired with the Sixty-Fifth Congress, Lucking's formal petition for a contest and recount (there was no provision for this in Michigan election law) waited for the Sixty-Sixth Congress.[4]

The more pressing business of peace took priority over the contest in the Senate, while Lucking went to work on Ford's libel suit against the *Chicago Tribune*. President Wilson had approached the negotiations with the hope that the war would lead to a progressive victory, with his Fourteen Points as the basis for a lasting and just peace. In Versailles, America's allies had gutted most of Wilson's plan but retained in Article X his League of Nations. After Wilson personally delivered the treaty to the Senate in July, he testified before the Foreign Relations Committee, demonstrating how much the treaty—especially the League—meant to him. The Senate was divided four ways. A group led by Henry Cabot Lodge, chair of the Foreign Relations Committee, was willing to sign off on the treaty if Wilson obtained revisions. Others, mostly Democrats, backed the plan without reservations. Even revisions would not satisfy a group largely made up of progressives, including some Democrats, who saw the League as an unacceptable breach of the principle of national sovereignty. A group of Republicans would have been satisfied with weak reservations that probably would not require reopening negotiations with the Allied powers. In November, progressives and supporters of the unmodified treaty defeated Lodge's amended version. The vote on the treaty without reservations was lost by an even larger margin.

Newberry supported the Lodge position. "Like every one else," he explained to friends and constituents who asked about his intentions, he was "strongly in favor of any League or Agreement which would insure the world against any further war and which would provide for some considerable amount of disarmament," but he rejected "any league which in any way diminishes the independence of the United States." With a businessman's distaste for wasted motion, he turned down Arthur Vandenberg's request for a letter for the *Grand Rapids Herald*. "To sit down in cold blood and write an essay on the League of Nations is beyond my ability," he wrote. Already the "best minds in the world are now being devoted to this very work, and the matter has already been so thoroughly discussed by Senator Lodge and Senator Knox and many others much better qualified than I am, that I hesitate to even try to write a letter worth publishing." This vote was his only significant act as a senator, and from it the legend was born that his tainted election defeated the League of Nations.[5]

While the drama of the treaty debate occupied the Senate, Lucking was busy with Ford's lawsuit. The circus came to Mount Clemens, Michigan, and stayed for three months, as experts such as historian William A. Dunning offered testimony on whether the utterances on war attributed to Ford might be called anarchistic and whether his views more resembled those of Plato and Diogenes or of Emma Goldman. Lucking failed to confine the trial to the headline's characterization of Ford as an anarchist, opening the whole offending editorial to questions. So for seven days Ford fidgeted on the stand, answering questions about political theory and American history. He demonstrated that he wrote nothing credited to him; that he may not have been able to read or write much at all; that his grasp of history was uncertain (Benedict Arnold was a writer, according to Ford, and the American Revolution happened in 1812); and that while he knew quite a bit about birds, he did not know much about World War I or the preparedness issue. The jury found for Ford, awarding him damages of six cents. Ford retained the affections of many Americans who would not have wanted to pass a history quiz themselves. But in much respectable opinion there was a sense of relief that Ford was not in the Senate. He was, according to the *New York Times*, "a genius in his own business," but "his qualifications as an instructor of the people are not too manifest, and he must feel that his appearances in that role are at an end."[6]

As it happened, Ford did not feel that way at all. To keep his ideas before the public, he was preparing to launch the *Dearborn Independent,* edited by E. G. Pipp, former editor in chief of the *Detroit News*. And his views about the Michigan election would be heard through another criminal trial and Senate debate.

In late December 1918, Bernard Robinson handed Ford's attorney, Alfred Lucking, and Ford assistant Ernst Liebold the two-inch-thick "Report of Private Investigation of U.S. Senatorial Primary and Election in Michigan in 1918," which he and his investigators had been assembling since the primary. Covering the state county by county, they assumed fraud if the Newberry vote of a county was "disproportionate to the sentiment before the election," and took every bit of local bragging and complaining as encapsulating a kernel of fact. Ford loaned Robinson the detective force that "set up Dictaphones in hotel rooms" and "hid themselves under the beds" in hotels, hoping to overhear some juicy gossip. In Flint, one agent "got pretty close" to a woman who worked at a Western Union office, and she liberated copies of telegraph messages to the Newberry organization. When she lost her job, there was one waiting at Ford. Liebold believed the report confirmed his and his boss's suspicions about huge sums spent on the campaign (Liebold thought it was $2 million) and its evil Wall Street and Jewish sources. "The money was brought in here by William [sic] Cody," who worked for the Newberry-connected American Book Company in New York, he concluded. "We had reports from our operators and various sources that Mr. Cody came from New York on frequent occasions and on such trips brought large sums of money in cash with him. That money was used as part of the campaign expenses."[7]

When angling for his paycheck, Robinson, later the chief counsel and secretary at Firestone, crowed that he had "defined the crime, outlined the procedure, and named the defendants" and even picked the prosecutor and venue:

When I began work in Michigan, the Government had lost the New York case and tabooed further effort, Newberry's crowd brazenly derided the mere suggestion of guilt or prosecution, the public was indifferent and even Mr. Ford's friends merely hoped against hope that something would save an apparently defeated cause. I took *rumors* and within eight weeks, personally directing, twenty-four hours of every day, a state wide investigation in the camp of the enemy, with forty men in the field, ran these rumors into a *case*.

He would have liked to have prosecuted it himself, but his relationship with Firestone and Ford might have damaged the case. So he "did the next best thing," recommending an old friend, Frank C. Dailey. As a former federal prosecutor in Indiana, Dailey had successfully prosecuted Republican politicians. Lucking went to Washington to secure Dailey's appointment "with the thought in mind that the President had gotten Mr. Ford into this thing [and] . . . [i]n order that Mr. Ford could clear himself and that the corruption and everything else could be exposed and Newberry could be shown up, we felt that the President ought to lend his assistance and his influence toward prosecuting this thing." The prosecutors chose Grand Rapids, in the Western District of Michigan, as the venue, safely outside of Newberry's circle of influence in Detroit, with the crusty and crusading Judge Clarence W. Sessions, who had broken the bathtub trust, presiding. "Within a few months Newberry and his co-conspirators will stand convicted," Robinson predicted a month before the trial began, "a United States Senator will go to Federal

Prison for the first time in American history, and Mr. Ford will stand vindicated, honored and further beloved before the whole country."[8]

Robinson's self-congratulation overstated his role, but only a little. After the New York grand jury failed to return an indictment, Rush received the attorney general's approval to try again, this time in Michigan. His theory of the case had not changed—the prosecution would allege perjury. Rush wanted access to the Newberry Western Union accounts in order to develop evidence of Newberry's contact with his campaign and its finances, which the postmaster general refused to provide without a warrant. (A DNC official found such superciliousness hard to fathom.) Ford agents stepped forward with stories about potential discrepancies in the campaign's account of how much was spent. Rush was cautious. "I note what you say as to private parties making an investigation," he wrote to a field agent. "I sincerely hope they will keep it up and furnish us all the information they can get, but, of course, you will have to be up on your guard as a great many parties would make pretenses."[9]

Despite Rush's reservations, Robinson believed he had built a winning case. As soon as he completed his report, he met with Special Assistant Robert D. Ramsey of the Bureau of Investigation, along with Lucking and Liebold. Ramsey was dazzled. Repeating Robinson's claims, he reported that the Newberry campaign was "a gigantic scheme" to "flood the State of Michigan with money . . . and to indulge in various kinds of illegitimate practices to secure his nomination." Newberry not only participated in the vast conspiracy but likely visited Detroit to aid the plot. The Ford detectives had covered the ground so effectively that it would not be necessary to "send a great force of special agents." Their evidence of deceit (the Newberry campaign spent a lot more than it reported) and fraud usefully added "'color' and 'punch'" to a case about spending too much on advertising and organization, which jurors might find to be "no crime at all." Ramsey argued for locating the trial in the Western District, with the "fearless" and "absolutely fair" Sessions. The judge demonstrated that fairness when he told a former assistant U.S. attorney ("a most loyal Democrat") that he was "disgusted with the Newberry crowd and that they should be brought to account." True, Sessions was a Republican appointee, but his nomination came through former senator William Alden Smith, whose Grand Rapids newspaper was denouncing Newberry.[10]

Rush worked on the case at least until January 1919. When and why he was replaced are unclear. Lucking sent a coded message to Attorney General

Thomas Watt Gregory in February 1919, after Gregory had announced his resignation from Wilson's cabinet. Then the case went silent. E. G. Pipp claimed that A. Mitchell Palmer, who replaced Gregory in March, pulled the plug on further effort. But in September the case was back, with Dailey in the lead. Dailey seemed satisfied with what he had, which was what Robinson provided. So he busied himself with politics (urging, as Ramsey had before him, that a friend of Sessions be hired as an investigator) and public relations arrangements, requesting a specific Associated Press reporter to cover the trial.[11]

With the Ford evidence and publicity in hand, on October 18, 1919, the Justice Department announced it would seat a grand jury to hear complaints about excessive spending and fraud connected with the Newberry primary and general election campaigns. The Ford team hovered over Grand Rapids. "Of course, we had several of our men up there around the Court . . . look[ing] after anything that Dailey wanted," Liebold recalled. He was both excited and alarmed by the rumor that the grand jury was going to indict 150 Republicans. He advised Ford that Dailey was "overstretching the thing." "Better see what you can do about it," said Ford, and Liebold hurried to Grand Rapids, rousing Dailey at 1:00 a.m. "Heavens, you are going too far on this thing! That will react against us. . . . If you can cut it down to about fifty, it wouldn't be so bad," he urged. The number came down, but just a little: the grand jury indicted Newberry and 134 others on November 29.[12]

The first four counts of the indictment dealt with the FCPA, alleging that the defendants conspired to "give, contribute, expend, use, promise, or cause to be given, contributed, expended, used, or promised" more than the $3,750 for a U.S. Senate seat. The federal law limited spending to $10,000, unless the state limit was lower, as it was in Michigan. The fifth charged the group with conspiring to violate the Gerry Act by bribing voters, newspaper editors, and opinion leaders. The sixth count charged a conspiracy to use the U.S. mail to defraud contributors, a charge that Dailey had used successfully in the Indiana cases. The prosecution declared that it had "revealed a political scandal that in many respects was without parallel in American annals," with up to $1 million spent to bribe voters and buy up election boards, newspaper editors, and movie theaters. Privately Newberry distanced himself from the campaign, telling a college friend that the mess emerged "through no act or fault of my own, unless it be that I did not have time to go back and run the

campaign, just as I have always conducted my own business, that is with attention to detail and regularity." Newberry's public statement dismissed the
allegations as "lies made out of whole cloth" inspired by "political animus"
and promised "to expose that source, to show the malignity behind it as well
as the use of unlimited money in the attempt to cast a cloud upon my good
name and that of my supporters." He also urged the Senate Committee on
Privileges and Elections to move "immediately" to its investigation.[13]

There was no chance of that happening. A recount of the Michigan vote
and the results of trial would determine whether there would be an investigation. Meanwhile, the defense team, which included Ford critic and former
judge in Michigan's Third Circuit James O. Murfin, presented a series of preliminary motions for the defense. They asked for the list of witnesses who
had testified before the grand jury. Sessions denied the motion, saying that
doing so would hinder the prosecution. The defense filed a demurrer, which
claimed that Congress did not have the power to regulate primary elections.
Sessions rejected the argument with a profession of faith that must have
brought knowing smiles to the prosecution team. If Congress was "impotent
to enact laws to prevent a candidate for the office of United States Senator
from procuring his nomination and election by the lavish expenditure of
huge sums of money," he wrote, "then money rather than fitness and ability
becomes the controlling political force and . . . the very life of the Nation is
threatened." Money perverted democracy. "Because of its hidden and insidi-
ous character and the difficulties of discovery, conviction and punishment,
the corrupting influence of money . . . is infinitely more to be feared . . . than
the terrors of the Ku Klux Klan. . . . To deny this Government the right to
protect itself from such evils is to deny its right to continue to exist." If Congress was powerless to regulate primary elections, it was "helpless to prevent
the dumping of filth and poison into the spring at its source."[14]

In February 1920 the trial began, with the Newberry campaign having
filed paperwork that showed spending of about $195,000, adding in the late
invoices, a prosecution team that thought much more had been spent to corrupt opinion leaders and voters, a judge who believed any of the defendants
who participated in spending more than $3,750 were guilty, and a defense
team that denied a crime had been committed. The prosecution would try
to show that Newberry's campaign was not a modern media production but
an old-fashioned buy-up-the-voters affair. Given Sessions's understanding of

the law, anyone with significant responsibility in the campaign was already guilty, but fraud would have to be proved.

With the exception of Helme, the Democratic primary candidate, the Republican Party chairmen, state party leaders, campaign workers, and elected officials wedged into the courtroom resembled a state party convention. Someone thought to form the "One Hundred and Thirty Five Republicans Club," with blue buttons reading, "I Helped Keep Henry Ford Out of the United States Senate," as a badge of honor. The number of full members of the club decreased, with ten pleading nolo contendere and one pleading guilty. The rest believed they had been part of an uncommonly hard-fought campaign, not a criminal conspiracy. Helme denied being paid for his effort and asserted that it was not a crime to be "worked" in politics. The prosecutorial logic that imagined a candidate in the Democratic primary conspiring with Republicans to spend "over the speed limit" escaped him. King remained proud of the campaign he ran. It was costly, but necessarily so, given Ford's name recognition and repugnant views, and the money paid for advertising, not corrupt practices. Most of all, the Newberry team's lawyers believed the campaign operated fully within the laws. The state limit did not apply to independent committees—even Osborn hoped to spend as much as $15,000 in his primary campaign—and the federal law, whatever it meant, did not apply to primaries.[15]

Team Newberry would not have a chance to make those arguments. Judge Sessions's early warning reliably predicted his rulings on evidence. Out went witnesses who could talk about Newberry's initial reluctance to run and the committee's reasons for spending and questions about the credibility of prosecution witnesses. Dailey's investigators had spent the months after the indictment recovering the ground Robinson's report had mapped and extending it to cover office boys in New York and potential witnesses now as far away as Montana and Alabama. Dailey called, among others, the entire clerical staff of the Newberry committee, newspaper publishers, theater owners, and party activists (including Osborn) in his attempt to prove a conspiracy that began with Newberry and extended down to the tiniest hamlet. Taken together, the testimony of secretaries who reported that they were indeed paid, sometimes with cash and sometimes by check; reports of invoices never sent to Detroit; and lurid tales of work among Indians, railroad workers, and Poles (including the sighting of a pile of money on a table at Newberry headquarters, which Dailey helpfully described as $1 million) was designed to show that the campaign spent much more than $195,000. Osborn, who had supported Newberry in the general election, testified that some Detroit politicos told him that he would be the next senator if he came up with $150,000 to $200,000. Dailey sought to leave the impression that the campaign bribed newspaper owners and movie theater operators, the last with the free distribution of "Our Navy" (the testimony of a theater owner who blurted out that he also showed the weekly free Ford film was stricken). Dailey aimed to show through the testimony of bank employees and an accountant that unrecorded cash coursed in and out of the campaign coffers. Finally, there were stories of misbehavior away from headquarters—county organizers slipping a few bucks to their assistants, another organizer threatening to withhold his support of a local candidate who backed Osborn. Dailey trimmed his presentation, but still the transcript ran 5,312 pages.[16]

Dailey beat the defense to a motion to dismiss charges against twenty-three of the indicted men. Judge Sessions dismissed fifteen more, along with the fifth charge of fraud, since the Gerry Act was passed after the primary. With what Sessions called the "rubbish" cleared away, the defense presented its case. Their sole witness was King, who described the circumstances of his joining the campaign, produced his correspondence with Newberry, and outlined his work, which included nothing on finances. When King took ill with a nervous breakdown, the defense rested.[17]

Sessions instructed the jury on the law relevant to charges one through four, now consolidated into one:

If you are satisfied from the evidence that the defendant, Truman H. Newberry, at or about the time that he became a candidate for United States Senator was informed and knew that his campaign for the nomination and election would require the expenditure and use of more money than is permitted by law and with such knowledge became a candidate, and thereafter by advice, by conduct, by his acts, by his direction, by his counsel, or by his procurement he actively participated and took part in the expenditure and use of . . . an unlawful sum of money, you will be warranted in finding that he did violate this statute known as the Corrupt Practices Act.

Even with guidance that drew a straight line to a guilty verdict, a jury drawn from Grand Rapids, home of William Alden Smith and Arthur Vandenburg, was not blown away by the prosecution's case. One juror reported that if not for Paul King, whose correspondence documented Newberry's engagement in the campaign and who testified that he told Newberry that a campaign could cost as much as $50,000, the jury might have acquitted the group. With that testimony they found seventeen of the defendants guilty on the first count, including Truman, his brother John, and the top tier of the campaign committee. Truman Newberry, King, and Cody received the stiffest sentences (two years at Leavenworth and a $10,000 fine). They returned a not-guilty verdict on the last count, dealing with mail fraud. The next stop would be the Supreme Court, with Charles Evans Hughes joining the Newberry defense.[18]

While the Grand Rapids trial was still in progress, Lucking pressed Ford's case before the Senate. "There is a large amount of additional evidence and different testimony to be laid before your honorable body in this contest," he promised. A subcommittee of the Privileges and Elections Committee conducted a recount before hearing the evidence. Ford and Newberry men gathered ballots from the 1,700 city and township clerks. Lucking saw sinister purpose in random local glitches: a Saginaw janitor's habit of selling used ballots to a junk dealer (recovered by a Ford agent), a shortage of ballot boxes in one township that caused election officials to unseal the Ford-Newberry ballots, and confusion about who was responsible for custody of the ballots in another township. The sacks of ballots, minus the missing few, arrived in Washington, where ten teams of counters found 264 additional votes for Ford and 2,962 fewer for Newberry. Newberry still had a plurality of 4,334.[19]

The recount confirmed Newberry's election, but his promise to become an "efficient and useful Senator" went unmet, since it seemed prudent to stay out of Washington while he awaited the appeal of his conviction. And he was broke in the way that rich people can be. He had spent more than the cost of the campaign—$250,000—on legal fees. His bank account had enough to pay his taxes and not much else. Murfin accepted stocks in partial payment, but Newberry's New York–based lawyer wanted cash. He examined a list of stocks to sell, looking for those with a "ready market." Bills for the next phase were on the way.[20]

In January 1921, the Supreme Court heard arguments in the Newberry appeal. The Court had three questions before it. The most fundamental was a federalism question: Was the FCPA an unconstitutional extension of federal power into primary elections, which were properly left to the states? The second concerned the meaning of the FCPA, especially whether its spending limits applied to candidates—the literal reading of the text—or also to the actions of independent (at least technically) committees. Finally, the Court reviewed Sessions's controversial interpretation of a statute that previously had not been tested in court. What exactly did "causing to have spent" mean?

Neither Hughes nor Solicitor General William Frierson (assisted by Dailey) took his full time for argument, even with plenty of interruptions from the bench. Hughes's brief highlighted the federalism question, arguing that since the primaries were a recent invention unknown to the framers, and parties and factions had used a number of different mechanisms to nominate candidates, primaries were not "elections" in the meaning of article 1, section 4 of the Constitution. His oral argument pounded Sessions's "grotesque" interpretation of the statute that resulted in Newberry's conviction. "Never did a candidate have less to do with his nomination and campaign," Hughes insisted, reminding the justices that Newberry himself had contributed nothing. If Newberry's knowledge that his campaign would spend more than state law allowed was conspiracy, then the law was a "trap which would take in every senator and representative in congress today." The solicitor general (a Wilson appointee) argued that Congress had the power to limit campaign spending: if Congress could not, it was hard to see how the states could. And if Newberry knew (as he certainly did) that his campaign was going to spend more than the law allowed, a conspiracy to break the law existed.[21]

The murky, multipart decision, announced in May 1921, freed Newberry to take his seat in the Senate but left important questions hanging. Three justices joined James McReynolds, later famous for his opposition to the New Deal, in the opinion of the Court. McReynolds tracked Hughes's brief, finding that Congress did not have the power to regulate primary elections, since they were "merely methods by which party adherents agree upon candidates," not elections under the meaning of the Constitution. It was a classic McReynolds opinion, turning on the literal, narrow meaning of words and insistent on the limited power of the federal government. The wonder was not his opinion but the concurrence of Oliver Wendell Holmes

Jr., long a critic of legal formalism. The vote was so out of character that legal scholar Benno C. Schmidt speculated that Holmes found the FCPA to be such "legal and economic humbug" that he sided with the otherwise "absurd" opinion. Justice McKenna concurred in part, making a majority to reverse the lower court's decision. He argued that since the Seventeenth Amendment took effect after the FCPA, the law did not apply to Senate races, but he left open the question of whether Congress had the power to regulate primary elections.[22]

Two dissenting opinions took issue with McReynolds's narrow understanding of congressional power but would have reversed Newberry's conviction because of Judge Sessions's defective interpretation of the statute. Chief Justice White maintained that Congress had the power to regulate elections to federal offices; to say otherwise was "suicidal" to any reasonable view of federal power. The Pitney dissent, joined by Justices Clarke and Brandeis, argued that McReynolds's restrictive interpretation would "leave the general government destitute of the means to insure its own preservation." But as much as Congress rightly concerned itself with the "harmful influences resulting from an unlimited expenditure of money in paid propaganda and other purchased campaign activities," Sessions misread the statute. By White's reading, it intended "not to restrict the right of the citizen to contribute to a campaign" but to curb the spending of candidates. If the law also applied to others, a candidate would have to withdraw or face prosecution if he heard that supporters had contributed or spent more than the law allowed. The Pitney dissent criticized Sessions's expansive interpretation of "causing to have spent," which amounted to as little as agreeing to run and suspecting the effort might cost more than the limit.[23]

The decision had consequences for the federal regulation of campaign finance, and more broadly for election law and the Court itself. Together the opinion of the Court and the dissents left little of the FCPA standing. If the FCPA applied only to general elections and to the spending of candidates, it regulated nothing. In practice, candidates and their committees spent money in primary elections. Parties raised and spent funds in general elections, and party activities were not covered by the FCPA. In 1922, Attorney General Daugherty issued his informal opinion that the decision invalidated the law, bringing a flood of questions to the Justice Department about whether candidates had to file reports. White southern Democrats suffered no confusion about what the decision meant. Some southern senators had opposed the FCPA in 1912 because it implied that Congress could regulate primary elections. Anxious to build redundancy into the disfranchisement of African Americans, some state parties closed primary elections to blacks. Although the Court did not muster a majority in favor of the proposition that Congress lacked the power to regulate primary elections, southern Democrats constructed whites-only primaries confident that the rule did not conflict with the Fourteenth and Fifteenth Amendments. Finally, the decision outlined the broad constitutional arguments about federal power that would occupy the Court until 1938.[24]

Newberry and his lawyers celebrated what they saw as vindication, or at least the setting right of an injustice. Newberry assembled a scrapbook of congratulations, with some glad for the defeat of Ford, some for the clearing of Newberry's name, and one "even more pleased at the final collapse of the last great conspiracy of Woodrow Wilson against ordered civil government in this country." "Somehow the air seems purer, and the sun brighter, and the world a better place to live in," wrote a constituent. Marvin Littleton, Newberry's pricey New York lawyer, "so rejoiced over the result" that he "sat down and recounted all of the events of the trial, from beginning to end," which he would share in an address to the bar association. He challenged Newberry to a game of golf, "wagers to be made at the first tee and odds not to be asked for."[25]

Newberry would have been better off had he lost on the federalism question, with what would have been a unanimous Court sending the case back for rehearing. The critique of Sessions's reading of the law got no attention, and his opponents charged that he had evaded the penitentiary on a technicality. But Justice McReynolds had reminded Congress that it had a remedy at hand. It could "protect itself against corruption, fraud or other malign influences" by exercising its authority to act as judge of its own members. Lucking was ready with a telegram from Ford sent on May 19, 1921, to members of the Committee on Privilege and Elections urging that the Senate take up McReynolds's suggestion. Ford claimed that he "personally care[d] little or nothing for the seat for myself" but "insist[ed] upon the investigation, in order to have it forever established that a seat in the United States Senate may not be purchased and that seats are not for sale to the highest bidders." A subcommittee acting as a grand jury would hear testimony, with Lucking as prosecutor (with the help of some of Dailey's assistants) and Murfin, Newberry's Detroit attorney, trying to prevent damage to his client.[26]

Newberry went into the hearings with distinct advantages. It was risky precedent for senators to argue that they knew better than a state's voters, who were fully aware of the Newberry expenditures when they elected him. The 1920 elections had made Warren G. Harding president with a largely united party behind him and, more important to Newberry's case, had padded the Republican majority. Before a word was spoken on the Senate floor, one head counter believed the Republican's comfortable 59 to 37–seat lead translated into a likely 3 to 7 vote margin for Newberry, factoring in progressive Republican defections. In Selden P. Spencer of Missouri, a former circuit court judge who graduated from Yale a year before Newberry, he had a committee chair ably guarding his interests. Together with Charles E. Townsend, Michigan's senior senator who had worked with Paul King, Spencer guided Newberry's defense. Help also came from an unusual source: Kathleen Lawler, a Michigan native, clerk to the Committee on Privileges and Elections. A specialist on election contests, she had served in this capacity since the turn of the century, maintaining records and overseeing "all the working, mechanical details" of cases. Lively, opinionated, and staunchly partisan, she updated Newberry, Murfin, King, and others interested in the case on the whats and whys of senators' behavior. "You may depend upon what I write you," Lawler instructed Newberry, contrasting her good information with the "fragmentary conversations, newspaper gossip, and guesses, personal conclusions and inferences" that filled other reports.[27]

Although the Grand Rapids trial had not uncovered fraud, Lucking pushed that angle in the committee hearings, since it could surmount senatorial reticence about overturning the will of voters. He sought to prove that the financial report filed by the Newberry committee was "faked." Without direct evidence, he played up the papers and people that had disappeared since the Grand Rapids trial, which surely would have converted innuendo to fact. The Newberry family ledgers had been examined by the grand jury, but Fred Smith, the overseer of the family's accounts, said they since had been lost in a break-in. Benjamin F. Emory, the finance director, presumably could have explained the accounting, but he was recuperating in Canada. His skull was fractured in an accident that occurred while he was a passenger in a car driven by a Ford agent; he had a $100,000 suit pending against Ford. Lucking badgered witnesses who did appear. "You've been living off Newberry and his friends ever since that campaign, haven't you?" he snapped at the assistant finance director. Murfin objected to the "nasty, dirty" nonquestion. "Aw, shut up," retorted Lucking, clearing space to take a swing at the Newberry attorney.[28]

Lucking perhaps had run out of patience, since Murfin spent most of the hearing objecting to repetition of material covered at Grand Rapids. The new witnesses generated little fresh information. John S. Newberry and the other major donors to the campaign related the same story: they were devoted friends or family members moved to contribute heavily, without coordination or consultation with the candidate, by their admiration of Truman or distaste for Ford. Lucking lost ground by calling campaign chairman Templeton. Lucking leaped up, shouting, "No! No!" to object to Murfin's question to him about a discussion with Ford. "Never mind," Lucking sighed, as Templeton told of Ford's harangue about how "a gang of Jews had a general conspiracy to control the senate and the government," putting up $1 million to elect Newberry in furtherance of the plot.[29]

The one crack came in Fred Smith's testimony. The man who had handled the family accounts for decades described the context of a telegram that reminded Newberry that the primary was in August, not July. He explained that Newberry had been "kicking about the balances." Lucking did not succeed in clarifying what Smith meant. But he had extracted a phrase that would ring through the floor debate and the hint that maybe Truman had paid for the campaign after all.[30]

Lawler was not impressed. "I have never experienced such disrespect, and such frivolity of showing; it has been ridiculous to go through this performance," she told a Michigan contact. "After screaming for three years to be heard, and making brave claims of exposure of dreadful crime and wrong doing they have simply re-hashed and jockeyed for time." Liebold agreed that Lucking had "failed to support [the charges] with definite evidence before the Senate committee." But it scarcely mattered. Lawler had advised Newberry to "forget the whole matter, because in the classic language of our temporarily (at least) dear departed (politically) democratic brethren—WE HAVE THE VOTES." The Republican majority recommended rejecting Ford's claim: he had lost the recount and had not proved the fraud that would justify overturning the choice of Michigan voters. The Democratic minority, led by Ohio's Atlee Pomerene, up for reelection in 1922 and with his eye on the 1924 presidential nomination, agreed that Ford had not won the seat but returned to the suspicions Lucking had raised in his contest. "The proposed minority report is really disappointingly weak—it is not even wicked!" Lawler wrote in relief to Spencer, leaking the report before it went to the printer.[31]

In November 1921, the Senate opened the floor to debate on the Republican resolution. It continued in fits and starts until January 1922, interrupted by actual legislation on such matters as the tariff and the railroads, and an investigation of U.S. military behavior in Haiti. This was not a mere vote on a colleague's fitness for office. Rather, it was war, declared Alabama Democrat J. Thomas Heflin, requiring "every senator here to fight to the death to protect this body from the corrupt use of money." It was "possibly the bitterest fight waged in a generation over the title to a seat to that body," according to the *Baltimore Sun*. The debate was vicious because it was partisan and factional but also because senators defending or attacking Newberry's right to a seat had to make sense of their business as politicians, of what had happened to political campaigns in the wake of Progressive Era reforms, the Great War, and commercial culture.[32]

Ohio Democrat Atlee Pomerene, the ranking minority member of the Privileges and Elections subcommittee that ran the hearings, promised "a considerable number of speeches" from his side of the aisle. His colleagues delivered. In this war, southerners were the infantry, and progressive Republicans the snipers, with Thomas Walsh, a Montana Democrat ("very vain and regards himself as a great lawyer, which is a very bad combination," in Wilson's estimation), providing the legal logistics. They reviewed the testimony given at Grand Rapids and the Senate hearing, but their rhetorical ambitions soared far higher than the record before them. They refought the Civil War and Reconstruction, reviewed the arguments about World War I and the League of Nations, traveled through the history of the Roman Empire, and revisited investigations past, including the decision to vacate Illinois senator Lorimer's seat and to accept Isaac Stephenson of Wisconsin. Even if their oratory swayed no votes, senators speaking against Newberry's continued presence among them sought to establish his guilt and the potential of big campaign budgets to "destroy the very rock upon which rests the destiny of the Republic."[33]

Neither the FCPA nor the Michigan law prohibited much beyond candidates' own spending, and the fraud charges against Newberry's campaign never even made it to the jury in Grand Rapids. But unconstrained by courtroom niceties, senators freely filled in the gaps in the record and the law. For Idaho's William Borah, an insurgent Republican ever alert to the power of moneyed interests, simple arithmetic made Newberry guilty and unworthy of the Senate: the "amount expended in the Michigan election was such as to lead to the conclusion that it was intended to and did corruptly affect the result of the primary election." Because the correspondence between Paul King and Newberry demonstrated Newberry's contact with his campaign, it seemed a short leap to the conclusion that he directed it, or at the very least knew exactly what was being done in his name. Missouri's James A. Reed, a wicked debater, made the point with sarcasm: "To argue that candidate Newberry did not know what was going on is to argue that he is without sufficient mental capacity to find his way from this Chamber to his hotel." For Borah, Newberry's knowledge was beside the point, since by picking a committee chairman the committee's illegal "acts became his acts." Newberry's Senate critics asserted that Newberry violated Michigan election law—a crime missed even by the aggressive Dailey and Robinson—by hiring campaign workers. Alabama's Oscar Underwood found the facts and the legal interpretation so compelling that the only question left was "whether or not the Republican Party as a party intends to obey the law of the land." The detail-oriented Lawler, observing the proceedings for Newberry and his supporters, sputtered about inaccuracies, such as Helfin's guess that the campaign spent between $700,000 and $1 million, upping the estimate, itself based on rumors, in Lieutenant Governor Dickinson's letter.[34]

Even if legal, the campaign's spending offended decent people, speakers claimed, and if left unpunished, it endangered the nation. Heflin predicted that if "money bags control elections in this country then the day of revolution will not be far away." Wall Street and "the money interests, the corrupt money interests of America," ignored the people's real problems and demanded that Newberry keep his seat. Henry Ashurst of Arizona, part of the Democratic class of 1912, worried about the future of the nation, since the Roman Empire fell "because it permitted without rebuke just such scandals as that which we are facing to-day." Insurgent stalwart William Kenyon railed against a "social lobby" that was using friendship, dinner invitations, and visits to the White House to swing votes for Newberry. It had gotten so bad, Heflin claimed, that "Senators can not attend a reception unless wealthy women of the East besiege them and ask them to support Mr. Newberry." The Senate, republican government, the common people of America, and Washington receptions had been tainted by the money spent on Newberry's election.[35]

Classic moments of personal and partisan bickering enlivened what soon became a repetitious debate. The ailing Pennsylvania boss Boise Penrose gathered himself up uncertainly from his seat, joining others who had walked out on another Heflin speech on Newberry's corruption. When Heflin complained about the vacant Republican chairs, the Pennsylvanian's retort—"I am surprised that the Senator expects any one to listen to his speech"—brought everyone scurrying back from the cloakrooms to join the pandemonium. Mississippi's elegant John Sharp Williams, a Senate wit whose long twirled mustache gave him the look of the Bourbon planter he was, stomped out of the chamber after his argument with fellow Democrat Tom Watson about Ford's wartime profits and the League. Perhaps he lost patience because he had replaced James Vardman, Watson's race-baiting, populist Mississippi counterpart, in a campaign that turned on whether white supremacy was better protected by a man of culture and learning or one who riled up the white lower classes with false claims such as Williams having forced a white and a black servant to eat together. (In fact, Williams, protested, he had fired the white employee for eating with a black servant.) The most pointed defense of Newberry, from George H. Moses of New Hampshire, skewered Ford ("an amiable and somewhat narrow minded wizard of Industry . . . the possessor of a huge fortune, however slender his intellectual capital") and southern Democrats who fretted about the purity of elections in Michigan but denied the vote to African Americans in their own states. Moses asked why Wilson's Justice Department had such a keen interest in Newberry's race—and in his own—but had shown no concern about elections Democrats had won in 1918 where rumors flew about excessive spending and election irregularities. Thaddeus Caraway of Arkansas elicited chuckles with a catalog of Republican spending on notoriously rotten presidential nominating conventions in southern states, some of it directed by Moses.[36]

The protracted debate left plenty of time to line up votes. Alfred Lucking remained active in Ford's interest, focusing on progressive Republicans and using his connection with Tumulty to shore up support among potentially wavering Democrats. Watson was likely lost, and until Reed, an anti-League Democrat and critic of Wilson, lambasted Newberry from the floor, Lucking worried about him, too. To reduce suspicions that Ford was plotting to be installed in Newberry's place, a telegram from Ford headquarters indicated that he had no interest in the seat, and that it was up to the Senate to "clean its own skirts." Ford's team pressured senators by distributing newspapers in Indiana, New Jersey, and Missouri that denounced Newberry's corruption, and by hinting that Ford would spend freely in 1922 to defeat those who voted for the Republican resolution. Newberry got as far as inquiring about the cost of distributing a best-of collection of critical articles by E. G. Pipp, the former editor of Ford's *Dearborn Independent* and author of much of Ford's 1918 campaign material. (Pipp had broken with his boss over the incessant new focus on the "international Jew.")[37]

At the beginning of the contest Newberry's friends anticipated that Newberry's TR connections would minimize the defections of progressive Republicans. That hope evaporated, as Newberry's slender record in the Senate (largely in connection with a veterans' bonus and farm state–backed changes to the Federal Reserve) signaled regular rather than progressive instincts, giving insurgents little reason to support him. The only remaining mystery was Hiram Johnson's vote, which he had apparently promised to both sides. No one knew what the Californian would do when he returned from a West Coast trip. Everyone monitored the health of senators from Pennsylvania and fretted about how William E. Crow would be paired if he lived long enough for a vote and who would replace Crow, Penrose, or both if they died before it. Crow remained hospitalized, but Penrose's death on New Year's Eve generated enormous pressure on the governor of Pennsylvania to quickly name an acceptable replacement.[38]

Since the trial, observers, including Newberry, wondered when and if he might speak for himself. It was sound strategy to keep him mute in

Grand Rapids, since the defense argued that he knew only what the men in charge told him. He was not straining to defend himself. While summering in Watch Hill, he tweaked a speech drafted by Murfin and King, to have ready, Murfin said, if "the right psychological moment" arose in the Senate committee hearings. Newberry vetted the statement with his Senate allies, but while Spencer found it "a frank, manly, and strong statement, he was firmly convinced that I should not make it and I gladly concur in this as I believe . . . any statement I make would only supply ammunition to my political opponents." If a statement had to be made when the resolution moved to the floor, Newberry asked Townsend to deliver it. It would be a great relief, he wrote, "if there is any practicable way of making this personal statement without doing it in person." Newberry's allies divided over the wisdom of a Newberry speech, but Lawler joined Spencer, seeing more risk than reward, "and my rule of life is—when in doubt, don't act!" But Newberry's silence had become a talking point for his critics. Characterizing Newberry either as a liar or as too stupid to sit in the Senate if he knew nothing about his own campaign, they clamored for him to appear for questioning. "Can it be possible that the other side is afraid to talk to this money king?" cried Missouri's Reed.[39]

The day came on January 9, 1922. Murfin was worried. "Personally, I deplore the thought that Senator Newberry is going to assume to make a speech," even one he drafted. "Unfortunately, however, he went away without consulting me on the subject," he complained to Lawler. After a hostile speaker finished, Newberry emerged from a cloakroom and read his statement, without deviation from the text and, by prearrangement, without interruption. He told the packed chamber about how his friends induced him to run, how they tapped King to organize the campaign, and how he knew King's publicity "cost a considerable sum," but he did not have "the faintest idea" about the amount until the report filed after the primary. Learning that King had spent $195,000 filled him with "astonishment and regret," even if it was legal and paid for permissible goods and services. Walsh, the Montana Democrat, was the only senator to ask questions, and they were surprisingly mild and disjointed, focusing on such matters as who paid the New York hotel bills of visiting members of the Newberry committee. He, too, failed to get a clear explanation of what "kicking about the balances" meant. It was over in a bit more than an hour. Lawler judged Newberry's performance "strong, and convincing, wonderfully pleasing to all his friends. . . . I regretted more questions were not asked him. Even Jay Hayden admitted and volunteered he was fine and handled himself more than well."[40]

The speech was carefully balanced: Newberry defended himself while expressing distaste for big-spending campaigns, professed ignorance while not blaming Michigan Republicans and his campaign team, and provided an explanation without harsh partisanship. Pomerene's wife, listening from the gallery, surmised it was written by a "'smart' lawyer," guessing wrong only at the number. Newberry aimed it at his supporters and the few who could be convinced. "The senators who are skulking behind the cloak of his silence, in my opinion, will find another excuse when he speaks," Lawler correctly predicted. Mississippi's Williams wasted no time, turning on his heels to face his colleagues after Newberry left the chamber. "Is there a man within the sound of my voice who believes it?" he asked. "It is a horrible thing to accuse a gentleman of perjury. Do you believe it? You know it is as false as hell." Walsh introduced a substitute resolution declaring the seat vacant and another sending the case back to committee. Lawler anticipated both resolutions, dismissing them as "the same as every tactic employed," designed "to drag this case along and bring it as near as possible to the next election."[41]

Both sides worked furiously to nail down votes. The day Newberry spoke, George Wharton Pepper, a distinguished patrician Philadelphia lawyer friendly with Harding, was sworn in. While everyone expected he would support Newberry, he held off declaring his intentions until he digested the record. (That left time enough for Democrats to accuse Harding of romancing Pepper with White House invitations.) To secure the vote of Ohio's Frank B. Willis, a masterful campaigner (he died a good death, on the stump, in 1928) who was feeling some heat on the issue at home, Spencer allowed an amendment to the Republican resolution. Newberry would keep his seat. But the additional language "severely condemned and disapproved of" expensive campaigns as "contrary to sound public policy, harmful to the honor and dignity of the Senate and dangerous to the perpetuation of free government."[42]

The last-minute amendment capped a day of rehashing familiar points. When Heflin added poetry to his dark rumblings about Newberry's corruption, cries of "Vote!" grew louder. Republicans had no Byron, but they did have numbers. The resolution passed 46 to 41, with all Democrats and a dozen Republicans against and Watson, Johnson, and Newberry not voting. (Johnson claimed he was delayed by a snowstorm in the Midwest, which the unfriendly *Los Angeles Times* observed was "a purely Johnsonian blizzard, observable to him and no one else.") Irvine Lenroot, once a close ally of progressive Robert La Follette but by this time trending toward regularity, was the closest Newberry came to the support of a progressive Republican.[43]

Much about the debate had been theater, but in discussion of some of the details senators confronted how reform and commercial advertising had changed politics. Was it not only legal but necessary and normal for a candidate's campaign to pay workers? This question generated tendentious arguments about the correct interpretation of Michigan's election laws, but also about the practice itself. "These things are not only done but ought to be done in every election," Spencer claimed, suggesting that the experienced politicians in the room knew this fact of political life. He was no doubt right, but few senators admitted it. Only the most powerful incumbent or most unserious challenger could trust a primary race conducted by no workforce or a band of volunteers. But how large could a paid campaign workforce be before it became "stench in the nostrils of the public"? Candidates routinely bought advertising space in newspapers, at least since the demise of nineteenth-century "party organs." How much advertising was too much? Oscar Underwood proclaimed that "when newspaper advertising is carried to the extent . . . that it carries the newspaper, it is a way of purchasing the paper." (Buying newspapers outright to gain favorable coverage remained, as in the nineteenth century, unremarkable.) When Paul King bought advertising late in the primary in a labor newspaper in order to shore up support among workers, was he using the space to communicate with the public, as any advertiser would do? What was the appropriate extent? Or was he purchasing editorial support, which mattered in this period, when newspapers were the only available medium?[44]

How much was too much in total, even if candidates spent campaign funds legally? Already, Norris pointed out, it was "more and more difficult to secure a seat" without outlandish spending. "What amount would receive our condemnation?" he asked in exasperation. Townsend wondered whether it was possible to fix an amount that was defensible. "Can we draw a moral line or a legal line, and say that the amount of advertising, the amount of publicity, the amount of canvassing, must be limited to the amount of my means, a poor man?" he asked. "Will that be the limit? . . . [O]r shall we say—'It is legal to do this, and anybody can do little or much of it, as he sees fit.'" These questions pointed up the irony in Progressive Era reforms that required candidates to raise and spend money for organization and advertising, even as politicians denounced the evils of money in politics. The pages of talk about the Newberry case failed to provide a solution. In the immediate aftermath of the *Newberry* decision, Pomerene proposed to limit spending to $10,000, including advertising and workers, with the cap enforced by a Senate rule. It was a clever idea that bypassed the courts. It went nowhere. The Senate was not willing to attach a real number to limits on political spending. Senators could not know how much was enough. The questions would only grow more pressing as the cost of campaigns continued to rise.[45]

If this vote had not settled the practical and ethical questions surrounding campaign finance, neither did it allow Newberry to settle comfortably into his role as senator. "The adoption of that resolution was the most stupid piece of business that ever disgraced any body of men, whether pirates sailing the seas under the black flag or statesmen here seated in this body," said Reed, H. L. Mencken's favorite lawmaker. In the same speech Reed put Newberry in the political lexicon: "Newberryism" in popular usage came to mean big-money campaigns with implications of corruption. Divided on liquor and the League and other foreign policy issues, Democrats united in their opposition to "Newberryism" and the Harding administration, and they intended to ride those issues in 1922 and beyond. Republicans were terrified that it was 1910 or 1912 all over again. Progressives such as Kenyon and La Follette campaigned for insurgent candidates running against regulars; there were rumors that the Republican Congressional Campaign Committee might return the favor by cutting off support for successful insurgents. If so, there were savings to be had. Unrest persisted along with an agricultural depression in the Great Plains and parts of the Midwest, and progressives Albert Beveridge and Smith W. Brookhart deposed regular Republicans in the Indiana and Iowa primaries.[46]

Reports had Ford, poised to exact revenge, backing Republican insurgents in primaries against Newberry supporters, and Democrats in general elections. Lucking denied that a Ford friend was executing the strategy in New Jersey, but he was on his way out of Ford's inner circle and into membership in the ever growing Ford executive alumni group. Ford's help was not necessary. It was a gloomy election day for Republicans, especially the regulars. The party lost ten seats in the Senate. Their only good news came in the defeats of Democrats Hitchcock in Nebraska and Pomerene in Ohio and Republican Beveridge in Indiana, who had been deserted by regulars sore about his primary win. The results should not have been a surprise: this was, after all, a midterm election conducted as parts of the country were just coming out of a sharp recession (agricultural and mining regions remained mired in it). As always in midterm elections, dynamics peculiar to individual races created a national trend: in some states foreign policy issues mattered, in others, legalization of light beer and wine, and in still others crop prices and veterans' bonuses.[47]

Democrats and progressive Republican candidates invoked Newberry-ism in their campaigns. Democrat Clarence Dill of Washington credited his defeat of Miles Poindexter to his relentless discussion of Newberry. If voters had forgotten who Newberry was, Charles Evans Hughes, now secretary of state, reminded them with a letter replying to a New Jersey minister, made public by the RNC and published in August. "A more extraordinary misconstruction of a statute has never come under my observation," he wrote, citing the dissenting opinions in explaining the miscarriage of justice that swept up Newberry. Cordell Hull, chair of the DNC, pounced. Hughes's letter was both a Republican attempt to defang the Newberry issue and a "desperate effort to check the rising tide of popular indignation" over the "monstrous tariff," the recession, and general failure of Republican policies. If Hull correctly divined Republican strategy, he misread the punctilious Hughes. The former and future Supreme Court justice continued to defend the distinctions between an unreasonable prosecution and substantive complaints about money in politics. Writing to Walter Lippmann two years later, he repeated that Newberry's conviction was "as gross a miscarriage of justice as had ever come under my observation," which was not to say anything about Newberry's character, money in politics, or the Michigan campaign. But only regular Republicans at this point had a stake in separating the legal from the moral.[48]

Despite the Hughes letter and the stump speeches, there is little that suggests that Newberry mattered in most races. Except in Michigan, that is,
where the long-running party fights broke out again, this time with Newberry and his organization as the focus. Senator Townsend overcame two
primary challengers; the most serious was, ironically, a Newberry supporter
in 1918. Townsend lost in the general election to Woodbridge Ferris, who
declared his win "a victory of political righteousness." Ferris promised to unseat Newberry when he joined a new Senate that surely would not condone
the lesson that "if you commit a crime, violate the law, plead ignorance . . .
if you are high-up and you have the money, you can go free." Townsend had
defended his support of Newberry on legal principles and had distanced his
organization from the group that had worked for Newberry. This was all too
wordy and abstract for Kathleen Lawler, the committee clerk still connected
in Michigan political circles. She thought that Townsend's campaign had
erred in not tackling "Newberryism" directly, by fighting rather than explaining. So "all over the state, first voters, and new voters, young girls, and young
mother's [sic] with their babes in their arms would say—'Oh! I don't know
anything about what it all means . . . but we must help stamp out this terrible
scourge of Newberryism which is destroying our state and our nation.' When
asked—'What is Newberryism?' . . . [t]hey did not know whether it was a
new dance, or a personality."49

Talk began immediately about Newberry's resignation. Given the
makeup of the incoming Senate, another committee hearing, another floor
debate, and a majority voting to unseat Newberry were certain. The Republican leadership had to be concerned about prolonging an issue that
united Democrats. But Newberry already had made his way to the exit in
the spring of 1922. Movers packed up his Massachusetts Avenue rented
mansion, formerly housing the Swiss legation, hauling the ornate furniture,
artwork, and Packards back to Grosse Pointe. After consulting with Harding and Michigan governor Groesbeck, he officially resigned on November
19, 1922. In what was for him a flourish, Newberry defended his own character, honesty, and patriotism, dismissed his enemies as partisan hacks, and
thanked those who had stood by him. The time had come to give up his
seat, he explained, because his work in the Senate "has been and would
continue to be hampered by partisan political persecution." Townsend
had lost, Newberry claimed, because of "over four years of continuous

propaganda of misrepresentation and untruth." And he took credit for one accomplishment, since his vote had helped to keep the United States out of the League of Nations.[50]

Right on cue, a few of his foes declared that his decision was a victory for the virtue of the Senate and goodness itself. Arkansas senator Thaddeus Caraway announced that the removal of Newberry would help restore the "honor and dignity" of the Senate. More grandly, Pat Harrison of Mississippi predicted that Newberry's resignation "will prove glad tiding to the people generally and will send a thrill of joy into every American home." Most of Newberry's opponents—and supporters—expressed relief, except for the diehards. "I am sorry he did it," said Caraway. "He has cheated the senate of a chance to vindicate itself before the nation." Townsend thought Newberry's campaign had spent too much, "most of it foolishly," but that "most of the opposition to him came from senators from states which have held no honest elections since the civil war." Even before the vote, Williams could muster only resignation. "Like everybody else, I am a little tired of it, especially the pretense of virtue while having others buy voters, which seems to be a sort of salient characteristic of modern politics."[51]

Newberry had asked for Governor Groesbeck's assurance that his replacement would stand for "cardinal Republican principles," a sort of progressivism that fell within that, and opposition to the League of Nations. Groesbeck appointed James Couzens, mayor of Detroit, former Ford executive, and decidedly irregular Republican. The appointment bothered Newberry enough that he refused to contribute to President Coolidge's 1924 campaign unless assured that none of his funds would help Groesbeck and Couzens. But his anger was not consuming. He got on with things, writing long letters of thanks to those who had fought his case for him, paying for his staff's salary through January, having his door and desk nameplates sent to him. On January 6, he and his wife boarded the RMS *Majestic* for London, the first stop on a trip around the world.[52]

Contrary to the images created in the 1918 campaign, Ford turned out to be more of a politician than Newberry. While Newberry returned to his businesses, family, yacht, and clubs, Ford continued his erratic public career. There was talk of a run for the presidency in 1920 and again in 1924, which got as far as the formation of Ford-for-president groups. The presidential buzz fit his scheme to extract a 100-year lease (costing Ford $5 million) on the Wilson Dam, at Muscle Shoals, Alabama, which he promised would produce cheap power and fertilizer, benefiting all of mankind. Defeated by progressives opposed to the privatization of the federal asset, a campaign led by George Norris that included Couzens, Muscle Shoals was later the core of the New Deal showcase, the Tennessee Valley Authority. There was a new libel suit, this one lodged against Ford by Aaron Shapiro, an organizer of agricultural cooperatives, charging that Ford had defamed an entire race in the *Dearborn Independent*'s series on Jews. At first intending to fight the suit with Senator Reed as his attorney, Ford eventually settled. His apology blamed Liebold and a ghostwriter for the offensive ideas published without his knowledge or consent. Personal relationships, now without public importance, improved. Although Violet Newberry could not abide Henry, Phelps and Edsel became Grosse Pointe friends and business associates.[53]

By 1935, Truman had mended relations with Henry enough to extend a well-mannered apology for the publication of Spencer Ervin's book on the 1918 election controversy. Newberry did not spot "any unfriendly references to you but I wanted to assure you that I had nothing whatever to do with the publication, and regret that the book has been published. I earnestly hope you will let nothing now or hereafter interfere with what I trust is a real friendship existing between us." Yet he liked the book well enough to send copies to a few old Senate colleagues. In his autobiographical sketch he described it as the place to go for accurate information about that phase of his life. Written by an attorney, it characterizes the Grand Rapids prosecution and the Senate hearings as miscarriages of justice, deliberate misreadings of the Michigan and federal statutes and the common law shaped by partisanship and Ford's vengefulness.[54]

Ervin was right about the legal errors, most of which owed to Sessions's overly broad reading of a badly drafted law. There never was real evidence of fraud or spending above the $195,000 reported. Rumors abounded about Newberry's campaign—and those of many candidates that year, whether the Justice Department tracked them or not—but a truly assiduous search produced nothing solid. And partisanship mattered—a lot—in the prosecution of Newberry. Michigan senator Townsend got the history right when he summarized the case as "a political job from beginning to end. Its genesis was in politics, and its exodus will be politics very largely." Persuading Ford to run took the effort of the DNC and Wilson; keeping Newberry in the race took the acquiescence of the RNC. Democrats in the Senate managed a level of party discipline generally unfamiliar to them, while the Republicans could not close ranks. Politics also guided Wilson's most partisan aides who wanted prosecutable cases in the event that the Democrats lost their majority. The Justice Department obliged with political investigations.

The politics went beyond partisanship. The Newberry campaign highlighted the strains created by reform in the business of running campaigns—in politics as a career. It took real talent for Paul King to turn a little-known businessman who made no campaign appearances and took no positions into a senator against the famous and popular Ford. For those who had grounded their careers on the dangers of money in politics—senators such as Kenyon and Norris and perhaps La Follette and Heflin, whose politics still owed much to populism—King's magic trick just seemed evil. Electing Newberry proved what money could do in politics, and it should be stopped before it got worse. But everyone knew that as much as denouncing money in politics made for good speeches, campaigns in the real world cost money. Newberry's race raised the bar on what a first-class primary organization looked like and how much it cost. It was the future, and few senators, even those who voted for Newberry keeping his seat, could not find much to like about it.

But without Ford's and Newberry's persistence, there would have been no case to argue and no speeches to make. Their motives are hard to tease out. Ford's close associates could only guess at his plan, if there was one. Pipp thought Ford's eye was on the presidency, and even a little time in the Senate (Lucking imagined that he would carry out the day-to-day chores) would, with proper publicity, fix the damage of the *Tribune* trial. He also suspected that Ford felt cheated. The "downright cruel" assurances of victory by the yes-men around Ford left him believing that fraud was the only possible explanation. Liebold, whom Pipp counted among those who knew that their livelihood depended on anticipating what Ford wished to hear, offered a string of explanations. There was the corruption of the Newberry campaign. There was Newberry himself. Presumably echoing his boss, Liebold believed Newberry "was very instrumental in getting young Jewish boys appointed to the Navy to avoid the selected draft. That's about the only activity we found he was connected to down there. Mr. Newberry wasn't Jewish. They used their influence with him, and that's about as far as his activity in the Navy ever went." But Ford's vengeance, or attention span, also had limits. Pipp reported that Ford had promised to go to Grand Rapids during the trial to "lend at least the influence of his presence" in Newberry's support. Liebold talked him out of it. He also was not happy about spending money on distributing copies of a publication critical of Newberry in New Jersey and Missouri, but Lucking wheedled $2,000 from Ford, rather than the requested $10,000.[55]

Newberry's second thoughts were more serious than Ford's. He explained to a friend that he was ready to quit on three occasions: after he won the nomination and learned what it cost, in the spring of 1921, and finally after the 1922 election, when "regardless of the results" he would have earned "some measure of independence and as the Declaration says, to 'the pursuit of Happiness.'" He claimed TR persuaded him to stay in after the primary lest the seat go to the pacifist Ford. While there is no evidence of TR's intervention, Republicans certainly wanted Newberry in the race at that point. Evidence for Newberry weakening is in a speech that he drafted in longhand, probably in 1919. It was heavy on his horror at learning his campaign had spent so much and admitting that his brother, through Fred Smith, temporarily borrowed money from him, although without his knowledge or approval. Newberry's explanation to his friend had a self-serving spin, describing himself as duty-bound through the whole "hideous" affair and unwilling to sell out Fred Smith or Paul King. But there was something to it. Newberry was not an ambitious politician or really much of a politician at all. Resignation was a relief. "I am happier than I have been in five years," he told Townsend. "The Senate Chamber never had any attraction for me and I am thankful every hour that I do not have to stay and associate with many of the personalities and mentalities that infest that room."[56]

Through the tangle of motives, the fact remained that Paul King spent $195,000 building a frighteningly efficient organization and advertising campaign for Newberry. Had he spent the projected $50,000, well above the figures mentioned in the state and federal laws, it is unlikely that complaints would have gained much traction, as it fell within expectations for statewide races. Newberry's defense—that he merely rooted from the sidelines, without detailed knowledge much less direction of the game—had to have rankled senators. It had the air of class privilege if not deceit, as if Newberry could not be bothered with what the help was up to. Ford was indeed a dangerous man in politics. But senators knew there was only one Henry Ford, one man with his fame and peculiar tics. There were many deep-pocketed empty suits like Truman Newberry who could supply funds to organizers like Paul King. There were bound to be primary challengers who would spend heavily on advertising and workers. The Senate would decide, ad hoc, how much was too much. Newberry's fate was fair warning.

6

Scandal

Toward the end of 1926, a *Washington Post* political writer imagined a conversation in a Senate cloakroom, in which one senator asked another, "What have you ever done to be ashamed of?" "I am not going to tell you," was the reply, since a resolution and investigation would surely follow. It was an "age of inquisition," in which the Senate crowded the calendar with inquiries into businesses and trades, the executive branch, foreign governments, and each other. The *Post* writer counted nearly fifty resolutions and investigations in various stages of ripeness. "The majority of these investigations are political," he observed, pointing out that this "weapon is primarily one to be used by the minority [Democrats, insurgent Republicans, and Farmer-Laborers] in harassing the majority." Republican regulars usually acquiesced, since doing otherwise seemed an omission of guilt, but occasionally responded with a "feeble blow" of their own, such as Kentucky Republican Richard P. Ernst's resolution to examine the disfranchisement of African Americans in the South. The "thumbscrew and the rack" were at home in the Senate.[1]

The author should be forgiven for his cynicism. This was the period's journalistic style, and his eccentric boss had a stake in spinning the investigative fervor as nothing more than witch-hunting. A friend of the Hardings, the owner of the *Post* was implicated in one of the period's major scandals. But the writer did have the politics right. With little hope of setting a progressive agenda, Democrats and insurgent Republicans harassed and blocked regular Republicans throughout the 1920s. In doing so they helped make "scandal" one of our first impressions of the decade's politics. The Harding administration in particular usually settles at the bottom of presidential rankings, given chase only by the presidency of James Buchanan. While some of Harding's appointees certainly took advantage of their positions for personal gain, corruption variously defined over time is a more or less constant political fact, especially as what counts as corrupt has expanded. Scandal is something that happens to corruption that turns it into a major public event. Corruption became scandal because while the insurgent Republican-Democratic coalition in the Senate did not have the clout to make policy, it successfully targeted both the executive branch and the fitness of its own members.[2]

In the course of these investigations, Democrats and insurgent Republicans tried to return the nation's attention to the depredations of wealth and power in what seemed to them to be a conservative, cynical, materialistic age. But despite this group of senators' inquisitiveness about a range of issues, they revisited federal campaign finance law without much curiosity or crusading zeal. The revised FCPA was, like the original, unenforceable legally but useful politically. The spending of some primary candidates later in the 1920s far superseded the Newberry total. Those campaigns fired up indignation and investigations but not the will to craft effective legislation. The investigatory flurry, however, did raise questions about the fate of the Constitution's limits on power and civility in a democratic polity.

In the classic story, the 1920s was a comfortable Republican decade. Presidential elections leave the impression of Republican unity, with the party's organizing and fund-raising machine purring behind its electable if stolid candidates. Think of the Republicans as either business-oriented purveyors of corruption or as forgotten progressives building an "associationalist" state, and the political story remains the same. The Republicans recovered from the schisms of the 1910s and advanced a political agenda that swamped insurgent hostility toward big business. The Democrats appear to be a mess by contrast, divided by liquor and other cultural issues, their big-city base chafing against their rural southern constituency, barely able to nominate a presidential candidate at all. The party convention rule (sacrosanct to southerners) requiring their presidential candidate to gain the vote of two-thirds of the delegates meant that party factions bloodied each other before starting national campaigns. Demography may have been on their side—the Democratic base in the North was getting larger, unlike the Republicans'—but the party was not able to take advantage.[3]

The relative strengths and weaknesses of the parties reversed in the Senate. The Republicans maintained a numerical majority, but a governing one only when their candidates rode the coattails of presidential nominees. In off-year elections, Republican regulars lost control. Western and midwestern progressives retained the balance of power and bargained with both parties for whatever they could get. Meanwhile, the by-and-large progressive Democratic Senate delegation acted with relative unity, occasionally siding with regular Republicans but usually attracting the insurgents. In the Democratic-insurgent Republican coalition, a people-versus-the-interests brand of progressivism persisted in the 1920s Senate.[4]

Finding agreement within this coalition on positive policies, even legislation that would support the sagging agricultural sector, proved difficult. The prices of southern agricultural staples had not tanked as corn and wheat had, so southern Democrats felt little urgency about supporting price-fixing schemes. The Democratic and progressive Republican coalition found it easy to unite around attacks on regular Republican corruption. Teapot Dome was the signature scandal of the 1920s, which is odd in some respects. Unlike the straightforward theft in the Veterans Bureau, the Teapot Dome story was murky. It began in a long-running policy dispute that pitted western congressmen, the Interior Department, and the oil companies against conservationists, easterners, and the Navy Department over how the federal government would handle (presumably productive) oil land set aside for military use. Oil had won out over coal as the fuel of choice for the navy, and military demand competed with consumers who needed to fill their cars' gas tanks. Supply fluctuated as there were new fortunes to be made and older ones augmented in finding and exploiting new fields in the West and Southwest. In 1909, the Taft administration set aside three areas of the public domain, two (proven) in California and one, the unproven Teapot Dome in Wyoming, for the navy's exclusive use. While the courts sorted out the legalities of withdrawing land through executive action, Congress, the Interior Department, and the Navy Department dealt with the specific claims of harm lodged by oil companies.[5]

At a number of junctures, the interested parties nearly agreed to lease the reserves to oil companies. Even with war imminent, Montana Democrat

Thomas Walsh led an effort (defeated by southern Democrats) to pass legislation to create a leasing system. Oil companies claimed that shortages and high prices loomed once existing fields were exhausted, which made access to government reserves imperative. Josephus Daniels, Wilson's secretary of the navy, was not impressed. With the support of Gifford Pinchot and other conservationists who had been watching closely for any deviation from Taft's reserve policy, Daniels insisted that the best way to guarantee supply for military use was to keep the oil safely stored underground, where nature had put it. Wilson's interior secretary, Franklin Lane, a Californian sympathetic to western pro-development sentiment, could not be trusted to ignore the pleas of his region. So Daniels had decisions about drilling in the reserves moved from the Interior Department to the Navy Department. Enacted in the waning months of the Wilson administration, Daniels's move won the applause of conservationists but not of western representatives, who saw this as yet another barrier to the region's growth thrown up by easterners who had no understanding of the country west of St. Louis.[6]

Daniels's plan sounded simple, but it was not. A deep and tangled pile of private claims to the federal reserve remained, along with fears that commercial drilling at the edges of the navy's land would drain the fields. The new secretary, Edwin Denby (Newberry's *Yosemite* shipmate who had beaten Newberry in the 1904 congressional race), was interested in ships and organization, not oil and land policy. Uncertain about what to do with the ongoing mess, he was more than happy to hand the problems back to Interior. That department's new secretary, Albert Fall, was an enthusiast toward the development of western resources. A Democrat turned Republican and a poker buddy of President Harding, he had left his native Kentucky for the Southwest as a young man hoping to recover his health and make his fortune in mining. While the big strike eluded him, he practiced law and developed expertise in southwestern and Mexican mineral rights. His pugnacious approach to politics served him well in New Mexico, where nasty, personal fights over narrow interests were the norm. After serving two terms in the Senate, where his blunt partisanship and take-no-prisoners debating style created enemies, Fall had planned to return home to repair his family's strained finances. It took persuasion to get him to accept the Interior job, and it was a decision he would regret.[7]

Conservationists such as Pinchot distrusted the Interior Department as a matter of faith, and Fall even more because of his pro-development Senate record. Alarmed by rumors that Fall had struck a leasing deal on one of the California reserves with Pan-American Petroleum, Pinchot and his allies encouraged Robert La Follette to launch an investigation. While that got under way, Fall signed without public announcement a leasing deal for the Teapot Dome reserve, with Mammoth Oil agreeing to build a pipeline, to construct a storage facility at Pearl Harbor, and to transport the oil. Edward Doheny (Pan-American), Harry Sinclair (Mammoth), and Fall claimed that the leases were a good deal for the government, which got royalties and storage, while the companies, Sinclair's in particular, took the risks. A spike in the price of oil seemed to add urgency to tapping the reserves. La Follette and the conservationists did not see it that way, and talk, originating with Fall's Republican adversaries in New Mexico, that the cash-strapped Interior secretary's ranch was undergoing huge improvements added a whiff of bribery to their suspicions.[8]

The Senate opened hearings in 1923, chaired by Senator Walsh. Neither the Senate nor the public found the leasing contracts all that exciting at first. The Senate had been through the complexities of federal land policy and oil many times, and Fall's contracts were legal, even if his department had not provided for competitive bidding. But Fall's newfound good fortune provided the hook for public attention. That some senators had scores to settle with their less-than-beloved former colleague intensified interest, as Walsh assembled evidence that strongly hinted that Fall (who, frozen out of the Harding inner circle and the focus of attack, resigned as Walsh's hearings began) received a sizable "loan" from Doheny. When the hearings ended in May 1924, Walsh called for the leases to be broken (the oil companies would eat the costs of the work completed) and for the president to appoint a special prosecutor to handle bribery charges, since Attorney General Harry Daugherty could not be trusted.

By that time, Harding had died, and Calvin Coolidge, intimating that the scandal touched both parties, moved to appoint two special prosecutors, one from each party. After one false start and some (mostly Democratic) grumbling, Congress approved Harding's appointees: Atlee Pomerene, the former Ohio senator, and Owen Roberts, a Pennsylvania Republican and future Supreme Court justice. The trials that followed their investigations, including criminal cases against Fall and Doheny, dragged on through the decade. The prosecutors won the conviction of Fall, the alleged bribed party, but not of Doheny, the apparent briber. The grievously ill Fall served time in a Texas prison.

Teapot Dome was a big story in the 1920s, but despite the hopes of Democrats and insurgent Republicans, it was inert politically. The taint of oil money was bipartisan. Doheny was a Democrat, and he had on his payroll Wilson administration cabinet members, including William McAdoo, Woodrow Wilson's son-in-law and former treasury secretary. McAdoo's sizable retainer for phantom legal work helped knock him out of running for the Democratic presidential nomination in 1924, even as he seemed to be the only candidate capable of resuscitating Wilson's coalition. By appointing the special prosecutors and moving Denby and Daugherty out of the cabinet, Coolidge effectively distanced himself from the corruption associated with the Harding gang. What began as a complicated story about oil policy had a headline-grabbing turn as a bribery morality tale, but ended as a complicated story about the oil industry and influence that implicated both parties.[9]

But Teapot Dome was a spur to a new FCPA. The investigations turned up interesting information about the size of the RNC's debt following the 1920 campaign and how the party covered it. Perhaps in an effort to combat the association between regular Republicans and "Newberryism," party chairman Will Hays had attempted to raise $3 million for the campaign through contributions of $1,000 and less. The RNC reached the goal, but campaign costs ran a good deal higher than the initial budget, leaving a $1.5 million debt when loans to the campaign were factored in. As Hays was preparing to leave the RNC for Hollywood, the debt disappeared. In the spring of 1924, Hays and Fred Upham, the RNC treasurer, testified as part of Walsh's Teapot Dome investigation that Harry Sinclair, who had made one of the $1,000 contributions during the campaign, also had retired a loan of $75,000 after the campaign. Both men asserted that Sinclair's contribution was not intended to cement friendships amid the ongoing Teapot Dome investigation. Upham claimed that the only "oil interest" contribution he had heard about was the $100,000 to $150,000 Doheny had given to the DNC against its debts.[10]

It later emerged that the $75,000 Hays mentioned did not capture Sinclair's full generosity. The total, including loans converted to gifts obscured through a complicated string of transactions, came to $260,000. These contributions pointed to one of the weaknesses of the existing FCPA: major contributions to the party committees arrived at times other than campaign season. This revelation triggered an overdue reevaluation of the FCPA. Here was a chance not only to publicize donations that retired party debt (parties typically ended elections in the red) but also to fix the problems with the legislation that both the majority and minority opinions in *Newberry* had highlighted and to address concerns about unreported interest group (especially the Anti-Saloon League) campaign spending.[11]

Congress let the opportunity pass. There was talk of a constitutional amendment that would undo the *Newberry* decision. A legal opinion provided by the Republican Party pointed out the obvious: four, not five, justices had signed on to the argument that primary elections were beyond the regulatory reach of Congress. A different case might well find the regulation of primaries constitutional. There were fulminations about the immorality of money in politics, with Doheny's contributions to both parties standing as the example of how a wealthy individual played both sides in the effort to buy influence. Senator Borah proposed putting a stop to the long-established campaign practice of raising money in large, wealthy states and spending it elsewhere. In order to combat the "campaign contribution evil" that was "gnawing at the very vitals of the Republic," Senator Kenneth McKeller, a Democrat from Tennessee, proposed contribution limits of $500, a ban on giving on the part of civil servants and those applying for such positions, and a cap of some sort on loans to party committees.[12]

None of this happened, or even came to a vote. A rider on the Postal Salary and Rate Act, the revised statute provided a formula that allowed spending up to $25,000 (on the specious theory that by doubling the electorate, women's suffrage had doubled costs) in the absence of state law to the contrary. The Teapot Dome scandal motivated a provision requiring more frequent reports. And a "political committee" for the purposes of campaign finance regulation included organizations such as the Anti-Saloon League, which were now obliged to report their receipts and spending. In deference to the *Newberry* decision and southern Democrats, the revised FCPA dropped reference to primaries. The new law retained the previous version's core approach to campaign finance, along with its artfully problematic language. It failed to address whether spending limits applied to "independent" committees. The House committee hearings were vague on whether its members thought that independent committees, the completely legal mechanism the Newberry campaign had used to raise money, were a problem, and if so, if it could be corrected by new legislation. (Because such committees usually operated only in primary elections, Congress would not have the ability to regulate them.) Nor did Congress define what "cause to have spent" meant. The law's reporting requirements remained just short of an honor system: candidates, committees, and groups would turn in reports (following their own muse on accounting practices) to the clerk of the House, who would file them away. What was essentially a publicity system had no mechanism for publicizing spending. The measure, vetoed by Coolidge once because he judged the increase in postal salaries to be wasteful, passed again by a vote of 69 to 12, with the dissenting votes coming from progressives upset about a one-cent increase in first-class postage. Coolidge signed the bill.[13]

If Congress had intended to limit spending on campaigns, it would need to have taken a much bolder approach, one that would have disturbed southern Democrats and challenged the *Newberry* restriction of the regulation of primaries. By keeping the framework that, at most, publicized contributions to congressional and national organizations, the new FCPA could not curb spending any more than the previous version had. No one could honestly believe that it might. Senate and House candidates determined that even the reporting requirements need not be taken seriously, and they rarely reported much spending, if any, since the law covered only general elections, which were usually run by the parties. Meanwhile, the cost of campaigns had not declined. Candidates' organizations needed money to buy advertising, mailings, headquarters, and, increasingly, radio time. Some wealthy individuals such as Doheny had good reason to contribute, since his business depended on the decisions of the federal government. And the federal government's expanded responsibilities meant that the oil business was not alone in its interest in politics. A variety of groups, those for and against prohibition most prominently, worked for and against candidates. The conditions that made for more expensive campaigns had become more entrenched, while the extent of groups seeking specific policies had grown. But the basics of the FCPA remained. Given the Supreme Court's warnings about the earlier statute, it is hard to escape the conclusion that Congress assumed no one would ever face criminal penalties for violating the FCPA and that enforcement would be arbitrary, arising in Congress rather than the courts.[14]

The political incentives that encouraged senators to investigate some campaigns remained alongside the legally ineffective FCPA. Regular Republicans rarely enjoyed a working Senate majority in the 1920s. They gained enough seats in presidential election years and lost enough in off years to make questioning the fitness of potential new members worthwhile politically. But there was more than partisan and factional politics. Just as the League of Nations vote created some of the furor over Newberry's seat, issues contributed to senators' calculations about new members. While no one believed that a big spender could be prosecuted for violations of the FCPA, the law was still useful in challenging senators' rights to their seats. In so doing, senators might shape the outcome of future votes or the balance of power in the Senate, and at the very least embarrass those deemed to have spent too much.

Most cases brought together the long-standing coalition between Democrats and insurgent Republicans. But Senate regulars had an unusual opportunity to get some payback in 1924. When the party nominated Calvin Coolidge, some progressives had determined that they had suffered enough. While they had grudgingly gone along with Harding's nomination in 1920, the corruption scandals of his administration, inattention to the persistent agricultural depression, and general drift in a business-friendly direction were enough to persuade them to nominate insurgent lion Robert La Follette for the presidency as a Progressive. Coolidge won handily, with only La Follette's home state, Wisconsin, breaking from the ranks of the normally Republican states. Coolidge carried with him a large enough Senate majority that the regulars would not have to worry about naming committee chairs. They had the votes to do some mischief themselves.

An unusual coalition of regulars and Democrats eyed incumbent Smith Brookhart's narrow 1924 victory over Democrat Daniel T. Steck in Iowa. Here was an opportunity for the regulars to punish a pseudo-Republican and for the Democrats to pick up a seat. Brookhart had joined the Senate in 1922, filling out the remainder of the term of William S. Kenyon, who had accepted an appeals court appointment. But the nominal Republican had signed on with La Follette as the 1924 general election neared. He barely squeaked to victory, while Coolidge handily carried the state. The spread owed to regular Republicans crossing over in the general election to vote for Steck. That race, not the forgone conclusion of the presidential election in Republican Iowa, incited "the savage interest" of party factions. Regulars went so far as to show voters how to cast their ballots for Steck. Newspapers printed what turned out to be a not-so-handy guide with an arrow pointing at Steck's name. Some literal-minded voters obediently drew arrows on their ballots.[15]

Tabulators in Iowa discarded those irregular ballots, giving the Senate a *Bush v. Gore* type of quandary. Should the Senate recount follow the intentions of voters (wiping out Brookhart's 776-vote lead) or the letter of Iowa's election laws (disqualifying the ballots using arrows to point to Steck's name)? While seating Steck would not alter the Senate partisan and factional balance, the vote still had political implications. Southern Democrats had to decide whether they preferred to seat a Democrat or to override (a somewhat unclear) state law, which might be a precedent for future federal meddling in state elections. Regular Republicans had the chance to punish the maverick Brookhart, who had loudly proclaimed his differences with the White House. But there were rumors of a deal, in which Brookhart would trade a promise of regularity for his seat. This would help Iowa's senior senator, Albert Cummins, an insurgent turned regular, since he would otherwise have to face Brookhart in 1926. But most regular Republicans together with most Democrats (a few southerners bailed) combined to create a majority for seating Steck instead of Brookhart.[16]

Eliminating Brookhart fit with the regulars' effort to regain control of their delegation—and perhaps the party. The carrots in the form of committee chairmanships they offered in 1919 failed to induce regularity among the progressives, who had combined with Democrats in naming some committee chairs in 1923. A few threw their support to La Follette in the presidential election of 1924. So in 1925, the regulars, having gained enough seats in 1924, picked up the stick. They read La Follette and three others who had backed him out of the party for the purpose of committee assignments. This time most Democrats cooperated with the regulars. "All Republicans look alike to us," said Virginia Democrat Carter Glass. Regulars had the votes on the Privileges and Elections Committee to unanimously reject the challenge of Magnus Johnson, a Farmer-Laborer, to the seating of Republican Thomas

D. Schall. Johnson claimed that Schall had violated the FCPA, had received $75,000 from bootleggers, and had lied about Johnson in his campaign (a misdemeanor in Minnesota, "it may startle Illinoisans to learn," reported the *Chicago Tribune*). After the committee rejected Johnson's contest, Schall blasted Johnson's attorney, hired "because of his cunning, rat-like tendencies, and his extensive association with crooks and perjurers," and the committee for airing "nefarious manufactured, hearsay slander." A regular such as Schall would not have such an easy ride in the next Congress.[17]

The 1926 midterm election again brought Republican losses, leaving them with forty-eight to the Democrats' forty-seven and one for the Farmer-Labor Party. Observers classed six Republicans as insurgents, joined by at least five on many issues. Regulars persuaded Lynn Frazier of North Dakota and Henrik Shipstead of Minnesota to join them for the purpose of organizing the Senate, but their reward of committee slots guaranteed neither their loyalty nor that of other insurgents. A series of seating challenges, the most important with campaign finance at their core, emerged as a result of the election returns.[18]

At first it appeared that the seating of North Dakota's Gerald P. Nye would be settled with the deal that confirmed a Republican majority. But Nye's appointment raised problems, both procedural and political. The North Dakota governor had appointed the thirty-three-year-old maverick newspaper editor (he had supported La Follette in 1924 and had run for Congress on the Farmer-Labor ticket) to fill the term of the late Edwin Ladd, an insurgent. But the state constitution indicated only that the governor had such power in the case of state officials. Should senators count as state officers? Senator Moses, the New Hampshire regular, offered his legal opinion to the governor of North Dakota before Nye's appointment, warning that the state legislature had not given the governor the power to fill the vacancy. Either North Dakota would have to run a special election, Moses argued, or, more likely, it would be down one senator for a few months, since seating Nye would mean breaking a long-standing practice.[19]

The insurgents howled. "How can you kick Nye out after you have welcomed Newberry with arms upraised to heaven, thanking God," despite "Newberry dripping with moral turpitude and burdened with rascality?" asked a West Virginia Republican. But concerns about rattling farm-state voters and, more important, Nye's announcement that he would vote against a pending resolution that would allow the United States to join the World Court swayed the votes of isolationist senators. Nye's vote might prove to be important. In "the first big political surprise of the present session of Congress," Nye took his seat on a vote of 41 to 39, with the support of western and farm-state Republicans and isolationist Democrats.[20]

This case, like other seating challenges urged on by regular Republicans, revolved around the technical details of elections and appointments. Intimations of scandal and immorality linked to campaign spending belonged to the insurgent Republicans and Democrats. The first up, the victory of Arthur R. Gould in a Maine special election, hinted at what was in store after the 1926 elections. Gould's opponent, joined by a leader of the state Ku Klux Klan, alleged excessive spending and moral unfitness, since a Canadian judge apparently had suggested more than a decade earlier that Gould had committed bribery in a railroad deal. Thomas Walsh, the Montana Democrat, stunned the gallery when he interrupted the swearing-in ceremony with a resolution demanding an investigation of the charges, which had been aired in the campaign. He acted on the belief that a simple majority was enough to reject the credentials of a senator-elect, while it would take two-thirds to remove a sitting senator. The motion was ruled out of order, but the case moved to Privileges and Elections. There it became tangled in the question of legal jurisdiction. What did it mean for the Senate to have the power to pass on the qualifications of its members? For David Reed, a Pennsylvania Republican, the authority stopped at assuring the minimum standards (age, citizenship, residence, and treason); it did not permit the Senate "to go back into the indefinite past of the individual who comes here as the solemn choice of his state." Gould, unlike Newberry, appeared before the committee to deny the charges and spar with Walsh, who failed to produce documents that would corroborate the story of a bribe. In March 1927, the committee deemed Gould of "good character" in a report recommending his seating; the full Senate adopted the recommendation without debate.[21]

Everyone knew the arguments about Gould and the Senate's jurisdiction were really warm-ups for the main event, the cases of William S. Vare of Pennsylvania and Frank L. Smith of Illinois. Both won Republican nominations in tough and spectacularly costly primary elections before defeating their Democratic rivals in normally Republican states. Progressive Republicans and Democrats had pushed through a resolution calling for the investigation of spending in all senatorial primaries, investigations to be carried out by a special committee consisting of two regular Republicans, two Democrats, and one insurgent Republican. With the resolution in hand, the Senate could bypass the procedural tangles that had knotted up the Gould investigation and the potential need for a two-thirds vote to undo the results of these elections.

Each case had peculiar wrinkles. In Pennsylvania, interest group politics and discontent with prohibition made statewide races, never cheap, more expensive than usual. By the mid-1920s, middle-class opinion on prohibition had begun to sour, as enforcement seemed to create criminals within their own ranks while failing to control violent gangs. Incumbent George Wharton Pepper, occupying the slightly moist position, lost to Vare, the wet candidate who claimed that prohibition had caused a spike in the crime rate, with the dry Gifford Pinchot, the conservationist and TR-connected reformer and governor, coming in third. The Anti-Saloon League divided its assistance between the Pinchot and Pepper campaigns. No one worked for free in the Commonwealth. The customary election day "watchers"—thousands of them—needed their cut, and in what appeared to be a kickback, members of the Woman's Christian Temperance Union received $200 per appearance for Pinchot. Add in advertising, and the costs were enormous. Pinchot spent as much as Newberry had. The cost of the Vare and Pepper campaigns was hard to calculate. Alongside organizations that worked for them, dueling gubernatorial committees lent support to Senate candidates. The total bill for the Vare team ran to $800,000 and for Pepper $1.8 million, excluding late bills. Both the activities of the Anti-Saloon League and the candidates' spending alarmed senators.[22]

Prohibition was an issue in Illinois, but there the direct primary combined with Chicago's intricate politics drove the costs of doing business. As in Lorimer's day, a Republican statewide candidate in the Land of Lincoln had to assemble a Chicago organization out of the shifting alliances among various factions, whose leaders demanded support for local elections, the only ones that really mattered to them. Frank Smith, an amiable fellow whose ambition for high office was as persistent as his talent for it was obscure, had served a term in Congress and had for years pined for either the Senate or the governorship. Chair of the Illinois Public Utilities Commission in 1926, he was a successful downstate businessman. Unlike his primary opponent, incumbent William B. McKinley, a retired utility magnate gradually cashing out his holdings, he lacked a great fortune and reputation for sharing it among worthy politicians. But he did hold a job with the potential to attract contributions. Utility magnate Samuel Insull, of Commonwealth Edison, saw in Smith the makings of a good enough senator, since anyone, as far as he was concerned, deserved the honor more than McKinley. Insull regularly contributed to all of Chicago's Republican factions as the cost of doing business in the city, but in this case he rashly went beyond his normal generosity. McKinley lost the primary, as the Chicago factions he thought were friendly had turned abruptly cold. As near as can be determined, McKinley spent $514,143, most of it his own, to Smith's $458,782, most of it Insull's, through personal contributions to the Smith organization and to an anti–World Court group formed for the campaign. Smith carried the general election over his Democratic opponent, who had purchased his own good-government organization for the occasion. A reform group chimed in with anti-Smith and anti-Insull publicity bought by a New York broker interested in handling Chicago street railway securities.[23]

McKinley died before his term was up. Smith was appointed to fill out the remainder, which allowed the Senate to reject his credentials twice. The Senate declined to seat Vare as well until hearings could determine both men's fitness for office. Reed of Missouri, the former prosecutor whose stock as a potential presidential candidate rose with press coverage of the campaign finance investigations, stumbled with his committee through the double-dealing and backstabbing of Chicago's ward politics and the local customs of the Pennsylvania machines. The most damning part of Smith's case was the impression of corruption once the investigation had established Insull's contribution. While Insull's operations had not received special treatment from state regulators, the suspicious appearance mattered. For Vare, it was the enormity of the cost of running a statewide election in Pennsylvania, where even the sainted Pinchot ran up a bill that in 1918 seemed shockingly large. Defenders of the two senators-elect could only argue that their state laws did not prohibit such spending (which local conditions demanded) and that the federal law did not apply to primaries. Reaching beyond its constitutional powers, the Senate was naming itself the judge of elections, arbitrarily overruling the preferences of voters. Progressive Republicans and Democrats described Vare and Smith as both embarrassments to the Senate and threats to democracy. For Gerald P. Nye seating them would mean that "every public office in the United States will be placed on the auction block." In deciding the fate of the two members-elect, the Senate "will determine the prospect of government being retained and restored in the interests of the people."[24]

The Senate rescued the people's interests by refusing to seat both men in 1928. The progressive Republican-Democratic coalition was poised to strike another blow for virtue in 1930, in the case of Republican Ruth Hanna McCormick's expensive Illinois primary. Gerald Nye headed a committee to investigate spending in Illinois and Pennsylvania primaries, including that of McCormick, the daughter of Marcus Hanna, William McKinley's campaign manager and Ohio senator and widow of the *Chicago Tribune*'s Medill McCormick. When called to testify after the primary, she claimed to have spent $252,572, most of it downstate, in the effort to combat Senator Charles Deneen's statewide machine. Nye believed that her campaign must have spent much more. The investigation took an odd turn when McCormick implied that Nye's investigators broke in and rifled through her office, wiretapping it to boot. But her loss in a Democratic landslide denied the Senate another crack at understanding Illinois politics. There seemed to be no end in sight to the factional warfare, but McCormick's was the last campaign finance investigation. Challenges disappeared with Republicans, as Democrats built a bulletproof majority in the 1930s. Seat contests returned in the 1940s, when the balance between the parties tightened. Although campaign spending by that time made the $25,000 limit as quaint as a Model T, violations of the FCPA never again figured in serious challenges.[25]

It is tempting to conclude that the defenders of Newberry and of the later targets of Senate FCPA investigations were right in arguing that the bleating about campaign spending was vindictive politics, pure and simple. Albert Jay Nock's magazine *The Freeman*, a heterodox publication for intellectuals who had lost faith in whichever political church they had once attended, took the point to its most cynical conclusion. Commenting on the sorry spectacle of the Senate Privileges and Elections Committee vote on the Newberry case in 1921, Nock thought the public had learned that "money talks." What it said spoke in a heavily partisan accent, since "if he had been a Democrat, a Democratic majority would have been found for him and a Republican minority against him." The lesson was "inescapable" if banal to those even moderately attentive to party politics. The Senate vote reminded those who had somehow forgotten that "embracery, bribery, and corruption take on a halo of gravity according to the party affiliations of the person accused and not according to the crime itself" and of "the kind of interests that politics serves, and the expectations that one may safely put upon politics and political action." Party politics, especially when it involved statements of principle, fell beneath the notice of serious people.[26]

Political scientist Jeffrey A. Jenkins offers a more sophisticated analysis of the politics of seat contests. Analyzing election contests in both the House and the Senate from 1787 to 2002, he found that partisanship goes a long way in explaining congressional action: when a seat or two could make a big difference, contests went forward. He also finds evidence of a party-building strategy, especially in the House and to a lesser extent in the Senate. During Reconstruction, Republican House members challenged the elections of some southern Democrats in order to highlight fraud and to strengthen the GOP in the former Confederacy. Senators were not quite as systematic as those Republican congressmen, but they seized opportunities to build majorities when they had the chance. Jenkins might have added factional interests to his analysis. In the 1910s and 1920s, election contests were a specialty of insurgent Republicans, who joined with Democrats. Although without national leadership after TR's (and Robert La Follette Sr.'s) death, unable to nominate one of their number for the presidency, and uncertain of the viability of a third party, they had not given up their claim on the Republican Party. They sought to redirect their party, even if they had to hook up with Democrats to do it.[27]

There was, of course, plenty of politics in the Newberry case and those that followed. There was politics, too, in the FCPA itself. A project of Democrats and insurgent Republicans, the first FCPA expressed their disapproval of large campaign budgets, which they saw as corrupting democratic institutions and, we can assume, damaging to the prospects of that party and faction. By insisting that any meaningful law would have to include primary elections, regular Republicans set off a bidding war that strengthened the law in some respects, or at least made it appear so. No partisan auction took place in the 1920s revision. The postal bill to which the new FCPA was attached roused much more insurgent energy and oratory. Congress was willing to let the campaign finance system stand with few revisions. Parties would continue to raise and spend funds for general elections, while Congress would investigate candidates' primary election spending when it suited.

The FCPA provided symbolic rather than real limits on campaign spending, but the rising cost of campaigns remained an available target for investigations in the 1910s and 1920s because of what Newberry called the "perfectly honest expenditures made necessary by the primary system." Primary elections had not destroyed political organizations, but they did make candidates spend more for support, and it took some years for many state party organizations to regain control over nominations. And primary elections increased the number of competitive races, at least for a time. After a further spike in primary contests in the 1930s, however, House members, and to a lesser extent senators, settled into safe seats. Newberry and the others rode into a freak political storm between the calm of the late nineteenth-century bosses and of the southern-accented club that gained control in the 1930s.[28]

Special circumstances were not necessary to increase the amount of money spent on politics. All Senate candidates facing primary elections were forced to raise and spend money on their elections. All but the safest incumbent with an existing statewide network of supporters had to buy advertising, build an organization, and communicate with voters. Some had to spend quite a lot. Anyone running a statewide election in California, a large state with weak party organizations, could count on the necessity of a substantial budget. Candidates running against incumbents (who could use franking privileges for free mailings to constituents) or against an opponent with a state organization had to compensate for such disadvantages with cash. Both Isaac Stephenson in Wisconsin, running against the candidate who enjoyed the support of the La Follette organization, and Ruth Hanna McCormick, who aimed to defeat an incumbent who also had a long-standing statewide machine, learned how much a Senate election could cost. In New York, Illinois, and Pennsylvania, populous states with old-fashioned ward politics and expensive media markets, all statewide races were costly. Throw in a competitive primary, as Vare, Pepper, Pinchot, Smith, and McKinley discovered, and the expenditures skyrocketed. The case of Newberry, running against the most famous man in the state who also had an extensive dealer network that might be put to political work, was like no other. None of the investigations into these primaries uncovered much traditional corruption. They showed instead the price of running for office without the help of a party or personal organization.

Congress had no real answer for what to do about such rather common situations. Arkansas' Thaddeus Caraway suggested leaving blank the sum mentioned in Senator Frank Willis's resolution condemning the Newberry spending, with the amount filled in by regular Republicans who seemed to think no ceiling was high enough. Each presidential election also inevitably stirred outrage about costs and the intimation that the office was available to the highest bidder. Yet outspending opponents did not necessarily bring success, as Leonard Wood learned in the 1920 primary against Warren Harding. There was also no reason to believe that presidential campaigns had become more corrupt than they had been in the nineteenth century. Just the opposite: as both the Democratic and Republican parties announced that they hoped to spend some $4 million in 1928, a *New York Times* article described the costly, if expensive, accoutrements of modern campaigns. The lithographs, pamphlets, postcards, billboards, advertisements, and the staff to develop and distribute the materials did not come cheap. Even with $4 million to spend, managers complained about pamphlets they could not tailor for an overlooked group in the electorate, not about their inability to deliver boodle and bribes. "It's an expensive thing, this effort to elect a president," given "our typically American methods of inducing voters."[29]

Were campaigns inordinately expensive? It was certainly possible to make the case that they were not. The rising cost of living in the 1910s and 1920s, combined with the anything-but-corrupt educational approach to campaigning that emerged in the late nineteenth-century and twentieth-century advertising, raised the price of running for office. The case could be made that campaigns actually cost less than they should. The attempt to convince voters through "informative literature, powerful and persuasive argument, [and] illuminative human-interest personality stories" was necessary, and almost noble, in one account of spending on the 1920 presidential campaign. Anticipating some recent scholarship on campaign finance, the article noted how small the sums actually were given the stakes and the context. "Certainly a people who spend a billion dollars a year on candy, fifty millions for chewing gum, nigh a billion to see the 'movies,' and almost a billion and a half for smokes, and some nineteen more billions annually for various other *luxuries*" should not begrudge campaign managers a few million to elect a president.[30]

Indignation, or at the very least uneasiness, greeted the sums spent on campaigns. That disapproval might have been the public's, although how wide and deep that might have been is difficult to gauge before pollsters asked random samples of the adult population to rank their policy concerns. Anyone in Congress who represented a part of the country where primary elections mattered had reason to be worried, even if rising costs were not driven by classic corrupt methods. Candidates in competitive primaries had to raise money, the most unpleasant and potentially treacherous aspect of making a campaign. Those without long-standing political careers had to do this on their own, engaging the managers and staff who could organize a modern campaign. Although opening the way to a candidate like Newberry, whose stiff-backed propriety and lack of panache made him a better candidate for the nineteenth-century caucus system than for popular elections, professional managers, advertising, and the funds to purchase them were facts that primary elections and an independent press had created. It is easy to see why politicians would not like the new political world, even if they had made it.

There was more to the arguments about campaign expenses than politics. There was a moral point. At least some of the Democrats and insurgent Republicans who led the attack on big spending campaigns believed, we can grant, that large campaign budgets imperiled democratic institutions, just as some House Republicans in the Reconstruction period cared about violence and the rights of African American voters as well as party building. We can suppose that Nye and some of the other progressives (Democratic and Republican) believed that money subverted the people's will. They consistently proposed limits on spending or contributions. Suspicion of big money in politics fit their partisan and factional interests, but also their wider crusade against the power of the "special interests" in American politics.

Costly campaigns, in this view, were a menace even if the money bought legal goods such as commercial advertising. After all, product advertising had an unsavory reputation as deceptive, not informative, an impression that

SCANDAL [149]

the burgeoning advertising profession in the 1920s tried to shake off. Political advertising fell under the same suspicions. Some states, such as Michigan, expressed it by regulating the size of pictures (apparently more dangerous than words) used in political ads and requiring that ads carry labels, lest they be confused with news. As the investigation of Vare ground slowly toward a vote, Virginia Democrat Carter Glass expressed it with incredulity. "Do you think anybody in Pennsylvania knows more of William S. Vare through the advertising of the campaign?" he asked, adding a theatrical choke when a regular Republican said that voters did. For campaign finance hard-liners, an operation like Newberry's that rested on commercial advertising was worse than an old-fashioned purchase of state legislators or voters: by forcing citizens to encounter so much advertising, Newberry had "debauched" a whole state, not just a few men.[31]

Advertising, both commercial and political, may not have had a reputation for honesty, but it enabled a journalism free from party ties. Without commercial advertising the independent press that publicized progressive causes would have been thin and weak, dependent on the whims of a few wealthy individuals or a base of subscriptions deep enough to finance publication. Without product advertising, Michigan progressive Chase Osborn would have been forced to run his newspapers as a hobby. Small-town newspapers like Gerald Nye's *Fryburg Pioneer* would have been difficult to sustain without a subsidy. In the 1910s and 1920s, the growth of advertising for national brands made for good times even for rural weeklies and small city dailies. But the independence from party ties that advertising allowed opened the way for crusading journalism—journalism especially attentive to scandal, likely to offer more than one side of a story, and, by the 1920s with an air of hard-bitten skepticism. Expensive campaigns were part of the price to be paid for campaigns unhooked from parties, centered on candidates, and chronicled by an independent press.[32]

There were other costs, too. Those stuck with defending candidates charged with spending excessive amounts outlined some of the perils of the Senate prosecuting candidates who had conducted their business within the law. Their claims about an exercise of power that went beyond the Constitution's limits and civility in democracy identified some of the problems with the Senate's approach to campaign finance. Just as the concerns of critics of money in politics remain with us, the counterattack had effects beyond the specifics of Newberry's or Vare's or Smith's case.

Some who defended the election winners who spent too much asked whether there were any limits to the power the Senate gave to itself in the interest of righteousness. When Justice McReynolds suggested that Congress had the power to judge the fitness of its members in the *Newberry* decision, he referenced article 1, section 5. But what did it mean for each house to be "the judge of the elections, returns and qualifications of its own members"? The literal qualifications for the Senate listed age, citizenship, and state residence. During the debate over Arthur Gould's fitness for office, the horrified *Portland Express* quoted Democrat Thomas Walsh as claiming that if citizens of Montana found Gould lacking, that was reason enough to vote to deny Gould his seat. Defenders of Vare argued that the Pennsylvania politician had broken no laws—the FCPA did not apply to primaries, and the Commonwealth permitted such spending. Vare was more than thirty years old, a U.S. citizen, and resident of Pennsylvania. He won the primary and the general election; there was no dispute about ballots, and a recount confirmed his nomination. Could the Senate simply make up qualifications? If so, what were they? Congress did not clarify the point, and neither Vare nor Smith tested the case in court. Congress, it seems, preferred ambiguity, and the grounds for excluding someone elected to a seat was left to representatives' imaginations until 1969.[33]

Attorney James M. Beck, solicitor general under Harding and Coolidge, wrote a sustained treatment of how the Senate had overstepped its power. *The Vanishing Rights of the States* argued that the Senate was rewriting the Constitution in refusing to seat Vare and Smith. The Supreme Court took Beck's position when a case finally came to it. Meanwhile, for Beck and others the Senate's behavior was part of a larger, disturbing pattern in the extension of state power in the name of progressive ideas. They made their way to a new ideological conservatism—one based on fixed principles rather than respect for tradition or for benefits of capitalism. For Henry Joy, Newberry's brother-in-law who, unlike Newberry, maintained a long and lively interest in public issues, the turning point was the enforcement of prohibition. As federal agents stepped up their efforts in the late 1920s, a resident of Grosse Pointe could not help but be alarmed at the ability of the government to search individuals' property on the basis of suspicion and to wreak havoc in the otherwise quiet, tony suburb. He joined the Association Against the Prohibition Amendment. A Republican and former dry who could use his position at Packard to advance his views, Joy was a valuable member of the repeal organization. And like many of them, he slid easily from repeal to the American Liberty League's opposition to the New Deal, since both groups celebrated limited government.[34]

Ideological conservatism in the 1920s and 1930s tried to reach back to the founding in order to ground legalistic arguments into a wider American narrative. Beginning in the 1880s and growing worse in the Progressive Era, fundamental elements of the framers' wise design, especially the separation of powers and limits on the power of the executive branch, had worn away. "Each decade sees some principle of the Constitution either weakened or nullified," Beck wrote. His devotion to the Constitution was part of a wider celebration of the document and its framers in the 1920s. In Beck's hands it perhaps had some attractiveness: he was able to ride his new fame (and Republican machine support) to four terms in the House. It otherwise had a fairly narrow appeal. When another new conservative movement developed in the 1950s, it would ignore these American predecessors. But their attention to the rule of law, reverence for the Constitution and the founders, and hostility toward progressivism remain significant in American conservatism.[35]

Civility and respect for politics seemed to get lost in the 1910s and 1920s climate of investigation. For Charles Townsend, the Michigan senator who thought that Newberry's campaign had wasted a good deal of money but who was one of his chief defenders, the Senate's investigative fury in no way encouraged democracy. Instead, it destroyed faith in democratic institutions. "The country is in not so much danger from the use of extravagant sums in elections as it is from the betrayal of the confidence placed by the people in the Members of the House and Senate," he argued. "The people can and will change their representatives when they please and for what they please; but the influence of the promoter of class prejudice, of the time server who poisons the public mind with unjust reflections upon men in public life, inflicts a permanent injury upon society." Senators were destroying public trust in government and trust in each other. "I would rather be subjected to the influences of friendship," he said, against the claims that Newberry's and Harding's likability might override anger at the money spent on Newberry's campaign, "than to the influences of partisan hatred and contemptible self-serving politics."[36]

No one in this round of debate on campaign finance, or in later ones, found a way to bring together discordant goals of campaign finance reform. If the system was to be fair, to give candidates without wealth but with good ideas a chance, did that mean allowing them to find a way to spend what was necessary to promote their views or to limit spending? How could a challenger take on a powerful incumbent or a machine without money? If the system was to be beyond the suspicion of corruption, did that mean that the Senate should set the rules as it went along? Or that candidates should raise money in small amounts? Could that be done without the sort of organization that parties—or fame—provided? Campaign finance was a complicated issue, at once practical and moral. The realities of running campaigns involved not so much money per se but the labor and means to communicate with voters that money must buy. The moral implications included fears of corruption, of politicians doing the bidding of their wealthy supporters. But they also involved civility and trust. Politics understood as purity and politics treated, as Nock had done, as synonymous with mindless, narrow self-interest left little to respect in political institutions or their products. Just politics in both senses of the phrase discouraged the assumption of good faith that made democracy possible.

NOTES

ABBREVIATIONS
Benson Ford (Benson Ford Research Center)
Bentley (Bentley Historical Library, University of Michigan)
CR (*Congressional Record*)
CT (*Chicago Daily Tribune*)
DFP (*Detroit Free Press*)
DPL (Burton Historical Collection, Detroit Public Library)
LOC (Library of Congress)
NARA (National Archives and Records Administration)
NYT (*New York Times*)
THN (Truman Handy Newberry)
WP (*Washington Post*)

CHAPTER 1: JUST POLITICS

1. A wonderfully told account of one of Ford's later ventures is Greg Grandin, *Fordlandia: The Rise and Fall of Henry Ford's Forgotten Jungle City* (New York: Henry Holt, 2009). Ford's anti-Semitism is covered with varying persuasiveness by Ford biographers. An insightful overview is Leo P. Ribuffo, "Henry Ford and *The International Jew*," *Jewish American History* 69 (June 1980): 437–477.
2. I will use "insurgent" and "progressive" interchangeably here to describe a faction of the Republican Party, consisting mostly of western and midwestern senators who often broke with the regulars on such issues as the tariff and regulatory policy. "Progressive" is capitalized when referring to a period of time or a political party.
3. Spencer Ervin, *Henry Ford vs. Truman Newberry: The Famous Senate Election Contest* (New York, 1935). A law professor revisited the case in 1986; see Maurice Kelman, "Campaign on Trial: The Unnecessary Ordeal of Truman Newberry," *Wayne Law Review* 33 (1986–1987): 1573–1603. See Alan Nevins and Frank Ernest Hill, *Ford: Expansion and Challenge, 1915–1933* (New York, 1957), especially 116–124 for confusion about the Ford-Newberry campaign. Also note the photograph of someone labeled "Truman F. Newberry" speaking, as an illustration of campaign appearances that Newberry never made. An exception in the Ford literature is Donald Finlay Davis, *Conspicuous Production: Automobiles and Elites in Detroit, 1899–1933* (Philadelphia: Temple University Press, 1988). On campaign finance reform, see, for example, Louise Overacker, *Money in Elections* (New York: Macmillan, 1932); Anthony Corrado, "Money and Politics: A History of Federal Campaign Finance Law," in *The New Campaign Finance Sourcebook*, ed. Anthony Corrado, Thomas E. Mann, Daniel R. Ortiz, and Trevor Potter

(Washington, D.C.: Brookings, 2005), 13–16; Robert E. Mutch, *Campaigns, Congress, and Courts: The Making of Federal Campaign Finance Law* (Westport, Conn.: Praeger, 1988); Melvin I. Urofsky, *Money and Free Speech: Campaign Finance Reform and the Courts* (Lawrence: University Press of Kansas, 2005), and Raymond La Raja, *Small Change: Money, Political Parties and Campaign Finance Reform* (Ann Arbor: University of Michigan Press, 2008), 52–56.

4. La Raja, *Small Change*; and, for example, Bruce Ackerman and Ian Ayres, *Voting with Dollars: A New Paradigm for Campaign Finance* (New Haven, Conn.: Yale University Press, 2002); Frank Pasquale, "Reclaiming Egalitarianism in the Political Theory of Campaign Finance Reform," *University of Illinois Law Review* 642 (2008): 599–625; and Lawrence Lessig, *Republic, Lost: How Money Corrupts Congress—and a Plan to Stop It* (New York: Twelve, 2011).

5. See, for example, Bradley A. Smith, *Unfree Speech: The Folly of Campaign Finance Reform* (Princeton, N.J.: Princeton University Press, 2001); John Samples, *The Fallacy of Campaign Finance Reform* (Chicago: University of Chicago Press, 2006); Rodney A. Smith, *Money, Power, and Elections: How Campaign Finance Reform Subverts American Democracy* (Baton Rouge: Louisiana State University Press, 2006); Peter J. Wallison and Joel M. Gora, *Better Parties, Better Government: A Realistic Program for Campaign Finance Reform* (Washington, D.C.: AEI Press, 2009); Stephen Ansolabehere, John M. deFigueiredo, and James M. Snyder Jr., "Why Is there So Little Money in American Politics?" *Journal of Economic Perspectives* 17 (Winter 2003): 105–130; and Jeffrey Milyo, David M. Primo, and Matthew L. Jacobsmeier, "Does Public Financing of State Election Campaigns Increase Voter Turnout?," in *Public Financing in American Elections*, ed. Costas Panagopoulos (Philadelphia: Temple University Press, 2011), 225–237.

6. The classic analysis of the impact of the rules of the game is Douglas W. Rae, *The Political Consequences of Electoral Laws* (New Haven, Conn.: Yale University Press, 1967).

7. On the independent press, see Paul Starr, *The Creation of the Media: The Political Origins of Modern Communication* (New York: Basic Books, 2004), chaps. 4 and 7; Gerald J. Baldasty, *The Commercialization of the News in the Nineteenth Century* (Madison: University of Wisconsin Press, 1992); Timothy E. Cook, *Governing the News: The News Media as a Political Institution* (Chicago: University of Chicago Press, 2005); and Michael Schudson, *Discovering the News* (New York: Basic Books, 1978). On the commercial press and politics, especially helpful is Richard L. Kaplan, *Politics and the American Press: The Rise of Objectivity, 1865–1920* (New York: Cambridge University Press, 2002).

8. Walter Lippmann's *Public Opinion* (1922) and *The Phantom Public* (1927) are the classic statements about the limitations of the public's grasp of public events and, by 1927, the capacity of experts. Progressive Era movements also made good use of campaign stunts to generate media attention. See Margaret Finnegan, *Selling*

Suffrage: Consumer Culture and Votes for Women (New York: New York University Press, 1999). On progressives and intelligence, see Michael Schudson, *The Good Citizen: A History of American Civic Life* (Cambridge, Mass.: Harvard University Press, 1998).

CHAPTER 2: DETROIT

1. Particularly good in capturing Ford's contradictions are Warren Susman, *Culture as History: The Transformation of American Society in the Twentieth Century* (New York: Pantheon, 1984); David E. Nye, *Henry Ford: "Ignorant Idealist"* (Port Washington, N.Y.: Kennikat Press, 1979); and Steven Watts, *The People's Tycoon: Henry Ford and the American Century* (New York: Vintage, 2005). On Ford's unusual commitment to inexpensive cars, see Donald Findlay Davis, *Conspicuous Production: Automobiles and Elites in Detroit, 1899–1933* (Philadelphia: Temple University Press, 1988).

2. Helen Bourne Joy Lee, *The Newberry Genealogy* (Chester, Conn.: Pequot Press, 1975), 86; M. A. Leeson, *History of Macomb County* (Chicago: M. A. Leeson, 1882), 522, 614, 626; Robert L. Root Jr., *"Time by Moments Steals Away": The 1848 Journal of Ruth Douglass* (Detroit: Wayne State University Press, 1998), 46–47; and John Bersey, *Cyclopedia of Michigan, Historical and Biographical* (New York: Western Publishing and Engraving, 1890), 144–145.

3. Charles Moore, *History of Michigan*, vol. 2 (Chicago: Lewis Publishing, 1915), 674–675; Davis, *Conspicuous Production*, 47–51; Olivier Zunz, *The Changing Face of Inequality: Urbanization, Industrial Development, and Immigrants in Detroit* (Chicago: University of Chicago Press, 1982), 212–213.

4. Zunz, *Changing Face of Inequality*; and Willis F. Dunbar, *Michigan: A History of the Wolverine State*, rev. ed. by George S. May (Grand Rapids, Mich.: Eerdman's, 1970), 461–483.

5. Richard Jules Oestreicher, *Solidarity and Fragmentation: Working People and Class Consciousness in Detroit, 1875–1900* (Urbana: University of Illinois Press, 1986), 148–163.

6. *DFP*, September 1 (quote), November 15, 1878; September 29, December 4 and 10, 1880; and *NYT*, May 25, December 13, 1879.

7. Stephen B. Sarasohn and Vera H. Sarasohn, *Political Party Patterns in Michigan* (Detroit: Wayne State University Press, 1957); Geoffrey G. Drutchas, "Gray Eminence in a Gilded Age: The Forgotten Career of Senator James McMillan of Michigan," *Michigan Historical Review* 28 (Fall 2002): 78–113; Mary K. George, *Zachariah Chandler: A Political Biography* (East Lansing: Michigan State University Press, 1969); and Marin J. Hershock, *The Paradox of Progress: Economic Change, Individual Enterprise, and Political Culture in Michigan, 1837–1878* (Athens: Ohio University Press, 2003).

8. Bersey, *Cyclopedia of Michigan*, 145; and Thomas A. Arbaugh, "John S. Newberry and James H. McMillan: Leaders of Industry and Commerce," in *Tonnancour:*

Life in Grosse Pointe and along the Shores of Lake St. Clair, ed. Arthur M. Wood-
ford (Detroit: Omnigraphics, 1994), 77–79.

9. Lee, *Newberry Genealogy*, 86, 112; and Arbaugh, "John S. Newberry and James H. McMillan," 75–76.

10. Newberry Autobiography, 4–5, THN Papers, DPL; and CL-1883–1884, THN Papers, DPL.

11. Newberry Autobiography, 1–5, THN Papers, DPL; Leonard Schlup, "Newberry, Truman Handy," *American National Biography Online*, February 2000, http://www.amb.org/articles/06/06-00470.html; Lee, *Newberry Genealogy*, 86, 132; and *Grosse Pointe News*, March 20, 1958.

12. *NYT*, October 4, 1945; Newberry Autobiography, 10, THN Papers, DPL; and Joy, *Newberry Genealogy*, 132. The genealogy claims that Harrie joined the diplomatic service after being passed over, not before. Truman P. Handy's death in 1898 added to the family's wealth, since Truman Newberry's mother was the primary beneficiary. *DFP*, March 30, 1898.

13. Davis, *Conspicuous Production*, 57–60, quote on 59. Arthur W. Einstein, *Ask the Man Who Owns One: An Illustrated History of Packard Advertising* (Jefferson, N.C.: McFarland, 2010); Beverly Rae Kimes, ed., *Packard: A History of the Motor Car and the Company* (Princeton, N.J.: Princeton Publishing, 1978); and Pete Davies, *American Road: The Story of an Epic Transcontinental Journey at the Dawn of the Motor Age* (New York: Henry Holt, 2002).

14. Newberry Autobiography, THN Papers, DPL; and Ann Marie Aliotta and Suzy Berschback, *Grosse Pointe* (Mount Pleasant, S.C.: Arcadia Publishing, 2007), 11.

15. Michael E. McGerr, *A Fierce Discontent: The Rise and Fall of the Progressive Movement in America, 1870–1920* (New York: Oxford University Press, 2003).

16. The biographical paragraphs rely upon Douglas Brinkley, *Wheels for the World: Henry Ford, His Company, and a Century of Progress* (New York: Penguin, 2003); Alan Nevins and Frank Ernest Hill, *Ford: The Times, the Man, the Company* (New York: Scribner's, 1954); and Watts, *People's Tycoon*.

17. Brinkley, *Wheels for the World*, 21.

18. Davis, *Conspicuous Production*, 60–63.

19. There is a vast literature on Ford and the Model T; the comparison in this discussion relies on Davis, *Conspicuous Production*.

20. Davis, *Conspicuous Production*, 129–130; David L. Lewis, *The Public Image of Henry Ford: An American Folk Hero and His Company* (Detroit: Wayne State University Press, 1976), 20–21.

21. Davis, *Conspicuous Production*, 130; and Lewis, *Public Image of Henry Ford*, 24.

22. Davis, *Conspicuous Production*, 131–132; and Samuel S. Marquis, *Henry Ford: An Interpretation* (Boston: Little, Brown, 1923), 108–109.

23. See *Wall Street Journal*, September 26, 2009, on the life and times of one of the lots Newberry sold.

24. *DFP*, March 7, July 7 and 16, 1895; July 29, September 26, 1897.

25. *DFP*, July 19, 1897.

26. *DFP*, April 27, 1898; Miguel Hernandez, "The Crew of the USS Yosemite," Spanish-American War Centennial Website, http://www.spanwar.com/yosemitecrew.htm, accessed August 22, 2011.

27. A. B. Feuer, *The Spanish-American War at Sea: Naval Action in the Atlantic* (Westport, Conn.: Greenwood Press, 1995), chap. 12.

28. Newberry Autobiography, 7, 27, THN Papers, DPL; *DFP*, January 5, 1899; March 30, 1904. In 1899, Newberry would have been setting himself against James McMillan, whose lieutenants in the state Senate blocked the Atkinson Bill that revamped railroad taxation. Allying with Pingree would have meant joining with one of his father's old enemies in city politics. Melvin G. Holli, *Reform in Detroit: Hazen S. Pingree and Urban Politics* (New York: Oxford University Press, 1969), 58–62, 203–214.

29. *DFP*, September 7 and 27, October 1 and 21, 1904.

30. Newberry Autobiography, 27, THN Papers, DPL. Denby took at least one position in the general election, supporting the ship subsidy bill that Lucking had described as a "steal." October 31, 1904, Edwin Denby Papers, Box 1, Bentley.

31. Newberry Autobiography, 9, 27–28, THN Papers, DPL; *WP*, September 9, 1906; November 9, 1907; Matthew M. Oyos, "Theodore Roosevelt and the Implements of War," *Journal of Military History* 60 (October 1996): 631–655; and Ronald Spector, *Professors of War: The Navy War College and the Development of the Naval Profession* (Newport, R.I.: Naval War College Press, 1977).

32. *WP*, November 2, 1905; May 27, 1908; and *NYT*, April 18, 1906.

33. Newberry Autobiography, 9, THN Papers, DPL; *NYT*, November 14, 1908; April 19, 1909; *WP*, January 19, 1909; *DFP*, November 19, 1908; and *Ironwood (Mich.) News Record*, November 14, 1908.

34. Lewis L. Gould, *Four Hats in the Ring: The 1912 Election and the Birth of Modern American Politics* (Lawrence: University Press of Kansas, 2008), is a fine overview of the election.

35. *NYT*, February 2, 1912; *DFP*, February 2, 1912; and *Washington Herald*, May 30, 1912.

36. *DFP*, March 13, 1912; Edwin W. Sims to Osborn, Osborn Papers, Bentley; and *CT*, March 1, 1912.

37. Henry B. Joy, "Price Maintenance: Discussion before the National Advertising Managers, Hotel Astor, Wednesday, May 14, 1913" (Detroit: n.p., 1913); and "Hearing in Ford Case Adjourned," *Horseless Age* 33, no. 16 (October 15, 1913): 606. Even Senator Charles Townsend, who had defeated the conservative Burrows in the Republican primary and won the seat in the state's first direct election in 1910, was puzzled by the Roosevelt boom. He assigned Taft's unpopularity in Michigan to his support for the reciprocity treaty with Canada, which Townsend also favored. So did Osborn, who was pursuing all angles to get Michigan's convention votes for Roosevelt. Townsend to Osborn, February 12, 1912; and Osborn

to Townsend, February 24, 1912, Box 28, Osborn Papers, Bentley. Osborn was upset with Taft for, among other reasons, his failure to appoint James Murfin and Frank Knox to government posts, instead hiring "the cheapest lot of clerks."

38. A. C. Millspaugh, *Party Organization and Machinery in Michigan since 1890* (Baltimore: Johns Hopkins University Press, 1917); *Sault Ste. Marie (Mich.) Evening News*, April 3, 1912.

39. *Grand Rapids Herald*, April 12, 1912, quoted in Millspaugh, *Party Organization and Machinery in Michigan*, 86; *NYT*, April 12, 1912.

40. Taft to King, William Howard Taft Papers, Reel 511, LOC.

41. Medill McCormick to E. A. Vanvalkenburg, April 8, 1912, TR Papers, Reel 136; TR to THN, undated, TR Papers, Reel 382; THN to TR, April 10, 1912, Papers of Theodore Roosevelt (hereafter TR Papers), Reel 136; THN to Knox, May 20, 1912; Knox to THN, May 27, 1912, and Knox to Frank Harper, May 28, 1912, TR Papers, Reel 142, LOC; Knox to George H. Moses, March 31, 1920, Box 3a, George H. Moses Papers, New Hampshire Historical Society; Osborn to Knox, April 12, 1912; Beveridge to Knox, April 13, 1912, Box 29, Osborn Papers, Bentley.

42. *DFP*, June 14, 19, and 27, 1912. Newberry continued to follow and fund the campaign; THN to TR, May 29, 1912, TR Papers, Reel 143. The postelection statement is THN to TR, November 6, 1912, TR Papers, Reel 156, LOC.

43. *WP*, March 31, 1912, for the announcement; on the broken engagement, see *Washington Herald*, May 30, 1912; *NYT*, June 7, 1912 (quote); *WP*, June 8, 1912; and *NYT*, June 24, 1912. Also, Newberry's mother died in 1912; *DFP*, December 17, 1912. Carol Newberry divorced her husband and remarried in 1937; *NYT*, December 8, 1937.

44. *NYT*, April 12, 1912; and Newberry Autobiography, 5, THN Papers, DPL.

45. Alan Nevins and Frank Ernest Hill, *Ford: Expansion and Challenge, 1915–1933* (New York: Scribner's, 1957), 99.

46. Ford quoted in Davis, *Conspicuous Production*, 127; Nevins and Hill, *Ford: Expansion and Challenge*, 86–111; and Charles K. Hyde, *The Dodge Brothers: The Men, the Motor Cars, and the Legacy* (Detroit: Wayne State University Press, 2005), 56–60, 83–84.

47. Davis, *Conspicuous Production*, 128; Leibold quoted in Neil Baldwin, *Henry Ford and the Jews: The Mass Production of Hate* (New York: Public Affairs, 2001), 61.

48. Watts, *People's Tycoon*, 258–265; Charles Sorensen, *My Forty Years with Ford* (New York: Norton, 1962), 18; and Lewis, *Public Image of Henry Ford*, 214–215.

49. Marquis, *Henry Ford*, 55; Nye, *Henry Ford*, 79–80 (quote), 60–69; Lewis, *Public Image of Henry Ford*, 218–219; and Cassandra Tate, *Cigarette Wars: The Triumph of "The Little White Slaver"* (New York: Oxford University Press, 1998), 55–56.

50. Nevins and Hill, *Ford: The Times, the Man, the Company*, 561–562. The real increase in the African American workforce came after World War I, and while their pay equaled that of whites doing the same jobs, most found themselves trapped in the worst jobs. Christopher L. Foot, Warren C. Whatley, and Gavin

Wright, "Arbitraging a Discriminatory Labor Market: Black Workers at the Ford Motor Company, 1918–1947," *Journal of Labor Economics* 21 (2003): 493–532.

51. Nevins and Hill, *Ford: The Times, the Man, the Company*, 533; Stephen Meyer III, *The Five Dollar Day: Labor Management and Social Control in the Ford Motor Company, 1908–1921* (Albany, N.Y.: SUNY Press, 1981), 72; Watts, *People's Tycoon*, 180–194; and Davis, *Conspicuous Production*, 134.

52. Meyer, *Five Dollar Day*, 115, and, on the investigations, chap. 6.

53. Barbara S. Kraft, *The Peace Ship: Henry Ford's Pacifist Adventure in the First World War* (New York: Macmillan, 1978); Nevins and Hill, *Ford: Expansion and Challenge*, 23; Alfred Lucking to Joseph P. Tumulty, November 20, 1915; and Woodrow Wilson to Tumulty, undated, 1915, Woodrow Wilson Papers, Reel 74, LOC.

54. Watts, *People's Tycoon*, 229, 235–236; Nevins and Hill, *Ford: Expansion and Challenge*, 30, 51.

55. Harry Barnard, *Independent Man: The Life of James Couzens* (New York: Scribner's, 1958).

56. Watts, *People's Tycoon*, 240–242; Lewis, *Public Image of Henry Ford*, 97–98; *NYT*, April 5, 1916; and Liebold Reminiscences, 284–288, Benson Ford.

57. *CT*, June 23, 1916; Lewis, *Public Image of Henry Ford*, 104; Davis, *Conspicuous Production*, 136; Nevins and Hill, *Ford: Expansion and Challenge*, 36; *DFP*, August 22, 1915 (Ford's statement); Henry Bourne Joy, "Millions for Tribute, Not One Cent for Defense: A Reply to Henry Ford" (Detroit: n.p., n.d.); *New York Herald*, January 9, 1916; and, in general, Henry Bourne Joy Scrapbook, vol. 26, 1913–1916, Henry Bourne Joy Papers, Bentley.

58. Watts, *People's Tycoon*, 243; E. G. Pipp, *Henry Ford, Both Sides of Him* (Detroit: Pipp's Magazine, 1926), 55.

CHAPTER 3: LAWS AND EFFECTS

1. *NYT*, June 6, 1920.

2. Ibid.; and Melvyn H. Bloom, *Public Relations and Presidential Campaigns: A Crisis in Democracy* (New York: Crowell, 1973), 13.

3. This discussion of electoral reform relies on John F. Reynolds, *Testing Democracy: Electoral Behavior and Progressive Reform* (Chapel Hill: University of North Carolina Press, 1988); Michael E. McGerr, *The Decline of Popular Politics: The American North, 1865–1928* (New York: Oxford University Press, 1986); Mark Lawrence Kornbluh, *Why America Stopped Voting: The Decline of Participatory Democracy and the Emergence of Modern American Politics* (New York: New York University Press, 2000); and Alexander Keyssar, *The Right to Vote: The Contested History of Democracy in the United States* (New York: Basic Books, 2000).

4. On the progressive revamping of citizenship, see Michael Schudson, *The Good Citizen: A History of American Civic Life* (Cambridge, Mass.: Harvard University Press, 1998), especially chap. 4.

5. Peter Argersinger, "'A Place on the Ballot': Fusion Politics and Anti-fusion Laws," *American Historical Review* 85 (April 1980): 268–297; and John F. Reynolds and Richard L. McCormick, "'Outlawing Treachery': Split Tickets and Ballot Laws in New York and New Jersey, 1880–1914," *Journal of American History* 72 (March 1986): 835–858. On primaries, see John F. Reynolds, *The Demise of the American Convention System, 1880–1911* (New York: Cambridge University Press, 2006); and Alan Ware, *The American Direct Primary: Party Institutionalization and Transformation in the North* (New York: Cambridge University Press, 2002).

6. Reynolds, *Demise of the Convention System*; Ware, *American Direct Primary*.

7. Ware, *American Direct Primary*.

8. On overstating change in the Progressive Era, see Schudson, *Good Citizen*. On the impact of primaries, see Charles E. Merriam and Louise Overacker, *Primary Elections* (Chicago: University of Chicago Press, 1926); Stephen Ansolabehere, John Mark Hansen, Shigeo Hirano, and James M. Snyder Jr., "The Decline of Competition in U.S. Primary Elections, 1908–2004," in *The Marketplace of Democracy: Electoral Competition and American Politics*, ed. Michael P. McDonald and John Samples (Washington, D.C.: Brookings Institution Press, 2006); Stephen Ansolabehere, John Mark Hansen, Shigeo Hirano, and James M. Snyder Jr., "More Democracy: The Direct Primary and Competition in U.S. Elections," *Studies in American Political Development* 24 (October 2010): 190–205.

9. Michael Schudson, *Discovering the News: A Social History of American Newspapers* (New York: Basic Books, 1981); Michael E. McGerr, *The Decline of Popular Politics: The American North, 1865–1928* (New York: Oxford University Press, 1986); Richard R. John, *Spreading the News: The American Postal System from Franklin to Morse* (Cambridge, Mass.: Harvard University Press, 1995); Timothy B. Cook, *Governing the News: The News Media as a Political Institution* (Chicago: University of Chicago Press, 2005); and Gerald J. Baldasty, *The Commercialization of News in the Nineteenth Century* (Madison: University of Wisconsin Press, 1992).

10. Among the biographies of newspapers in the glory years of influence (if not journalism), see, for example, David Nasaw, *The Chief: The Life of William Randolph Hearst* (New York: Houghton Mifflin, 2000); David Halberstam, *The Powers That Be* (New York: Knopf, 1979); Dennis McDougal, *Privileged Son: Otis Chandler and the Rise and Fall of the Los Angeles Times Dynasty* (Cambridge, Mass.: Perseus, 2001); David Zacher, *The Scripps Newspapers Go to War, 1914–1918* (Urbana: University of Illinois Press, 2008); and Richard Norton Smith, *The Colonel: The Life and Legend of Robert R. McCormick* (Boston: Houghton Mifflin, 1997). On political coverage after the partisan press, see Richard L. Kaplan, *Politics and the American Press: The Rise of Objectivity, 1865–1920* (New York: Cambridge University Press, 2002).

11. James K. Pollock, *Party Campaign Funds* (New York: Knopf, 1926), 143–179.

12. Ibid., 161–162, on precinct and ward expenses.

13. Daniel Wirls, "Regionalism, Rotten Boroughs, Race, and Realignment: The Seventeenth Amendment and the Politics of Representation," *Studies in American Political Development* 13 (Spring 1999): 3–4.

14. Anne M. Butler and Wendy Wolff, *United States Senate Election, Expulsion, and Censure Cases, 1793–1990* (Washington, D.C.: Government Printing Office, 1995), 275–276; Jerry A. O'Callaghan, "Senator John H. Mitchell and the Oregon Land Frauds, 1905," *Pacific Historical Review* (August 1952): 255–261; Lewis L. Gould, *The Most Exclusive Club: A History of the Modern United States Senate* (New York: Basic Books, 2005); Robert Harrison, *Congress, Progressive Reform, and the New American State* (New York: Cambridge University Press, 2004), 29–33.

15. This discussion of Lorimer's career draws on Joel Arthur Tarr, *A Study in Boss Politics: William Lorimer of Chicago* (Urbana: University of Illinois Press, 1971).

16. *CT*, April 30, 1910; Tarr; *Study in Boss Politics*; Smith, *The Colonel*, 130–132; and Richard D. Hupman, *Senate Election, Expulsion and Censure Cases from 1793 to 1972* (Washington, D.C.: Government Printing Office, 1972), 101–102.

17. Tarr, *Study in Boss Politics*.

18. Isaac Stephenson, *Recollections of a Long Life, 1829–1915* (Chicago: R. R. Donnelley, 1915); and Nancy C. Unger, *Fighting Bob La Follette: The Righteous Reformer* (Chapel Hill: University of North Carolina Press, 2000), 124–125, 150.

19. *NYT*, January 12, 1911; David P. Thelen, *Robert M. La Follette and the Insurgent Spirit* (Madison: University of Wisconsin Press, 1985), 61–62.

20. *CT*, October 4, 1911; *WP*, October 11, 1911.

21. *CT*, February 20, 1912; *WP*, March 5, 1912. The *Tribune* cheered on those opposed to seating Stephenson, seeing this case in light of Lorimer's.

22. *NYT*, March 26, 1912; H. L. Mencken, "James A. Reed of Missouri," *American Mercury*, April 1929.

23. Butler and Wolff, *Election, Expulsion and Censure Cases*, 285–287.

24. Hupman, *Senate Election, Expulsion and Censure Cases*, 104–105; *WP*, February 29, 1912; *NYT*, February 27, 1912; and *CT*, February 29, 1912.

25. *WP*, January 22, July 16, 1911; March 4, 1913; *NYT*, January 22, 1911; Gary Jackson Tucker, *Governor William E. Glasscock and Progressive Politics in West Virginia* (Morgantown: University of West Virginia Press, 2008). One state legislator who had charged Watson and Chilton with vote buying changed his story, claiming that he had floated it in the interest of another candidate.

26. The standard treatment of the amendment is George H. Haynes, *The Senate of the United States* (Boston: Houghton Mifflin, 1938).

27. Wirls, "Regionalism, Rotten Boroughs, Race, and Realignment"; Ronald F. King and Susan Ellis, "Partisan Advantage and Constitutional Change: The Case of the Seventeenth Amendment," *Studies in American Political Development* 10 (Spring 1996): 69–102; and John D. Buenker, "The Urban Political Machine and the Seventeenth Amendment," *Journal of American History* 56 (September 1969): 305–322.

28. *CT*, October 4, 1911; *NYT*, January 15, 1912; Reynolds, *Demise of the American Convention System*, 190–192; and *NYT*, February 13, 1910.

29. Perry Belmont, "Publicity of Election Expenditures," *North American Review* 180 (February 1906): 181.

30. Louise Overacker, *Money in Elections* (New York: Macmillan, 1932), 235–238, 240; Anthony Corrado, "Money and Politics: A History of Federal Campaign Finance Law," in Anthony Corrado, Thomas E. Mann, Daniel R. Ortiz, and Trevor Potter, eds., *The New Campaign Finance Sourcebook* (Washington, D.C.: Brookings Institution Press, 2005), 13–14.

31. Robert E. Mutch, *Campaigns, Congress, and the Courts: The Making of Federal Campaign Finance Law* (New York: Praeger, 1988), 1–8; Stephen Kantrowitz, *Ben Tillman and the Reconstruction of White Supremacy* (Chapel Hill: University of North Carolina Press, 2000); Leon Burr Richardson, *William Eaton Chandler, Republican* (New York: Dodd, Mead, 1940), 90–107; Adam Winkler, "Other People's Money: Corporations, Agency Costs, and Campaign Finance Law," *Georgetown Law Journal* 92 (2004): 871–940; and *United States v. United States Brewers' Association*, 239 Fed. 163 (1916).

32. *NYT*, May 7, June 20, June 21, 1910; April 3 and 15, July 18, 1911; *CR*, 61st Cong., 2nd sess., pt. v (Washington, D.C.: Government Printing Office, 1910), 4927–4928, 4933; *WP*, September 7, 1916; and Mutch, *Campaigns, Congress, and the Courts*, 13–16.

33. *WP*, March 14, April 4, May 8, 1910.

34. Mutch, *Campaigns, Congress, and the Courts*, 12–16.

35. *WP*, August 17 and 25, September 7, December 7, 1916; *NYT*, December 7, 1916; and Mutch, *Campaigns, Congress, and the Courts*, 14–16. Owen brought the measure back after the election but failed to move it through the new Senate, which had a less progressive and Democratic cast.

36. Overacker, *Money in Elections*, especially 249–257; and Pollock, *Party Campaign Funds*, 186–196.

37. Pollock, *Party Campaign Funds*, 196–199; *NYT*, January 28, February 5, 1911; December 13, 1912; *WP*, December 4, 1911; July 19 and 20, August 13, 1912. For an overview of House cases, see Jeffrey A. Jenkins, "Partisanship and Contested Election Cases in the House of Representatives, 1789–2002," *Studies in American Political Development* 18 (Fall 2004): 112–135. The 1910 elections generated eight contests, three in districts covering St. Louis. *WP*, December 8, 1911.

38. S. Gale Lowrie, *Corrupt Practices at Elections* (Madison: University of Wisconsin Press, 1911), 15; and Overacker, *Money in Elections*, 289–316.

39. Pollack, *Party Campaign Funds*, 256, 257; *NYT*, December 14, 1910; *WP*, February 5 and 13, 1915; and *NYT*, January 7, 1915.

40. *WP*, January 19 and 25, 1915; *NYT*, January 13, 1915; and *Indianapolis Star*, November 22, 1916; October 28, 1917. A judge dismissed the ninety-nine indictments in Ohio because the federal government lacked jurisdiction, *WP*, May 23, 1917.

41. *Bluefield (W.Va.) Daily Telegraph*, January 13, 1917; *Indianapolis Star*, November 14, 1916; and *Waterloo (Iowa) Evening Courier*, November 14, 1916.

42. *NYT*, December 6, 1916; *WP*, November 15, 1916; *Indianapolis Star*, January 26, 1917; on Bleakley, *WP*, December 10, 1916; March 31, 1917; and *NYT*, April 2, 1917. Congress moved on to new investigations of its members, now concerned about statements critical of the nation going to war. The most famous of these was La Follette, although others seemed to merit investigation. *CT*, October 2, 1917; and Unger, *Fighting Bob*, chap. 14.

CHAPTER 4: MICHIGAN

1. Melvin Holli, *Reform in Detroit: Hazen Pingree and Urban Politics* (New York: Oxford University Press, 1969); Geoffrey G. Drutchas, "Gray Eminence in a Gilded Age: The Forgotten Career of Senator James McMillan of Michigan," *Michigan Historical Review* 28 (Fall 2002): 78–113.

2. *NYT*, January 10, 1907; Robert M. Warner, "Chase S. Osborn and the Presidential Campaign of 1912," *Mississippi Valley Historical Review* 46 (June 1959): 19–45; Stephen B. Sarasohn and Vera H. Sarasohn, *Political Party Patterns in Michigan* (Detroit: Wayne State University Press, 1957), 8–19.

3. A. C. Millspaugh, *Party Organization and Machinery in Michigan since 1980* (Baltimore: Johns Hopkins University Press, 1917), chap. 5.

4. *NYT*, March 2, 1918; *DFP*, January 31, March 17, April 20, 1918.

5. *NYT*, November 22, 1923; May 19, 1931; February 5, 1948; April 12, 1949; *Kalamazoo Evening Post*, December 29, 1919, quoted in Richard P. Jennings, "A Rhetorical Analysis of Chase S. Osborn's 1910 Primary Campaign," *Michigan Historical Review* (Fall 1991): 40; *CT*, November 21, 1923; and Robert M. Warner, *Chase Salmon Osborn, 1860–1949*, Michigan Historical Collections, Bulletin No. 10 (Ann Arbor, Mich., 1960), 3. Couzens was elected mayor of Detroit in 1918.

6. Spencer Ervin, *Henry Ford vs. Truman H. Newberry: The Famous Senate Election Contest* (New York: Richard R. Smith, 1935), 3–8; Roger M. Andrews to Truman Newberry, November 17, 1917; Newberry to Andrews, November 22, 1917; and Burt D. Cady to Newberry, November 28, 1917, Box 3, THN Papers, DPL. The Thumb, the three-county area with Saginaw Bay to the west and Lake Huron to the east, gets its name from the mitten shape of Michigan's Lower Peninsula. Because Michigan had not sent a senator from Detroit since the death of Russell A. Alger in 1907, some in the state's largest city felt it was time to address the gap. Donald Finlay Davis, *Conspicuous Production: Automobiles and Elites in Detroit, 1899–1933* (Philadelphia: Temple University Press, 1988), 177.

7. Cody, one of the defendants in the Newberry conspiracy trial, did not testify. Biographical information is sketchy, but see his obituary, *NYT*, December 28, 1936. Cody went on to become a vice president of McCann-Erickson, a Madison Avenue advertising firm. On Newberry's musings, THN to George Miller, January 29, 1918, Subcommittee on Privileges and Elections, U.S. Senate, 67th Cong.,

1st sess., *Senator from Michigan, Hearing Pursuant to Senate Res. 11, A Resolution Authorizing the Investigation of Alleged Unlawful Practices in the Election of a Senator from the State of Michigan,* Appendix, Bill of Exceptions, Error to the District Court of the United States for the Western District of Michigan, Southern Division (Washington, D.C., 1921) (hereafter Bill of Exceptions), 643.

8. Newberry, Michigan, in the Upper Peninsula, was laid out with streets named after John S. Newberry's children, none of whom had any connection, other than the estate, with the village.

9. *DFP*, June 6, 1915.

10. Frank W. Blair to THN, February 14, 1918, Box 1, THN Papers, DPL; George B. Catlin, ed., *Local History of Detroit and Wayne County* (Dayton, Ohio: National Historical Association, 1928), 543–545.

11. THN to George Miller, April 6 and 12, 1918, Bill of Exceptions, 651, 652, 654.

12. THN to George Miller, April 6, 1918, Bill of Exceptions, 651; THN to Allan Templeton, February 15, 1918; THN to Templeton, March 2, 1918, Box 1, THN Papers, DPL.

13. Newberry was specifically concerned with whether a candidate's expenses before the primary papers were filed could be counted toward the total. Fred Smith to A. G. Angell, May 16, 1918, Box 2, THN Papers, DPL. On the Michigan law, see Millspaugh, *Party Organization and Machinery in Michigan,* 133–144.

14. Henry W. Rose to THN, April 8, 1918, Box 1, THN Papers, DPL; campaign organization and minority report folders, Box 35, THN Papers, DPL; Bill of Exceptions, 469, for King described his organization at the Grand Rapids trial; see also Ervin, *Henry Ford vs. Truman Newberry,* chap. 1.

15. THN to King, May 12, 1918, in reply to King to THN, May 5, 1918; THN to King, June 15, 1918, Bill of Exceptions, 718–722, 777, and, in general, the King-Newberry correspondence, 684–899.

16. King to THN, July 26, 1918, Bill of Exceptions, 848.

17. Chase S. Osborn to John C. Shaffer, June 2, 1918; Osborn to W. P. Kemp, June 3, 1918; Merlin Wiley to Osborn, June 8, 1918, Box 42, Osborn Papers, Bentley.

18. Merlin Wiley to Osborn, June 8, 1918, and F. L. Westover, June 14, 1918, Box 42, Osborn Papers, Bentley; THN to Congressman Nichols, June 1, 1918, Box 1, THN Papers, DPL; King to THN, June 17, Bill of Exceptions, 792–794, quote on 793.

19. Bill of Exceptions, 703; *NYT*, May 19, 1918; Josephus Daniels, *The Wilson Era: Years of War and After, 1917–1923* (Chapel Hill: University of North Carolina Press, 1946), 293–297.

20. *NYT*, June 13, 1918; Daniels, *Wilson Era,* 297–298.

21. Keith Sward, *The Legend of Henry Ford* (New York: Reinhart, 1948), 116; Daniels, *Wilson Era,* 296; *NYT*, June 23, 1918; and Box 163, Folder 15, Acc. 1, Fairlane Papers, Benson Ford.

22. King to THN, June 17, 1918, Bill of Exceptions, 792, 793; Osborn quoted in Warner, *Chase S. Osborn,* 26; *NYT*, June 16 and 24, 1918; and on Osborn's opposition

research, Osborn to Helen L. Earle, June 3, 1918; William Oates to Osborn, June 17, 1918; Raymond Benjamin to Osborn, June 28, 1918; Kathleen Lawler to Osborn, August 13, 1918, Box 42, Osborn Papers, Bentley; and *CT*, June 15, 1918.

23. *CT*, May 3 and 5, 1918; *WP*, May 5, 1918; *NYT*, June 20, 1918; *DFP*, June 20, 1918; John H. Blodgett to THN, July 10, 1918, Box 1, THN Papers, DPL; King to THN, June 17, 1918, Bill of Exceptions, 793; Osborn to Will Hays, June 19, 1918, Box 42, Osborn Papers, Bentley.

24. Bill of Exceptions, 793.

25. Nathan F. Simpson to Osborn, July 8, 1918; John F. Dodge to Will Hays, July 12, 1918; Osborn to William H. Field, July 13, 1918; Osborn to Will Hays, June 19, 1918; Osborn to John C. Shaffer, June 19, 1918, Box 42, Osborn Papers, Bentley; Albert J. Beveridge to Will Hays, July 16, 1918, Box 1, Will Harrison Hays Papers, Indiana State Library.

26. Box 1, Hays Papers, Indiana State Library; Ralph M. Goldman, *The National Party Chairman and Committees: Factionalism at the Top* (Armonk, N.Y.: M. E. Sharpe, 1990), 287–297.

27. TR to John Shaffer, June 10, 1918, Box 42, Osborn Papers, Bentley; and THN to TR, August 1, 1918, TR Papers, Reel 287, LOC. Roosevelt's policy of staying out of Republican primaries was not as hard-and-fast as he suggested. He did work behind the scenes in Wisconsin to clear the way for Irvine Lenroot. Herbert F. Margulies, *Senator Lenroot of Wisconsin: A Political Biography, 1900–1929* (Columbia: University of Missouri Press, 1977), 238–239.

28. TR to Hays, Box 1, Folder 32, Hays Papers, Indiana State Library. Further discussions of the problem include *NYT*, July 23, 1918; *DFP*, July 23, 1918; Chase Osborn to Mary Osborn, August 6, 1918, Box 42, Osborn Papers, Bentley; and THN to King, August 9, 1918, Bill of Exceptions, 880–881. According to the report in the *Detroit Free Press*, there was to be a meeting in New York including Smith, Newberry, Osborn, and Hays. It did not come off, since Smith backed out, insisting that Ford be part of the discussion—a request sure to doom a meeting designed to settle on a single candidate against Ford. *NYT*, July 19, 1918, on the possibility that Newberry would withdraw.

29. Helme had been a party maverick and had been secretary of a Ford-for-Governor committee in 1916. For Helme's statement, see notebook, Helme Papers, pp. 6, 81, Bentley; and on King's connection, Ervin, *Henry Ford vs. Truman Newberry*, 226–271; and John D. Mangum to THN, July 27, 1918, Box 1, THN Papers, DPL. Helme and his favored gubernatorial candidate were among the original Wilsonians and were miffed that those who supported Champ Clark for president in 1912 nonetheless got control of the state's share of federal patronage.

30. Merlin Wiley to Osborn, August 5, 1918; and Wiley to Osborn, August 6, 1918, Box 42, Osborn Papers, Bentley. Osborn might have held back because of worries that if he charged "Newberry with money crimes . . . they will charge that I

bought the Governorship." Chase Osborn to Mary Osborn, August 8, 1918, Box
42, Osborn Papers, Bentley. His 1910 race cost $35,000, much of it supplied by
Osborn himself. John F. Reynolds, *The Demise of the American Convention System, 1880–1911* (New York: Cambridge University Press, 2006), 201.

31. Arthur Vandenberg to THN, August 8, 1918, Box 1, THN Papers, DPL; Newberry's reply indicated that Newberry had no answers about spending, but that
he might contact Paul King. THN to Vandenberg, August 11, 1918, Box 1, THN
Papers, DPL; *Detroit News*, August 22, 1918.

32. THN to Hays, August 3, 1918, Box 1, THN Papers, DPL; Osborn to Mary F. Hadrich, August 13, 1918, Box 42, Osborn Papers, Bentley; THN to King, August 16,
1918, Bill of Exceptions, 889.

33. King to THN, August 16, 1918, Bill of Exceptions, 889; Vandenberg to THN,
August 26, 1918; THN to Murray Sales, August 24, 1918; and THN to Dickinson,
August 23, 1918, Box 1, THN Papers, DPL.

34. *DFP*, August 13, 1918; Osborn to Joseph E. Bayliss, August 16, 1918, Merlin
Wiley to Osborn, August 6, 1918, Box 42, Osborn Papers, Bentley. The *Free Press*
prepared its readers for an endorsement with an August 11, 1918, article titled
"Newberry Was Always Manly," which described incidents of his childhood.

35. Ervin, *Henry Ford vs. Truman Newberry*, 21–25. The Ford Building, Detroit's first
skyscraper, was an eighteen-story building designed by Daniel Burnham, the architect who created Chicago's skyline. With Burnham's characteristic clean lines,
the Ford Building was completed in 1909. It had nothing to do with Henry Ford
or his family, but rather with a Toledo, Ohio, glass business.

36. *Detroit News*, November 3, 1918; THN to Fred Smith, September 5, 1918, Box
6, THN Papers, DPL. On the problem on the *News*, also see H. A. Hopkins to
THN, September 7, 1918, Box 6, THN Papers, DPL; on the attempt to apply pressure on the *News* to lighten its attacks through visits paid its owner by Detroit
business leaders, see James O. Murfin to THN, September 12, 1918, Box 6, THN
Papers, DPL.

37. *Detroit News*, November 2, 1918. Examples of the materials can be found at Box
163, Folder 15, Acc. 1, Fairlane Papers, Benson Ford.

38. E. G. Pipp, *The Real Henry Ford* (Detroit: Pipp's Weekly Press, 1922), 3. Pipp
was Ford's choice to be editor of the *Dearborn Independent* in 1919, when Ford
decided that he wanted a venue for his views. Pipp broke with Ford when those
views came to consist of anti-Semitic rants.

39. Allan Nevins and Frank Ernest Hill, *Ford: Expansion and Challenge, 1915–1933*
(New York: Scribner's, 1957), 119–121, which emphasizes the Ford-Lucking view
of the campaign, including, oddly, a Newberry speaking tour; H. A. Hopkins
to THN on Lucking's organization, October 1, 1918, Box 7, THN Papers, DPL.
On Firestone and Robinson, see Henry S. Firestone to Henry Ford, October 22,
1918, and Bernard Robinson to H. S. Firestone, October 18, 1918, Acc. 62, Box 63,
Benson Ford.

40. *DFP*, October 28 and 26, 1918; *Ironwood News Record*, November 2, 1918. The attention the Newberry campaign paid to the press highlights the unusual importance of newspapers in this period, now free from direct party control and the only media game in town. Many newspapers still slanted news coverage to boost favored candidates. The Newberry campaign obsessed about the *Detroit News* and the *Detroit Free Press* and tracked rumors that William Randolph Hearst, at this point an ally of Ford, planned to launch a newspaper in Detroit if the unqualified support of the *News* was not forthcoming. The Booth family, which owned the *News*, was, in some renditions, upset by the (small) financial stake Newberry and some of his friends had in the *Detroit Saturday Night*, a paper that held to two cents. Ford had pulled his subscription on request; Newberry refused to do the same.

41. H. A. Hopkins to THN, October 2, 1918, Box 7, THN Papers, DPL; Henry Montgomery to Osborn, June 25, 1918, Box 42, Osborn Papers, Bentley; and *DFP*, October 26, 1918.

42. Liebold Reminiscences, 387, Benson Ford; additional anti-Ford campaign material, Box 10, THN Papers, DPL; William Cook to H. A. Hopkins, October 29, 1918, Box 4, Marshall L. Cook and William R. Cook Papers, Bentley; and THN to George T. Miller, August 16, 1918, Box 1, THN Papers, DPL.

43. Daniel Calhoun Roper to Joseph P. Tumulty, September 3, 1918; Woodrow Wilson to Josephus Daniels, September 6, 1918; Josephus Daniels to Woodrow Wilson, September 9, 1918, in *Papers of Woodrow Wilson*, ed. Arthur S. Link (Princeton, N.J.: Princeton University Press, 1985), 49:438–449, 461, 498; and *NYT*, September 8, 1918. Tumulty also asked the War Department to document Edsel's exemption; Benedict Crowell to Tumulty, September 9, 1918; E. H. Crowder, "Memorandum for the Acting Secretary of War," September 7, 1918; and Tumulty to Wilson, September 11, 1918, Box 1, Thomas Watt Gregory Papers, LOC.

44. *NYT*, October 25, 1918. Daniels praised the Eagle boats designed and produced by the Ford Motor Company as "next to the destroyer, the best weapon to exterminate the submarine." This was an odd claim, since the Eagle boat project was mired in problems, and only two boats made it to Atlantic coast docks by Armistice Day. Nevins and Hill, *Ford: Expansion and Challenge*, 70–74. Albert Lasker, *The Lasker Story* (Lincolnwood, Ill.: NTC Business Books, 1987), 55–59; *DFP*, October 28, 1918. The ad also included a more restrained statement by William Howard Taft. For a marked-up draft, see Hays to TR, October 18, 1918, Box 2, Hays Papers, Indiana State Library.

45. *DFP*, October 15, 19, 24, and 27, 1918. The ban was lifted on November 6.

46. *NYT*, September 18, 1918; and Ervin, *Henry Ford vs. Truman Newberry*, 27.

47. William G. Simpson to Robert Lansing and John E. Kinnane, July 24, 1918; Thomas Watt Gregory to Kinnane, September 10, 1918; Gregory to S. L. Rush, September 10, 1918, Department of Justice Central Files Classified Subject Files, RG 60, File 194917, NARA; *DFP*, March 1, 1916. On Rush, see James Sterling

Morton, *An Illustrated History of Nebraska* (Lincoln, Neb.: Western Publishing and Engraving, 1913), 3:575–576.

48. *NYT*, October 5, October 10, October 11, October 30, and November 1, 1918; Ervin, *Henry Ford vs. Truman Newberry*, 28; THN to Cameron, November 26, 1918, Box 9, THN Papers, DPL; John D. Mangum to Senator Charles Townsend, October 5, 1918, and John W. Blodgett to THN, Box 7, THN Papers, DPL. That the newspapers got the story caused some consternation, since such announcements were not made until the grand jury's term was up. The Department of Justice investigated the lapse; Statement of Charles F. White, October 31, 1918; and Francis G. Caffey to Gregory, November 2, 1918, Department of Justice Central Files Classified Subject Files, RG 60, File 194917, NARA.

49. U.S. Statutes at Large, 65th Cong., 2nd sess., P.L. 222, 40 Stat. 1013; Department of Justice, Circular 906, October 28, 1918; Homer S. Cummings to E. J. MacMillan, November 5, 1918; Cummings to W. R. Hollister, January 13, 1919, Box 47, Homer Stilles Cummings Papers, University of Virginia; Claude R. Porter to Summer Burkhart, September 27, 1918, Department of Justice Central Files Classified Subject Files, RG 60, NARA; case numbers 21164 and 21168, among others. Ironically, Democrats succeeded in erecting national oversight of the sort they had opposed in the Reconstruction years. Richard M. Valelly, "The Reed Rules and Republican Party Building: A New Look," *Studies in American Political Development* 23 (October 2009): 115–152.

50. *NYT*, February 12, 1919; Cummings to W. R. Hollister, January 13, 1919, Box 47, Cummings Papers, University of Virginia. A law professor has revived the idea of taxing large contributions; David S. Gamage, "Taxing Political Donations: The Case for Corrective Taxes in Campaign Finance," *Yale Law Journal* 113 (2004): 1203.

51. *NYT*, November 1, 1918.

52. *NYT*, November 2, 1918; Nevins and Hill, *Ford: Expansion and Challenge*, 78–80; *DFP*, November 3, 1918. Hayden also highlighted the Hughes report's discussion of the questionable dealings of a former Packard chief engineer; *Detroit News*, November 1, 1918.

53. Notebook, 80–81, James W. Helme Papers, Bentley; Rush to Gregory, November 1, 1918, Department of Justice Central Files Classified Subject Files, RG 60, NARA; Horace E. Dodge to THN, November 23, 1918, Box 10, THN Papers, DPL; and *Pipp's Weekly*, September 17, 1921.

CHAPTER 5: WASHINGTON

1. THN to Thomas P. Phillips, November 14, 1918, Box 8, THN Papers, DPL. Newberry was still talking about a trip in December; THN to Charles E. Townsend, December 12, 1918, Box 10, THN Papers, DPL. On the need to get out of the navy, see THN to Cameron, November 26, 1918; and Henry Cabot Lodge to THN, November 26, 1918, Box 9, THN Papers, DPL.

2. Seward W. Livermore, *Politics Is Adjourned: Woodrow Wilson and the War Congress, 1916–1918* (Middletown, Conn.: Wesleyan University Press, 1966); Robert Harrison, *Congress, Progressive Reform, and the New American State* (New York: Cambridge University Press, 2004); Lewis L. Gould, *The Most Exclusive Club: A History of the Modern United States Senate* (New York: Basic Books, 2005); Karen A. J. Miller, *Populist Nationalism: Republican Insurgency and American Foreign Policy Making, 1918–1925* (Westport, Conn.: Greenwood Press, 1999); and James Oliver Robertson, *No Third Choice: Progressives in Republican Politics, 1916–1921* (New York: Garland, 1983). Newberry declined to sign a letter circulating among insurgents urging that Penrose be denied a chairmanship; Gifford Pinchot to THN, February 17, 1919, Box 10, THN Papers, DPL. Some political scientists have quantified the effects of popular elections; see, for example, Scott R. Meinka, "Institutional Change and the Electoral Connection in the Senate: Revisiting the Effects of Direct Election," *Political Research Quarterly* 61 (September 2008): 445–457.

3. On Phipps, see, for example, R. Lee Craft, "In Re: Alleged Fraud in Congressional Election at Denver," December 17, 1918, Investigative Reports of the Bureau of Investigation 1908–1922, Miscellaneous Files, 1909–1921, RG 60 (hereafter BOI), Case 21168. On Spencer, Report, Louis Loebl, "In Re: Alleged Election Fraud," St. Louis, December 5, 1918, November 13, 1918 (quote), and November 20, 1918 (quote), BOI, Case 22176; and Steven L. Piott, *Holy Joe: Joseph W. Folk and the Missouri Idea* (Columbia: University of Missouri Press, 1997), 173–183. On Moses, see "Alleged Election Frauds in New Hampshire, Report of A. W. Levansaler, Special Agent," undated; Levansaler to Chief, Bureau of Investigation, December 7, 1918; Chief, Bureau of Investigation to Levansaler, December 11, 1918, BOI, Case 21164; and unsigned to Alexander Murchie, Chairman, Democratic State Committee, November 18, 1918, Box 3, George H. Moses Papers, New Hampshire Historical Society.

4. *NYT*, November 8 and 16, 1918; Spencer Ervin, *Henry Ford vs. Truman Newberry: The Famous Senate Election Contest* (New York: Richard R. Smith, 1935), 29–30; H. A. Hopkins to THN, November 15, 1918, Box 9, THN Papers, DPL.

5. THN to John W. Blodgett, March 7, 1919; THN to Arthur Vandenberg, March 19, 1919, Box 10, THN Papers, DPL. Newberry's friends at the time, and pro-League (and many Ford) scholars later, often portrayed Newberry's election as the key to blocking the League. Yet a great number of elections were close in 1918. But as Livermore points out, even under Democratic control a favorable vote without reservations was not certain. Livermore, *Politics Is Adjourned*, 236–241. Lodge pointed out that even if Newberry's case had been something other than "a gross case of persecution and of endless misrepresentation," there was no precedent for denying a seat to a duly elected and certified senator and that without Newberry, Republicans would have had a one-vote majority. Henry Cabot Lodge, *The Senate and the League of Nations* (New York: Scribner's, 1925), 149–150.

6. *NYT*, August 16, 1919. On support for Ford despite the trial, see Reynold Wik, *Henry Ford and Grassroots America* (Ann Arbor: University of Michigan Press, 1972); and on the trial, Alan Nevins and Frank Ernest Hill, *Ford*, vol. 2, *Expansion and Challenge, 1915–1933* (New York: Scribner's, 1957), 131–142.

7. "Report of Private Investigation of U.S. Senatorial Primary and Election in Michigan in 1918," Acc. 62, Box 63, Benson Ford. One example of the findings: "James F. McGregor, Asst. Secretary to Paul King, is reported as offering to H. S. Jennings, in August, 1918, $300.00 for his influence in behalf of Newberry campaign. . . . This information comes from L. A. Barry regarded as a reliable Democrat." On the investigation, see Liebold Reminiscences, 395–399, Benson Ford.

8. Robinson to Liebold, January 14, 1920, Acc. 284, Box 25, Benson Ford. Robinson was paid $6,000, although he wanted $10,000, Liebold Reminiscences, 397, Benson Ford. The Ford team and the Department of Justice sought to avoid Detroit, where Arthur Tuttle, who was close to Newberry's circle of friends, presided. On the stiff punishments Sessions handed out to the bathtub trust, see *WP*, January 5, 1913; *NYT*, January 5, February 15, and February 16, 1913.

9. Rush to Thomas Watt Gregory, November 1, 1918; Rush to R. E. Ferguson, December 13, 1918; Ferguson to Rush, December 16, 1918; Rush to Ferguson, December 18, 1918 (quote), Department of Justice (DOJ) Central Files Classified Subject Files, RG 60, Box 2946, File 194917, NARA.

10. Ramsey's report is attached to Claude R. Porter to Gregory, December 19, 1918, RG 60, DOJ Central Files Classified Subject Files, RG 60, Box 2946, File 194917, NARA. Porter had also worked on fraud cases related to the Gerry Act in 1918.

11. Porter to Rush, January 20, 1919; Lucking to Porter, February 8, 1919; Dailey to Attorney General, October 14, 1919, RG 60, DOJ Central Files Classified Subject Files, Box 2946, Folder 194917, NARA; *NYT*, January 13, February 5, and March 6, 1919. An indication that Dailey had picked up the case is P. J. Barry, "In Re: Investigation Alleged Perjury Senator Newberry of Michigan," September 6, 1919, BOI, Case 22176, NARA; *Indianapolis Star*, October 19, 1919.

12. Liebold Reminiscences, 404–405, Benson Ford.

13. *NYT*, November 29, December 3, 1919; THN to Charles P. McAvoy, November 9, 1919, Box 49, THN Papers, DPL; and Ervin, *Henry Ford vs. Truman Newberry*, 40–55.

14. Ervin, *Henry Ford vs. Truman Newberry*, 46–47, 336–357; *NYT*, January 13, 1919.

15. *NYT*, December 5, 1919; *WP*, March 4, 1920; Notebook, Helme Papers, Bentley; and Chase Osborn to John Shaffer, June 19, 1918, Box 42, Osborn Papers, Bentley.

16. *NYT*, March 21, February 11, 1920; BOI, Case 22176; and generally, Ervin, *Henry Ford vs. Truman Newberry*, chap. 18; and Bill of Exceptions.

17. *NYT*, March 4, 1920; *WP*, March 7, 1920. King's health issues were still a topic more than a year later; THN to King, May 21, 1921, Box 23, THN Papers, DPL.

18. *NYT*, March 21, 1920; for jury instructions, see *Newberry v. U.S.*, 256 U.S. 232 (1921).

19. *NYT*, February 3, 1921. Lucking claimed that 17,000 ballots had been lost or destroyed. Even if his conjecture were correct, it seems unlikely that those votes would have swung the election to Ford, given the small percentage of error that emerged in the recount. Ervin, *Henry Ford vs. Truman Newberry*, 67. Liebold followed his boss's interests closely, getting nightly updates. Liebold to G. E. Buckley, January 8, 1921, Acc. 284, Box 25, Folder 2; and William J. Cochran to Lucking, October 3, 1921 to Lucking, Box 132, Folder 1, Acc. 1, Fairlane Papers, Benson Ford.

20. Speech in Jackson, Michigan, February 10, 1919, Box 10, Fred Smith to THN, June 6, 1919; THN to King, Box 40; THN to Fred Smith, August 27, 1921, Box 52, THN Papers, DPL. Martin Littleton to THN, May 25, 1920, Box 23, THN Papers, DPL. Newberry choked on the Littleton bill. "If I had the ability to charge on the scale fixed . . . by New York lawyers, you and your entire family would owe money for forty years," Murfin wrote. Murfin to THN, May 11, 1921, Box 23, THN Papers, DPL.

21. *Newberry v. U.S.*; *NYT*, January 8, 1921; *CT*, January 8, 1921; and *WP*, January 11, 1921.

22. *Newberry v. U.S.*; Benno C. Schmidt, "Principle and Prejudice: The Supreme Court and Race in the Progressive Era, Part 3: Black Disfranchisement from the KKK to the Grandfather Clause," *Columbia Law Review* 82 (June 1982): 892–893.

23. *Newberry v. U.S.*; Ervin, *Henry Ford vs. Truman Newberry*, 358–370; Schmidt, "Principle and Prejudice," 893–895; and Maurice Kelman, "Campaign on Trial: The Unnecessary Ordeal of Truman Newberry," *Wayne Law Review* 33 (1987): 1589–1593.

24. Congress failed to challenge the idea that the federal government lacked the power to regulate primaries. It stood until the Court reversed *Newberry* in the 1940s white primary cases. On the arguments about the power of the federal government, see Schmidt, "Principle and Prejudice"; Charles L. Zelden, *The Battle for the Black Ballot: Smith v. Allwright and the Defeat of the Texas All-White Primary* (Lawrence: University Press of Kansas, 2004); and Jeff Schesol, *Supreme Power: Franklin Roosevelt vs. the Supreme Court* (New York: Norton, 2010). On the confusion for candidates, see Louise Overacker, *Money in Elections* (New York: Macmillan, 1932), 243–244; and BOI, Box 12378, RG 60, NARA.

25. William H. Hobbs to THN, May 4, 1921; John Jones to THN, May 9, 1921; Littleton to THN, May 11, 1921, Box 23, THN Papers, DPL.

26. Ervin, *Henry Ford vs. Truman Newberry*, 70–75, 269–270; *WP*, May 20, 1921.

27. Kathleen F. Lawler, "In Re Contested Election Cases in the Senate," Box 1, Folder 51; Lawler to THN, August 6, 1921, Box 2, Folder 31, Kathleen Lawler Papers, Michigan State University. Ford had his own insiders apart from Lucking; see, for example, Manton V. Wyvell to Liebold, April 12, 1920; Liebold to Lucking, April 19, 1920, Acc. 284, Box 32, Folder 7, Benson Ford.

28. *WP*, June 12, 1921; Subcommittee on Privileges and Elections, U.S. Senate, 67th Cong., 1st sess., *Senator from Michigan, Hearing Pursuant to Senate Res. 11, A Resolution Authorizing the Investigation of Alleged Unlawful Practices in the Election of a Senator from the State of Michigan* (Washington, D.C.: GPO, 1921), (hereafter *Senator from Michigan*); Ervin, *Henry Ford vs. Truman Newberry*, chaps. 8–12. Emery eventually won $10,000, after his attorneys tracked Ford for six months trying to serve a subpoena; *CT*, October 27, 1923; *NYT*, October 27 and November 24, 1923.

29. *CT*, June 10, 1921; *Senator from Michigan*, 419–420, 768–771; Ervin, *Henry Ford vs. Truman Newberry*, 136–154.

30. Ervin, *Henry Ford vs. Truman Newberry*, 139–140.

31. Lawler to Elbert Chilson, August 6, 1921, Box 1, Folder 25; Lawler to THN, August 6, 1921, Box 2, Folder 31; Lawler to Selden P. Spencer, September 13, 1912, Box 3, Folder 9, Lawler Papers, Michigan State University; Liebold Reminiscences, 402, Benson Ford. Senator Ashurst issued a separate minority report, characterizing Newberry's election as having "more of the character of an auction than an election." *WP*, September 30, 1921. Lawler sent copies of the report to Newberry, Murfin, and others before it was released. On Pomerene, see Thomas H. Smith, *The Senatorial Career of Atlee Pomerene of Ohio* (Kent, Ohio: Kent State University Press, 1966).

32. *Baltimore Sun*, January 7, 1922, quoted in LeRoy Ashby, *Spearless Leader: Senator Borah and the Progressive Movement in the 1920's* (Urbana: University of Illinois Press, 1972), 38; and *CR*, 67th Cong., 2nd sess., 774.

33. Notes, Monday May 31, 1920, Box 68, Homer S. Cummings Papers, University of Virginia; *CR*, 67th Cong., 2nd sess., 1043.

34. *CR*, 67th Cong., 2nd sess., 989, 1053, 1048–1049. Ervin, *Henry Ford vs. Truman Newberry*, 390–582, provides a careful analysis of the Senate debate, particularly on the various misleading allegations of fraud. Lawler maintained a log of inaccuracies, perhaps as a way to vent or perhaps as a reference for her correspondence and advice to Spencer and others; Box 1, Folder 50, Lawler Papers, Michigan State University.

35. *NYT*, January 7, 1922; *CR*, 67th Cong., 2nd sess., 775, 1000, 993. This was not the first time that Kenyon invoked the "social lobby." On this case, see *WP*, December 22, 1921; and in previous debates, *WP*, January 23, 1919, and *WP*, June 4, 1913. In the previous case he referred to lobbyists plying senators with dinners; in this one he perhaps meant the social circle around Newberry, particularly his wife, who was an ace at the Washington social scene. *WP*, April 2, 1922.

36. *NYT*, November 22 and 23, 1921; *CR*, 67th Cong., 1st sess., 218–229; George Coleman Osborn, *John Sharp Williams, Planter-Statesman of the Deep South* (Baton Rouge: Louisiana State University Press, 1943), chap. 8, especially 155–161; *CT*, January 7, 1922.

37. Lucking to Tumulty, August 31, 1921; Tumulty to Lucking, August 31, 1921; Lucking to Tumulty, October 3, 1921; Lucking to Tumulty, October 4, 1921; Lucking to Tumulty, October 31, 1921; and Lucking to Tumulty, December 22, 1921, Box 24, Joseph Tumulty Papers, LOC; Lucking to John Sharp Williams, October 22, 1922, Box 56, Williams Papers, LOC; WP, September 27, 1921; William J. Cochran to Lucking, October 3, 1921, Box 163, Folder 1, Acc. 1, Fairlane Papers, Benson Ford. On Ford's threat, Lawler to THN, August 2, 1921, Box 2, Folder 1, Lawler Papers, Michigan State University; NYT, September 28, 1922; and for Ford's statement, WP, September 27, 1921. On Newberry and Pipp, THN to Pipp, July 7, 192, Box 24, THN Papers, DPL.

38. On the Pennsylvania problem, WP, November 30, 1921, and January 2, 1922; and NYT, January 1, 1922. On Johnson, NYT, January 7, 1922; WP, January 13, 1922; Los Angeles Times, January 29, 1922; and James O. Murfin to Lawler, September 2, 1921, Box 2, Folder 29, Lawler Papers, Michigan State University.

39. THN to Lawler, September 1, 1921, Box 2, Folder 31, Lawler Papers, Michigan State University; Murfin to THN, June 23, 1921; THN to Murfin, June 25, 1921; Murfin to THN, July 26, 1921; THN to Townsend, August 3, 1921 (quote); Lawler to THN, September 6, 1921, Box 24, THN Papers, DPL; WP, September 27, 1921; NYT, September 29, 1921; CR, January 4, 1922, 775.

40. Murfin to Lawler, September 5, 1921; Murfin to Lawler, January 7, 1922; and Lawler to Murfin, January 9, 1922, Box 2, Folder 29, Lawler Papers, Michigan State University; NYT, January 10, 1922; CT, January 10, 1922; WP, January 10, 1922; Notes, Monday, May 31, 1920, Box 68, Cummings Papers, University of Virginia; and Ervin, Henry Ford vs. Truman Newberry, chap. 24. Murfin had concluded that unless those leading the fight for Newberry were solidly in favor of his speaking, he should "continue to maintain the splendid, dignified position" he had been taking. Murfin to THN, August 91, 1921, Box 24, THN Papers, DPL.

41. NYT, January 10, 1922; Diaries, January 9, 1922, Box 9, Atlee Pomerene Papers, Kent State University; and Lawler to Murfin, January 5, 1922; Lawler to Murfin, December 1, 1921, Box 3, Folder 29, Lawler Papers, Michigan State University.

42. Lawler to Murfin, January 5, 1922, Box 3, Folder 29, Lawler Papers, Michigan State University, describes the maneuvering on both sides; NYT, January 13, 1921, on the resolution, which neither side liked. On Willis, see Cleveland Plain Dealer, November 21, 1922; Cleveland Press, December 8, 1921; and Willis to John Alexander Hoover, December 12, 1921; Rau S. Ball, November 25, 1922; and Ethel I. Kirk, note, August 2, 1926, Willis Papers, Ohio Historical Society.

43. CR, 67th Cong., 2nd sess., 1089–1116; Los Angeles Times, January 16, 1922; and Herbert F. Margulies, Senator Lenroot of Wisconsin: A Political Biography, 1900–1929 (Columbia: University of Missouri Press, 1977).

44. CR, 67th Cong., 2nd sess., 1049–1051, 946.

45. CR, 67th Cong., 2nd sess., 990–992, 944–945; NYT, January 17, 1922.

46. *CR*, 67th Cong., 2nd sess., January 7, 1922, 1811; H. L. Mencken, "James A. Reed," *American Mercury*, April 1929; *NYT*, January 18 and 28, 1922; *NYT*, May 4, June 7 and 30, 1922; and Robert K. Murray, *The Harding Era: Warren G. Harding and His Administration* (Minneapolis: University of Minnesota Press, 1969), 314–321, on Republican divisions and economic unrest in 1922.

47. *NYT*, March 28, 1922; Keith Sward, *The Legend of Henry Ford* (New York: Reinhart, 1948), 192–193; and Pipp to THN, August 12, 1921, Box 24, THN Papers, DPL.

48. *St. Petersburg Independent*, November 11, 1922; *NYT*, November 9, 1922; August 22 and 25, 1922; *New Republic*, September 6, 1922; and Hughes to Lippmann, June 7 and June 15, 1924, Charles Evans Hughes Papers, Reel 4, LOC.

49. *NYT*, June 11, 1922; *Ironwood (Mich.) Daily Globe*, July 21, 1922; *CT*, November 9, 1922; *NYT*, November 9, 1922; and Kathleen Lawler, "The Issue in 1926," June 12, 1926, Box 3, Lawler Papers, Michigan State University.

50. THN to Charles Warren, December 14, 1922, Box 34, THN Papers, DPL; *WP*, September 19, 1919. The house had a dubious pedigree. It had just been vacated by Senator William A. Clark of Montana, one of the state's famed "copper kings," who once had his own problems (connected with charges that he had bribed state legislators) in persuading the Senate to seat him. For Newberry's statement, see *NYT*, November 20, 1922.

51. *NYT*, November 22, 1922; *WP*, November 9, 1922; *CT*, November 20, 1922; and John Sharp Williams to Morris Schaff, January 11, 1922, Box 57, John Sharp Williams Papers, LOC.

52. THN to Walter H. Dorsey, November 24, 1922; THN to George Moses, November 28, 1922; THN to Frank Kellogg, November 24, 1922; THN to Harding, November 25, 1922; THN to Townsend, November 25, 1922; THN to H. H. Chatfield Taylor, November 29, 1922; THN to Charles Warren, December 14, 1922, Box 34, THN Papers, DPL; THN to William M. Butler, October 7, 1924, Box 35, THN Papers, DPL; Harry Barnard, *Independent Man: The Life of Senator James Couzens* (New York, 1958).

53. Leo P. Ribuffo, "Henry Ford and 'The International Jew,'" *American Jewish History* 69 (June 1980): 43–77; and Victoria Saker Worste, "Louis Marshall, Henry Ford, and the Problem of Defamatory Antisemitism, 1920–1929," *Journal of American History* 91 (December 2004): 877–905.

54. THN to Henry Ford, December 18, 1935, Box 163, Folder 15, Acc. 1, Fairlane Papers, Benson Ford; THN to Frederick Hale, January 13, 1936, Hale Papers, Syracuse University; and Newberry Autobiography, THN Papers, DPL.

55. Sward, *Legend of Henry Ford*, 192–193; Liebold Reminiscences, 399, 403, Benson Ford; "The Inside Story of the Newberry Persecution," *Pipp's Weekly*, September 17, 1921; and Pipp to THN, August 12 and July 2, 1921, Box 24, THN Papers, DPL.

56. Undated 1919 fragment, Box 10, THN Papers, DPL. The loan troubled him. As late as 1921, he wanted legal reassurance about the status of loans, although he

denied knowing that Fred Smith had made the loans. THN to Murfin, June 2, 1921, Box 24; THN to H. H. Chatfield Taylor, December 29, 1922, Box 34; THN to Townsend, November 29, 1922, Box 34, THN Papers, DPL.

CHAPTER 6: SCANDAL

1. *WP*, December 26, 1926.

2. On the *Washington Post* backstory, see Donald A. Ritchie, *Reporting from Washington: The History of the Washington Press Corps* (New York: Oxford University Press, 2005), 243. The point on scandal and corruption draws on Frank Anechiarico and James B. Jacobs, *The Pursuit of Absolute Integrity: How Corruption Control Makes Government Ineffective* (Chicago: University of Chicago Press, 1996).

3. David Burner, *The Politics of Provincialism: The Democratic Party in Transition, 1918–1932* (New York: Knopf, 1967); Douglas B. Craig, *After Wilson: The Struggle for the Democratic Party, 1920–1934* (Chapel Hill: University of North Carolina Press, 1992); and Ellis Hawley, *The Great War and the Search for a Modern Order: A History of the American People and Their Institutions, 1917–1933* (New York: St. Martin's Press, 1979).

4. On the unity of congressional Democrats amid a growing ideological split, see Craig, *After Wilson*.

5. John Mark Hansen, *Gaining Access: Congress and the Farm Lobby, 1919–1981* (Chicago: University of Chicago Press); and J. Leonard Bates, *The Origins of Teapot Dome: Progressives, Parties, and Petroleum, 1909–1921* (Urbana: University of Illinois Press, 1963).

6. Bates, *Origins of Teapot Dome*, chaps. 11 and 12; and Paul Sabin, *Crude Politics: The California Oil Market, 1900–1940* (Berkeley: University of California Press, 2005), 28–41.

7. Bates, *Origins of Teapot Dome*, chap. 8; and David H. Stratton, *Tempest over Teapot Dome: The Story of Albert B. Fall* (Norman: University of Oklahoma Press, 1998).

8. Stratton, *Tempest over Teapot Dome*, chap. 7.

9. Craig, *After Wilson*, 35–63.

10. *CT*, March 23, 1924; *NYT*, March 23 and 25, 1924; and Louise Overacker, *Money in Elections* (New York: Macmillan, 1923), 147–149.

11. Overacker, *Money in Elections*, 147–153. Doheny had contributed $25,000 toward the Democratic debt; he had also supported the Republican campaign.

12. Hearings before the Committee on Election of President, Vice President, and Representatives in Congress of the House of Representatives, *Additional Publicity of Campaign Contributions Made to Political Parties, and Limiting Amount of Campaign Expenditures by Amending Corrupt Practices Act*, 68th Cong., 1st sess., February 21 and 28, March 13, 1924 (Washington, D.C.: Government Printing Office, 1924); *NYT*, February 13, March 30, 1924.

13. WP, February 27, 1925; and Robert E. Mutch, *Campaigns, Congress, and the Courts: The Making of Campaign Finance Law* (Westport, Conn., 1988), 18–21. The rider that passed, proposed by Congressman John Cable of Ohio, substituted for one proposed by Borah, which included a longer list of disclosures. There were no Senate hearings or committee reports on the rider. 68th Cong., 1st sess., *Additional Publicity of Campaign Contributions Made to Political Parties, and Limiting the Amount of Campaign Expenditures by Amending Corrupt Practices Act.*

14. Overacker, *Money in Elections*, 24–40, and 249–258, on campaign costs and whimsical bookkeeping and record keeping.

15. *Davenport (Iowa) Democrat and Leader*, November 9, 1924.

16. NYT, July 10, 1925; April 11, 1926; WP, July 20, 1925; Richard D. Hupman, *Senate Election, Expulsion and Censure Cases* (Washington, D.C.: Government Printing Office, 1962), 116–117; and Jeffrey A. Jenkins, "Partisanship and Contested Election Cases in the Senate, 1789–2002," *Studies in American Political Development* 19 (Spring 2005): 53–74. Cummins would lose his seat in 1926 to Brookhart.

17. WP, March 10, 1925; NYT, February 3, 1925, and March 23, 1926; CT, October 3, 1925; and NYT, June 17, 1926.

18. NYT, December 1, 2, and 12, 1925; Erik Olssen, "The Progressive Group in Congress, 1922–1929," *Historian* 42 (February 1980): 244–263.

19. CT, November 15, 1925, and January 8, 1926; NYT, November 22, 1925; and Wayne S. Cole, *Senator Gerald P. Nye and American Foreign Relations* (Minneapolis: University of Minnesota Press, 1962), 36–43.

20. WP, January 13, 1926.

21. NYT, December 7 and 8, 1926; WP, November 27, 1926; NYT, March 1 and 5, 1927; and *Oakland (Calif.) Tribune*, December 13, 1926.

22. George Wharton Pepper, *In the Senate* (Philadelphia: University of Pennsylvania Press, 1930), 131–136; William S. Vare, *My Forty Years in Politics* (Philadelphia: Rowland Swain, 1933); and Overacker, *Money in Elections*, 37–40, 61–65, 258–271. Had Pepper won the primary, the Senate would have had to decide whether to take seriously Pepper's claim that since the gubernatorial organization he supported was directed by an enemy of his, he actually derived no benefit from it.

23. This paragraph is drawn from the marvelous account of the campaign and its setting in Carroll Hill Wooddy, *The Case of Frank L. Smith: A Study in Representative Government* (reprint, New York: Arno, 1974); and Forrest McDonald, *Insull* (Chicago, 1962), 255–267.

24. Quoted in NYT, November 28, 1927.

25. Hupman, *Senate Election, Expulsion and Censure Cases*, 128–149; Jenkins, "Partisanship and Contested Election Cases in the Senate"; and Kristie Miller, *Ruth Hanna McCormick: A Life in Politics, 1880–1944* (Albuquerque: University of New Mexico Press, 1992), 224–229. Deneen, then governor, was Lorimer's antagonist for an Illinois Senate seat.

26. *Freeman*, October 19, 1921.

27. Jenkins, "Partisanship and Contested Election Cases in the Senate."

28. THN to Lawler, August 13, 1926, Box 2, Folder 31, Lawler Papers; and Stephen Ansolabehere, John Mark Hansen, Shigeo Hirano, and James M. Snyder, "More Democracy: The Direct Primary and Competition in U.S. Elections," *Studies in American Political Development* 24 (October 2010): 190–205. One reform that might have reduced the cost of politics—eliminating primary elections—failed to gain much traction. Alan Ware, *The American Direct Primary: Party Institutionalization and Transformation in the North* (New York: Cambridge University Press, 2002).

29. *NYT*, June 16, 1926; August 12, 1928; and Overacker, *Money in Elections*, 70, 88.

30. Alfred E. Keet, "The High Cost of President-Making: 'Educating the Voter' an Expensive Necessity," *Forum*, September/October 1920, 148. Recent work includes Stephen Ansolabehere, John M. deFigueiredo, and James M. Snyder Jr., "Why Is There So Little Money in American Politics?," *Journal of Economic Perspectives* 17 (Winter 2003): 105–130; and Bradley A. Smith, *Unfree Speech: The Folly of Campaign Finance Reform* (Princeton, N.J., 2001). On campaign styles, see Richard Jensen, "Armies, Admen, and Crusaders: Types of Presidential Election Campaigns," *History Teacher* 2 (January 1969): 33–50; and Michael E. McGerr, *The Decline of Popular Politics: The American North, 1865–1928* (New York: Oxford University Press, 1986).

31. Michael Schudson, *Advertising, the Uneasy Persuasion: Its Dubious Impact on American Society* (New York: Basic Books, 1984); T. J. Jackson Lears, *Fables of Abundance: A Cultural History of Advertising in America* (New York: Basic Books, 1994); *NYT*, December 9, 1927; and A. C. Millspaugh, *Party Organization and Machinery in Michigan since 1890* (Baltimore: Johns Hopkins University Press, 1917), 70, 154–155.

32. Maria Petrova, "Newspapers and Parties: How Advertising Revenues Created an Independent Press," *American Political Science Review* 105 (November 2011): 790–808; Richard L. Kaplan, *Politics and the American Press: The Rise of Objectivity, 1865–1920* (New York: Cambridge University Press, 2002).

33. *Daily Kennebec Journal*, December 20, 1926, reprinting *Portland Express*; *NYT*, December 9, 1927. The Senate never settled the question, no doubt because it was in no party's interest to do so. "Statutory Regulation of Political Campaign Funds," *Harvard Law Review* 66 (May 1953): 1259–1273. The case of Adam Clayton Powell Jr.'s right to his House seat settled the question on the narrow grounds preferred by defenders of Vare and Smith. Charles V. Hamilton, *Adam Clayton Powell Jr.: The Political Biography of an American Dilemma* (New York: Cooper Square Press, 1991), 447–471.

34. James M. Beck, *The Vanishing Rights of the States: A Discussion of the Right of the Senate to Nullify the Action of a Sovereign State in the Selection of Its Representatives in the Senate* (New York: George H. Doran, 1926); Henry B. Joy, comp.,

Appeal to President Coolidge's "Court of Last Resort" in Defense of the Constitution of the United States and the Bill of Rights against the XVIIIth Amendment (Detroit: n.p., 1930); *CT*, November 9, 1934; Craig, *After Wilson*, chaps. 12 and 13. Joy's opposition to Wilsonian progressivism likely did not extend to the targeting of radicals.

35. Beck, *Vanishing Rights of the States*, 14; and on the veneration of the Constitution, Morton Keller, *In Defense of Yesterday: James M. Beck and the Politics of Conservatism, 1861–1936* (New York: Coward-McCann, 1958).

36. *CR*, 67th Cong., 2nd sess., 940, 943.